Advance Praise

In this powerful book, the contributors draw our attention to the insidious and oppressive caste hierarchies that categorise humans and animals alike. They challenge the caste-imposed order, which relegates Dalits and tribals as inferior and impure because of their association with certain animals, occupations and food practices. The book examines how Dalit and tribal worlds are inextricably connected with the lives of animals in a relationship of care. By foregrounding anti-caste politics, the book offers a much-needed perspective of the marginalised voices in India's environmental discourse.

Dolly Kikon, University of California

This book, for the first time in environmental studies, examines the human–animal relationship from the perspective of marginalised populations – Dalits and tribals – and the marginal region of Northeast India, thereby addressing a historical gap in mainstream animal studies. The book offers a distinctive blend of positionality, lived experience, fieldwork and academic research to explore the intersection of caste, animals and Dalit identities, the animals in Dalit–tribal lives, the cultural representations of animal relationships, and animals as metaphors of identity and resistance. This multidimensional work envisions an alternative multispecies world rooted in dignity and justice.

Mukul Sharma, Ashoka University

A fabulous collection that covers literary, sociological and cultural frontiers in the emerging scholarship on caste and ecology. It will serve as a reference for new research in the fields of caste, South Asia, animal studies and media studies.

Suraj Milind Yengde, Harvard University

Beings and Beasts

A lot has been written about the need to 'decolonise' animal studies. However, there has not been any attempts to 'de-brahminise' them. Some animals and birds are positioned as superior in the Brahminical social order, while others seem to be subordinated and are associated with certain 'inferior' caste groups. *Beings and Beasts* discusses the relations between humans and animals of marginalised communities, especially Dalits and tribals. It analyses the various ways of perceiving their 'conjoint' living by examining texts, artwork, images, symbols and icons related to human–animal relations among marginalised groups, investigating their meaning-making processes to highlight differences in the social and natural orders. Its focus is on how social beliefs prioritise 'sacred' animals over oppressed communities, leading to exclusion and social injustice.

Ambika Aiyadurai, an anthropologist also trained in wildlife conservation, is Associate Professor at the Indian Institute of Technology, Gandhinagar. Her research examines the social dimensions of wildlife conservation with a special interest in human–animal relations. She has research degrees in natural and social sciences, and is the author of *Tigers Are Our Brothers*, an anthropological study of wildlife conservation in Northeast India. She has also co-edited a volume of essays, *Ecological Entanglements: Affect, Embodiment and Ethics of Care.*

Prashant Ingole teaches in the Department of Humanities and Social Sciences at the Indian Institute of Science Education and Research, Mohali. His research interests span Dalit Studies, Cultural Studies, Environmental Humanities, and interdisciplinary Social Sciences. His long-term academic work engages with the intersections of caste, visuality, representation and lived experience(s). He has contributed scholarly articles and opinion pieces to a wide range of academic journals and media platforms. He is the recipient of the Manju Deshbandhu Gupta Fellowship from Ashoka University for the translation of the Marathi nonfiction *Raghnak* by Shekhar G. Korde into English.

Beings and Beasts

Human–Animal Relations
at the 'Margins'

Edited by
Ambika Aiyadurai
Prashant Ingole

CAMBRIDGE
UNIVERSITY PRESS

Shaftesbury Road, Cambridge CB2 8EA, United Kingdom

One Liberty Plaza, 20th Floor, New York, NY 10006, USA

477 Williamstown Road, Port Melbourne, VIC 3207, Australia

314–321, 3rd Floor, Plot 3, Splendor Forum, Jasola District Centre, New Delhi – 110025, India

103 Penang Road, #05–06/07, Visioncrest Commercial, Singapore 238467

Cambridge University Press is part of Cambridge University Press & Assessment,
a department of the University of Cambridge.

We share the University's mission to contribute to society through the pursuit of
education, learning and research at the highest international levels of excellence.

www.cambridge.org
Information on this title: www.cambridge.org/9781009529938

First published 2025

Printed in India by Avantika Printers Pvt. Ltd.

Cover illustration: Jay Sagathia.

A catalogue record for this publication is available from the British Library

ISBN 978-1-009-52993-8 Hardback

Contents

HUMAN–ANIMALS RELATIONS IN THE NORTHEAST

ANIMALS AS COMPANIONS

Acknowledgements

We want to acknowledge and celebrate the many institutions and individuals whose support and intellectual deliberations have enriched the contributions in this edited volume, making for a truly collaborative effort. First and foremost, we would like to thank the Indian Council of Social Science Research (ICSSR) and the Department of Humanities and Social Sciences, IIT Gandhinagar, for helping us organise the online national seminar 'Human–Animal Relations at the Margins: A Quest for Social Justice', 17–18 August 2021, during the Covid lockdown. The chapters in this volume are an outcome of this seminar.

We would like to express our sincere gratitude to Mr Sajai Jose for his tireless efforts in editing the manuscript. We are thankful to Jay Sagathia and Jigar Sagathia for the wonderful illustrations that adorn the book cover as well as the individual chapters. We acknowledge the many excellent suggestions received from anonymous reviewers. We sincerely thank Anwesha Rana and Aniruddha De of Cambridge University Press for supporting and guiding us throughout our publishing journey.

From Prashant: I am grateful for the strong support extended by my friend Neha, at whose residence I completed editing this manuscript.

From Ambika: I thank Professor D. C. Baruah and Nihal Sharma of the Centre for Multidisciplinary Research (Tezpur University, Assam) for their constant support. The final stage of editing of this volume was completed at Ming House and Bamboosa Library at Tezu (Arunachal Pradesh). Thank you, Bapenlu Kri and Uncle Moosa, for your care and kindness.

Introduction

Human–Animal Relations at the 'Margins'

Ambika Aiyadurai and Prashant Ingole

> It is true that I have never felt any deep appreciation of nature. Nature
> seemed to be like a rich man with much property. I could only look
> down on the rich. The issues I had to confront left me with no space or
> time to stand and stare. Nature worship was for those whose stomachs
> are comfortably filled.[1]

The above quote is from *Baluta* by Daya Pawar, arguably one of the first
Dalit autobiographies in Marathi. Pawar recalls his childhood memories,
remembering how his mother would forage in the jungle for food, often
after paying off the forest guards, and how people from his community were
forced to survive on whatever they found edible in the forests or even on the
grains left behind in the fields after harvest. Pawar's powerful narrative is a
testament to Dalit lives and how they relate to their environment.

Meanings of and attitudes to nature, animals and the environment
vary across communities and cultures. They also generate different ideas
and feelings depending on the condition of the humans that relate to them.
Human relations with animals have always been multifaceted; animals are
worshipped, considered kin and also slaughtered as spiritual offerings.[2] Even
more complex is our relations with animals in the contemporary world,
where animals may be employed as performers in circuses, displayed in
zoological parks, recruited as research subjects in laboratories and kept as
companions and pets in homes. Ideas of morality are often attached to some
animals, which are idealised, venerated and 'used as models of order and
morality'.[3] Animals are seen with both admiration and disgust; some animals

are good, adorable and worthy of care, while some are represented as the 'other': cruel, shrewd and cunning. How do we evaluate our perceptions of animals that are associated with marginalised societies? Relations of animals with marginalised people, such as Dalits and Adivasis, reveal a lot not only about humans and their relations with nature but also about the complex sociocultural dynamics of Indian society.

Caste and Animality

In everyday conversations, the word 'animal' is associated with uncivilised or immoral behaviour. In Hindi, the word *jaanwar* (that is, animal) is used almost exclusively in negative or derogatory terms, and is never used to describe a person of privilege. Using the word 'animal' to refer to humans implies a disapproval of the particular behaviour of the latter. For example, the term 'animals' or 'beasts' is liberally applied to criminals of all stripes, indicating moral degradation. Our interest here is to assess the significance of the usage of certain animal metaphors as a tool for 'moral and social regulation'.[4] According to Serpell,[5] 'human conceptualisation, classification and theorisation of animals signify social thought'. Therefore, the social structure of human morality is routinely extended into the 'animal world' to give them an appearance of logical order consistent with universal reality. One of the aims of this book is to examine how in India caste identities are extended to the world of animals.

We cannot talk about animals in the Indian context without their roles becoming complex, disturbing and controversial. Indian society, given its geographical and ecological settings and sharply ordered caste hierarchy, plays a vital role in shaping distinctly different social fabrics for its mainstream and its margins. Among these, Dalit and tribal communities' lives especially are entangled with the lives of animals. They rear animals, graze them and take care of them. Animals also become essential food sources and are slaughtered when required.

The caste hierarchies in India have also ordered animals into certain hierarchies.[6] While some animals are positioned as 'superior' by the Brahminical social order, others seem to occupy a subordinate status as they are associated with certain 'inferior' caste groups. For example, cows and buffalos are both important for India's rural economy. However, the former is considered 'pure' and the latter 'impure'. Through the lens of caste, one can understand better how people's relations with animals, birds and nature, in general, are socially constructed in India. In Dalit writings, for instance, nature is almost never referred to in the romantic, almost reverential terms in which it is described in mainstream Indian literature, as Mukul Sharma[7] has noted. As the testimonies presented in this book reveal, across India Dalits are compared to animals by mainstream society, both at an abstract level, wherein they are rendered subhuman, and while referring to particular animals that are associated with their caste occupations. Focusing on marginalised people, we aim to unfold the question of what caste has to do with animals, while also exploring what role animals play in the lived experiences of Dalits and Adivasis.

In Indian society, many animals enjoy more elevated lives, both in real life and symbolically in culture, than many humans. For example, the importance attached to cows as 'pure' and 'spiritual' beings by upper-caste Hindus cannot be over-emphasised. The notion of some animals being 'sacred' and others 'polluting' creates deep divides and friction between communities. The 'sacredness' attached to cows has been increasingly used to incite violence against those who are outside the dominant caste, class and religious groups. Most of the victims in these rising incidents of violence in the name of cow protection have been minorities and poor, landless Dalits and Adivasis. The case of the flogging of Dalits in Una, Gujarat, for skinning a dead cow and the murder of several Muslims for trading in cattle have brought the questions of our social identities and our relations with animals to the forefront in the current political environment. 'Is a cow's life worthier than those of Dalits?' asks Kancha Ilaiah.[8] Similarly, in his autobiography *Joothan,* Omprakash Valmiki writes, 'I have asked many scholars to tell me why Savarnas hate Dalits and Shudras so much? The Hindus who worship trees and plants, beasts and birds, why are they so intolerant of Dalits?'[9] Suraj Yengde, in his essay 'Supreme Subalterns', writes that 'animals were subjugated and were declared as "beasts"' to justify human arrogance. Thereby, in the vertical hierarchy of the food chain, animals came to occupy the lowest position. In the Indian context of the dominant caste hierarchy, the 'lower' caste people occupy a similar position and are, in fact, considered lower than animals. In the Dalit collective consciousness, however, animals and plants are considered 'our non-human ancestors'.[10]

The reference to human relations with trees, birds and animals, and the question of how Dalits are treated as 'subanimals' and not just subhuman, is not unique to Valmiki's writings. Many Dalits have written about their experiences with animals and how specific animal names or terms that reflect a subhuman status are used for them. In *Baluta*, Pawar recalls names such as Kachrya (dust) and Gavyta (grass), which are employed by others sarcastically in the narrative to mock his community. Omprakash Valmiki writes how dominant castes called his community 'Chuhre key', which means 'pig-like'. He writes, 'They did not call us by our names. If the person were older, he would be called "Oye Chuhre". If the person were younger or of the same age, then "Abhey Chuhre" was used'.[11] While animals such as dogs and pigs are looked down upon as stigmatised, for many Dalit and tribal communities, pigs and pig rearing especially are not considered dirty or polluting, and often command important economic and cultural significance. Some communities even have names and identities that are linked to animals. Among the Dhangar, a pastoralist group in Maharashtra, the very name of their community is derived from the word *dhan,* meaning sheep, the animals they keep or are associated with. The name of the Musahars of Bihar is derived from the word *musa,* meaning rat, which refers to their traditional caste occupation as rat-catchers. The Maldhari of Gujarat are cattle rearers; the word *maldhari* comes from *mal,* which means cattle. The use of animal names as a slur by dominant castes is not new. The Kaikadi community in Maharashtra rear pigs as an occupation. Instead of calling them by their names, dominant-caste members often use the Marathi word for pig, *fandry,* to refer to the Kaikadi.

Many scholars have discussed how animals go through immense suffering and pain in human society. As Yamini Narayan[12] says, 'non-human animal lives are intricately enmeshed in the cultural, political, urban and technological worlds of humans, both in India and throughout the world'. At the same time, animals are also valued companions to humans. For Dalits and Bahujans, for instance, buffaloes are the 'most prized beasts', says Kancha Ilaiah,[13] producing richer milk than cows. Yet buffaloes never figure in the 'discourse of animal protection', whether in traditional society or that of the modern animal rights movement. He claims that the situation of Dalit–Bahujan groups is similar to that of the buffaloes, who have a subordinate status and whose labour and productive capacity are never acknowledged.[14] This systematic bias and neglect also extends to academia, where the intersections of the lives of animals and caste identities and lived experiences of the marginalised communities have not been given much attention, a historical gap which this book aims to fill.

In Dalit writings, animals are often discussed in the context of the writer's own identity; writing about animals for many of them is another way of writing about themselves, one often rooted in their personal experiences of having been treated like animals by *savarnas*.[15] Animality is yet another marker of social relations and power equations, designed to push Dalits into their 'assigned' positions forced upon them by the casteist Brahminical Indian society. The late economist and thinker M. Kunhaman[16] recalls in his autobiography an incident that happened when, as a fourteen-year-old boy in Kerala, he visited a landlord's house for gruel. As was the practice, a small hole was dug in the ground and covered with a leaf, into which gruel was poured. When he approached to drink the gruel, he was attacked by the landlord's dog. Kunhaman writes, 'It was not anything between a dog and a human; the relation was that of two dogs sparring with each other for a swig of gruel.'[17] Being forced to live in such dire social conditions gives one a feeling of being an animal or being treated like one. Many Dalits are also empathetic towards animals, as they can share their pain and understand what they are going through. 'When blood oozed out at the site of the bite, I had not felt any ire. Only an empathy with another being sailing in the same boat I was,' says Kunhaman about the dog he was forced to share his gruel with.

Such narratives associated with animals, especially those of Dalits, have been mainly ignored, hidden or avoided in academic literature and in animal studies. The stigma attached to certain marginalised peoples because of their association with particular animals, occupations and food places them in a disadvantaged position at all levels of their personal, social, economic and political spheres. Sharma argues that both live and dead animals mean different things to different people in a caste society and emphasises that dead animals are a crucial marker in Dalit autobiographies. It is a direct outcome of caste-imposed occupations and the social restrictions that most Dalits have been subjected to for generations.

In a historic speech delivered on 19 March 1927 at Mahad in support of the agitation demanding the right to draw water freely from the Chavdar tank, Babasaheb B. R. Ambedkar said,

The caste Hindus are so reasonable that they not only draw water from the lake themselves but freely permit people of any religion to draw water from it, nor do the caste Hindus prevent members of species considered lower than humans, such as birds and beasts, from drinking at the lake. Moreover, they freely permit beasts kept by untouchables to drink at the lake.[18]

In the same speech, he asks why caste Hindus treat the harmless cow kindly, and sometimes even sparing harmful creatures such as snakes, but continue to treat their fellow humans harshly, even rendering them untouchables?

Animals in the Tribal World

Animals are an integral part of the socio-cosmological networks of tribal communities.[19] Their knowledge systems are embedded in the social-cultural worldviews of forests; as Savyasaachi[20] shows, both human beings and non-humans in the forests are animated by *jiwa* – the life force generated by the self-activity of nature. For Koitor forest dwellers in Bastar, forests are living spaces to be shared by humans and all other beings. Emerging scholarship attempts to 'enable a deeper understanding of the specific ways that ideas about nature enter into processes of tribal identity formation'.[21] 'Tribal ecologies' focus on the relationship of tribal communities with animals and the wider ecosystem through established cultural-historical connections that continue to reflect in their day-to-day lives. The interconnectedness between humans and animals in tribal societies is underpinned by a deep sense of cultural mutuality. For example, for many tribal populations, the human and the non-human world are not separate. All nature is 'one', including the world of spirits.

For example, the Idu Mishmi, an eastern Himalayan indigenous group, believe that a mountain spirit (Ngolon) is the guardian of wild animals, and the Mishmi hunters both respect and fear this spirit. It is believed a hunt will become successful only if you maintain proper conduct in the forests. This association with spirits is a perennial one and can be observed during harvesting, healing rites and birth ceremonies. Among the Nayakas of south India, forests are seen as ancestors who unconditionally provide food and shelter in a 'giving environment'.[22] Nayakas believe that forests are their parents and they are the children of the forests. They refer to spirits that inhabit hills, rivers and forests as *doddappa* (big father) and *doddamma* (big mother). This 'giving environment' contrasts with the 'reciprocating environment', where successful food procuring depends on proper conduct.

Several local communities set aside some patches of the forests as sacred, and disturbing or extracting any resource from these sites is considered taboo.[23] These protected forests, known as sacred groves, are abodes of nature spirits. In Kerala, such sacred forests (*kavu*) are traditionally known to house pantheistic deities like snake gods (*naga devatha*, or *nagam*) or mother goddesses (various non-Brahminical forms of the mother, such as Bhagavati and Bhadrakali).

Members of tribal societies often act under rules that oblige them to receive material and spiritual goods, and pay reciprocally through a complex and dense network of exchanges that include both animals and spirits, along with humans. These examples represent common elements in the belief systems of indigenous groups across the world. In the context of India, deeply entrenched hierarchical social codes of mainstream society also influence tribal society, in addition to pressures brought on by development. Access to food, land and water by a community varies, depending directly on a community's position in Indian society. Tribals and other poor communities face a disproportionate amount of environmental burden in the face of extractive modern cultures.[24] The hierarchical and exclusionary social structure of Indian society is reflected in its economic policies and processes, forcing such communities to inhabit violent and toxic environments where they are exposed to dangerous forms of garbage, including animal waste. The issue is not just one of a health hazard – living in and next to such places makes one inhuman, subhuman and almost animal in the periphery of mainstream caste society. Animals, therefore, become a metaphor to voice their concerns or a reference point to share their lived experiences.

Adivasis especially, owing to their deep connections with forests, have many negative connotations attached to them by mainstream society which describe them as being 'primitive' and 'backward'. The Hindi word *jangli,* derived from *jangal* (woods, forest), is used as an insult, especially to refer to 'tribals' or 'forest-dwelling' people in a derogatory manner. They are frequently denigrated through comparison with animals, indicating their degraded and inhuman state of living – which condemns them to a subhuman status and as belonging to the world of forests and animals and not human society proper. Such references also have the effect of concealing Dalits' and tribals' deep knowledge of their landscape, water bodies, ecology and the animals they rear. For Dalits, such prejudices help enforce caste barriers that exclude them from mainstream society, whereas in the case of tribals, it leaves their land and resources vulnerable to be captured by 'civilised' society.[25]

Meaning-making in the Margins

In his book *Why I Am Not a Hindu*, Ilaiah[26] writes about his childhood as a shepherd boy. Each of the boys of his community would learn the specific language of the sheep and master sheep-rearing tasks, including how to cure diseases in sheep and how to shear wool. Many communities, labelled as 'marginalised' and 'stigmatised', are, in fact, highly productive social groups, argues Kancha Ilaiah. They are agriculturalists, potters, pastoralists, butchers, hunters and fishers. The toddy tappers know their trees by name, as the shepherds know their sheep or goats by name, and the peasants their cows. The Adivasis' and Dalits' deep knowledge of the land, animals and trees demands that their intimate relations with animals and other beings be acknowledged as epistemically important, a perspective that is often absent in academia. Increasingly, though, there is a growing engagement of scholars breaking barriers to bring forth the complex and less talked about aspects of the study of caste, especially as it relates to environmental studies and its allied areas. For instance, in his path-breaking book *Dalit Ecologies: Caste and Environmental Justice* (2024), Mukul Sharma describes that animals become markers of social relations, power formations and differences. Similarly, tribal ecology, as framed by Christopher et al.,[27] appeals to make space for the close study of how nature remains one of the primary means by which tribal identities are negotiated in contemporary India.

This book is an outcome of an online workshop held at the Indian Institute of Technology Gandhinagar (IITGN) titled 'Human–Animal Relations at the "Margins": A Quest for Social Justice' from 17 to 18 August 2020. The workshop was supported by the Indian Council for Social Science Research, Delhi (ICSSR, Delhi). The chapters in this book delve into how we use animals as species, metaphors and symbols, and how these are rendered in Dalit and tribal lives and also in the literary and cinematic representations of these communities.

We use the term 'margins' in the title in multiple ways (for example, both sociocultural and institutional). As our focus is on Dalits and other marginal groups, social margins are one of the areas of enquiry, and we examine the presence of animals in the lives of those considered marginalised. In addition to social margins, we look at the geographical margins of India, especially northeast India, where communities' relations to animals differ significantly from that of Hindu caste societies. Here, among the people of the eastern Himalayas, though placed on the country's margins, the animals stigmatised in mainstream Indian society (for example, pigs and dogs) are considered valuable both alive and dead, and continue to play a central role in the lives of tribal communities, economically and culturally.

There are compelling personal reasons why we conceived this book. Both of us are Dalits, and our positionalities play an important role in forming the ideas that shaped the book. Ambika Aiyadurai has had a long-term engagement with issues of human–animal relations in Arunachal Pradesh from a conservation angle. She has completed her BSc in zoology, MSc in wildlife science and a second master's in anthropology, environment and development. Her PhD focused on human–animal relations in Arunachal Pradesh. The part titled 'Human–Animal Relations in the Northeast' is an outcome of her research and interest in the region. Studies from the region provide crucial insights that can enrich the studies of similar issues elsewhere in the country, for instance, the importance placed by these communities on semi-domesticated cattle, dogs, pigs and other wild animals that are valued beyond economic reasons. Prashant Ingole has completed his BA and MA in English literature. His PhD research is in the broad area of Dalit and cultural studies, wherein he approaches his subject through the lens of representation and lived experience(s).

The contributors to this volume belong to diverse ethnic groups from across the country. The research backgrounds of these interdisciplinary scholars vary from literature, political science, social work, sociology, agricultural science and science-society and technology studies. Many are early career scholars, some of them first-generation learners from tribal, Dalit and pastoralist families. As a result, some of these thirteen chapters have been written from the lived experiences of the authors or of their family or community members who rear cattle or other animals and reflect their social positions. The new ideas of young scholars make this volume unique and a rare attempt to challenge the dominant narratives in the literature on human–animal relations. Writing from the social or political cultural perspective of the marginalised, and often in intensely personal terms, they directly challenge the dominant caste and class viewpoints that have hitherto dominated the subject. By bringing together the fresh outlook of young scholars and featuring research from across the country, this volume attempts to build a new scholarship on human–animal relations from the perspective of the marginalised, thereby casting new light on our understanding of Indian social dynamics.

Divided into four parts, the book examines the role of animals, their symbolic representations, and their significance and value in various domains across communities from various parts of the country. Through this text, we primarily attempt to make the connection between caste and tribal identities with animals visible. The volume argues that human–animal relations at the margins have strong socio-political and cultural connotations of significance to the downtrodden communities. The environmental–political paradox we aim to highlight is crucial to understanding the various ways of perceiving 'conjoint' living from multiple perspectives and disciplinary lenses. This is a relatively 'new' approach, since there are no significant works on this theme.

In this edited volume, we explore texts, artwork, images, symbols and icons related to the human–animal relations of Dalits and tribals and their meaning-making processes to elaborate on the differences in the social and natural order. We argue that despite the proliferating literature and research on environmental themes, there has been a loud silence combined with inordinate ignorance of anti-caste and marginal environmental perspectives, particularly as they relate to animals. We suggest that by deliberating about the varied forms in which these relations in the margins are present in the literature, culture, politics and society, while keeping 'animals' as its core focus, this book aims to trigger a much-needed discussion on caste and identity in India's environmental discourses, which often celebrate the grassroots while remaining unmindful of marginal perspectives.

The narratives in this book are not just stories of animals and their connections with Dalit and tribal identities but also stories of suppression that carry 'rebellion against the suppression'.[28] Some stories are individual narratives of pain and misery, but the 'content is essentially social'. Experiences are individual alone, but the suffering they describe is a shared one. In this book, we aim to discuss how humans and non-humans – in this case, non-human animals – mutually shape one another through social, cultural, emotional and political processes.

One can read *Beings and Beasts* metaphorically and also relate to peoples' lives and their relations to animals in multiple ways. For many cultures, animals play a significant role as pets, food, deities, symbols and icons. Many even see animals belonging not just to humans but also to spirits in a cosmological sense. In this book, we use 'beings and beasts' to encompass all animals, people, birds and even spirits that make our world and shape our relations with each other. By doing this: (1) We highlight multiple meanings that we attribute to animals that are sometimes 'beings' and sometimes 'beasts'. When does a being become a beast and vice versa can be understood more clearly from the margins. Here, certain animals and people who rear them are seen as 'inferior' beings and therefore, because of their association with certain occupations and livelihoods, are often branded as 'beasts' in a negative sense. (2) It helps to shift away from the anthropocentric view of the world where human dominance and its narratives take precedence. More importantly, *Beings and Beasts* challenges the dominant perspective of human–animal relations to particularly take into account the lives of Dalits, tribals and other societies, and how they see and understand themselves with relation to animals.

In the part titled 'Animals in Dalit Cinema', the scholars analyse three films that challenge the caste system through the symbolic representation of animals. Indian cinema has been extensively studied and written about, but stories from the margins continue to be absent or hidden in this voluminous corpus. 'Dalit Cinema'[29] particularly talks about the everyday life of the 'untouchable' castes. This volume extends this understanding through human–animal relations and how marginality positions animals socially, a view that has received little space in mainstream academia so far.

Purnachandra Naik, in his chapter, analyses *Fandry* (2013), a searing anti-caste Marathi film directed by Nagraj Manjule that highlights the absolute degradation that characterises the everyday life of Dalit communities. Naik articulates the political question raised by the symbolic content of the metaphors of the pig and the black sparrow, which articulate the desire to love and the quest for a sense of belonging. The next chapter by R. Samuel Gnanaraj examines *Pariyerum Perumal* (2018) and *Asuran* (2019), both Tamil movies, to understand how human identity is shaped through the relationship with animals and how it is impacted by the social structure. The close and loving relations of Dalits with hunting dogs are highlighted, but in stark contrast, the same animals become victims of violence by the upper castes. Along the same lines, Akshay Sawant, in his chapter 'Cast(e) ing Animals in Cinema: Exploring Human–Animal Relationships through *Fandry* and *Pariyerum Perumal*', analyses the concepts of fraternity, disgust, untouchability and forced labour through a discussion of human relations with various animals such as dogs, pigs and sparrows, eliciting fresh insights. Moving beyond this notion, Susan Harris, in her chapter 'Dalit Ecologies and Animal Rights: Caste, Body, Metaphor', offers alternative conceptions of environmental justice shaped by a language of experience and feeling towards certain animals, as well as their relations to caste markers such as purity, pollution and space. A phenomenology of animal life can then be located in the multispecies relations of Dalits with other species and humans.

Moving on from cinema, the next part of the book focuses on textual imagery and narratives of caste and animals. Shibangi Dash explores the construction of animalities in Dalit literature as a metanarrative of protest, an argument illustrated by the figure of the owl in Cho Dharman's novel *Koogai* (a Tamil word for owl). By doing this, she focuses on the role of avian metaphors in Dalit narratives as a way to liberate both the *koogai*s and Dalits from their mutually cloistered existence. Deepak, in his chapter '"Dhed and Bhedh": Caste and Animals in Ratan Kumar Sambharia's Short Stories', problematises human–animal dualism to examine the complex cultural economy and the interdependent lives of Dalit individuals and animals, both demographics on the margins of Indian society. Sambharia's four short stories, 'The Goat's Two Kids', 'The Buffalo', 'The Famine' and 'Salvation', argue for the possibility of a non-binary (transcending the natural and the artificial) space for human–animal interactions offered by marginal frontier cultures. Greeshma Mohan, in her analysis of Upamanyu Chatterjee's novel *The Revenge of the Non-Vegetarian*, looks at the attempt to police food practices as a political project. Mohan points to the rise of aggressive and muscular nationalism in India and asks how violence is imbricated with the discourse around vegetarianism and animal rights. She further finds that cow vigilantism is a project which serves the mythographic and enables the imagining of a newly muscular Hindu identity.

Case studies from the northeast are an important part of the book that challenges the dominant Hindu Brahminical order that designates certain animals and people as 'impure'. Therefore, even as tribal people acknowledge the differences and commonalities between Dalits and themselves, they stress how both communities have been marginalised by the dominant order. The part titled 'Human–Animal Relations in the Northeast' focuses on a region that often needs to be discussed much more in academia, especially in animal studies, from a socio-anthropological perspective. Unlike other parts of the country, relations between humans and animals take on multiple meanings in this region. A case study from Tawang by Khriengunuo Mepfhuo and Mihir Sarkar highlights the relations of the Brokpa tribe with their companion livestock, the yaks. The Brokpas and their yaks share space and undertake arduous, long journeys to high altitudes in search of pastures. The relationship between humans and animals in the trans-Himalayan landscape is rooted in care, trust and pragmatism. From the foothills of Assam, Rachan Daimary brings the story of pig sacrifice rituals among the Bodo. Pigs are integral to Bodo economy, livelihoods and social networks, but with the rise of right-leaning politics in Assam, pig sacrifice and the consumption of its meat are being stigmatised and contested. Abhishruti Sarma, in her insightful chapter, shares the cultural importance of a semi-domesticated animal, the mithun, around which several northeastern communities' lives revolve. This bovine is seen as a 'divine' and a sacrificial animal. Reared by several communities in northeast India, the mithun is also being appropriated by the Hindutva narrative owing to its 'sacred' status. In this immediate sense too, such perspectives from the margins take on an urgent importance and relevance.

One of the critical ways to understand the marginalisation, whether political or environmental, of any community is to examine how they stand up to power. The part titled 'Animals as Companions' focuses on particular communities and their relationships with animals. Identities are constructed culturally and politically using animal ecologies; while some reject these imposed identities, others take pride in them. In her chapter, Ashwini Labde narrates the social and human attitudes towards animals and the specialised knowledge of them displayed by the Dhangar community in Maharashtra. Written from her social position as a member of the community, the chapter explores their socio-economic dependency on animals and how they derive their cultural identity from the animals. On similar lines, Saravanan Velusamy explores this aspect of cultural identity as linked to animals through his chapter on the pro-Jallikattu protests in Tamil Nadu. His chapter argues that pro-Jallikattu protests were not just about the cultural sport but also proved to be an opportunity for the Tamils to communicate farmers' grievances to the federal power structure.

We could visualise the socio-spatial embeddedness of human–animal relations in several ways. Gautam Vegda's chapter takes an alternative approach by drawing heavily on his personal life and his experiences of living with vultures on the periphery of a village. The intensely self-reflexive writings of Vegda powerfully use animal and animal metaphors to raise a voice against the atrocities carried out on Dalits in contemporary society.

His poetry is a medium of resistance for him, and the liberal use of animal imagery its mainstay. Vegda claims that for him, poetry is a tool to sharpen his voice against injustice and to demand the right to be acknowledged as human and to be treated as one.

The significance of this volume lies in its giving a new direction to the field of environmental studies and its contemporary discourse at large. By bringing fresh perspectives into the discussion, this volume attempts to bridge the gap between exclusion and inclusion in the field – in other words, to generate fruitful conversation between mainstream and marginal discourses around environmental studies. It also attempts to re-evaluate and contribute to the theoretical and methodological premises of this discourse in an interdisciplinary and cross-disciplinary context. The book hopes to initiate a discussion about our relations with animals such as dogs, pigs, vultures, donkeys and buffaloes and how they relate to the marginalised existence of human communities through experiences of stigma, disgust and degradation. The encounters and experiences detailed here serve as a powerful reminder of the 'subhuman' status of underprivileged communities whose narratives are beginning to uncover the dark, inhumane, unsettling and hitherto neglected side to the mainstream discourse on animals and humans.

Notes

1. Daya Pawar, *Baluta*, trans. J. Pinto (Pune: Granthali, 1978).
2. Ambika Aiyadurai, *Tigers Are Our Brothers: Anthropology of Wildlife Conservation in Northeast India* (Oxford: Oxford University Press, 2021).
3. Richard Tapper, 'Animality, Humanity, Morality, Society', in *What Is an Animal?* ed. Tim Ingold (London and New York: Routledge, 2016), 47–62.
4. Steve Baker, *Picturing the Beast: Animals, Identity and Representation* (Chicago: University of Illinois Press, 2001).
5. James A. Serpell, 'Evidence for an Association between Pet Behaviour and Owner Attachment Levels', *Applied Animal Behaviour Science* 47, nos. 1–2 (1996): 49–60.
6. Narayan Yamini, *Mother Cow, Mother India: A Multispecies Politics of Dairy in India* (Stanford: Stanford University Press, 2023).
7. Mukul Sharma, *Caste and Nature: Dalits and Indian Environmental Politics* (Delhi: Oxford University Press, 2017).

8. Kancha Ilaiah Shepherd, *Why I Am Not a Hindu: A Sudra Critique of Hindutva Philosophy, Culture and Political Economy* (Calcutta: Samya, 2002).

9. Omprakash Valmiki, *Joothan: An Untouchable's Life*, trans. A. P. Mukherjee (New York: Columbia University Press, 2003).

10. Suraj Yengde, 'Supreme Subalterns', in *Subaltern Studies 2.0: Being against the Capitalocene*, ed. Milinda Banerjee and Jelle J. P. Wouters (Chicago: Prickly Paradigm Press, 2022), 191–206, 197.

11. Valmiki, *Joothan*, 2.

12. Yamini, *Mother Cow, Mother India*.

13. Ilaiah Shepherd, *Why I Am Not a Hindu*.

14. Kancha Ilaiah, *Buffalo Nationalism: A Critique of Spiritual Fascism* (Kolkata: Samya, 2004); Kancha Ilaiah, *Post-Hindu India: A Discourse on Dalit–Bahujan, Socio-Spiritual and Scientific Revolution* (New Delhi: Sage, 2009).

15. *Savarna* refers to the 'upper castes' or the dominant castes in India.

16. M. Kunhaman, *Dissent: Life Struggle of the Son of Cherona and Ayyappan*, 2nd ed. (Kerala: DC Books, 2023).

17. Kunhaman, *Dissent*, 19.

18. Arjun Dangle (ed.), *Poisoned Bread: Translations from Modern Marathi Dalit Literature* (Hyderabad: Orient Longman, 1992).

19. Aiyadurai, *Tigers Are Our Brothers*.

20. Savyasaachi, *A Tryst with Nature: Labour, Self and Language* (Hyderabad: Orient Blackswan, 2023).

21. Stephen Christopher, Matthew Shutzer, and Raile Rocky Ziipao, 'An Introduction to Tribal Ecologies in Modern India', *Journal of Tribal Intellectual Collective India* 7, no. 1 (2023): 1–18.

22. Nurit Bird-David, 'The Giving Environment: Another Perspective on the Economic System of Gatherer-Hunters', *Current Anthropology* 31, no. 2 (1990): 189–96.

23. Eliza F. Kent, *Sacred Groves and Local Gods: Religion and Environmentalism in South Asia* (New York: Oxford University Press, 2013).

24. Christopher, Shutzer and Ziipao, 'An Introduction to Tribal Ecologies in Modern India'; Dolly Kikon, *Living with Oil and Coal: Resource Politics and Militarization in Northeast India* (Seattle: University of Washington Press, 2019).

25. Virginius Xaxa, *State, Society and Tribes: Issues in Post-Colonial India* (Noida: Pearson, 2008).

26. Ilaiah Shepherd, *Why I Am Not a Hindu*.

27. Christopher, Shutzer and Ziipao, 'An Introduction to Tribal Ecologies in Modern India'.

28. Sharatchandra Muktibodh, 'What Is Dalit Literature?' in *Poisoned Bread: Translations from Modern Marathi Dalit Literature*, ed. Arjun Dangle (Delhi: Orient Longman, 1992), 267–70.

29. Suraj Yengde, 'Dalit Cinema', *South Asia: Journal of South Asian Studies* 41, no. 3 (2018): 503–18.

ANIMALS IN DALIT CINEMA

1

The Pig, the National Anthem and Anti-caste Belonging in *Fandry*

Purnachandra Naik

Birds and animals have distinctly marked and informed Dalit art and literature. Dalit literature effectively mines the imageries of birds and animals as motifs, metaphors and anthropomorphic devices, not only to express Dalit agony and degradation under the caste system but also to subvert the Brahminical sociocultural ethos and aesthetic conventions. Dalit life-writings, novels, short stories, poetry (across Indian languages) and paintings are some of the prominent forms that vividly illustrate this. In her memoir *The Prisons We Broke*, Dalit writer Baby Kamble affirms:

> Such was the condition of our people. We were just like animals, but without tails.... But how had we been reduced to this bestial state? Who was responsible? Who else, but people of the high castes!... We had to fight with cats and dogs and kites and vultures to establish our right over the carcasses, to tear off the flesh from the dead bodies.[1]

Baby Kamble's visceral imageries of animals, birds and Dalits vying for the raw meat of the carcasses strikingly portray Dalit precarity and destitution. The juxtaposition of Dalits with scavenging birds and animals shines a light on the dehumanisation of Dalits because of the caste system. Likewise, Telugu Dalit poet Gurram Jashuva exposes the Brahminical notions of purity and pollution in his poem 'Gabbilam' ('The Bat Messenger'), in which the Dalit poetic persona reassuringly addresses the nocturnal bird: 'You're a bad omen to them. / For me you are a friend.'[2] It is telling that the Dalit poetic persona confides in non-human species and relates to them, implying the severely limited scope for meaningful communion with humans because of the lack of social osmosis: 'He begins to speak to the bat / of his life and all his troubles. / Who else will listen to him / if not birds, beasts, and insects?'[3] In a similar vein, in the novel *Koogai: The Owl*,[4] Tamil Dalit writer Cho. Dharman projects the titular bird as a totem of Dalit pride, reappraising the 'ominous' owl from a markedly distinct vantage point.[5]

The distinction is unmistakable in the paintings by Dalit artists such as Savi Sawarkar and Malvika Raj, who repudiate the Brahminical hegemony in art[6] and sketch an aesthetically enriched alternative Dalit universe. Savi Sawarkar's 'Devadasi with Crow', for instance, graphically depicts the socially sanctioned sexual violence upon the *devadasi*'s body, bearing a surgical wound on her stomach,[7] while the crow sitting atop her head intensifies the haunting image. Malvika Raj's artwork, populated with birds, deer and elephants, portrays the life and legacy of the Buddha, Savitribai Phule and B. R. Ambedkar, illustrating Dalit aesthetic belonging beyond caste.[8]

Although relatively recent in their development, films made by Dalits share the aesthetic-cultural affinity with Dalit literature and art in drawing on and depicting birds and animals on screen, yielding a variety of effects.[9] In this chapter I examine the Marathi-language film *Fandry*[10] by the critically acclaimed Dalit filmmaker Nagraj Manjule.[11] *Fandry*, which means 'pig', follows Jambhuvant Kachru Mané, also known as Jabya – the adolescent Dalit who is secretly attracted towards his 'upper-caste' classmate Shalu. But Jabya is acutely self-conscious of their respective social identities in the caste-feudal landscape of Maharashtra. In an Indian society obsessed with 'fair' skin, Jabya's dark skin colour further undermines his confidence, and he keeps his feelings to himself, furtively stealing a glance at Shalu when he can. However, the shadowy cycle mechanic Chankya (played by Nagraj Manjule) encourages him to hunt the black sparrow whose feather ash, Chankya claims, could work as a magic charm on Shalu, instantly enchanting her towards him.

A major part of the film is devoted to Jabya's hunt for the black sparrow armed with a slingshot. Yet Jabya's search for the magical black sparrow remains elusive as the bird hops from branch to branch, always flying out of his reach. While the film draws a straightforward comparison between the black sparrow (which is like a 'Brahmin bird') and Shalu, the social stigma and predicaments that Jabya suffers are analogous to the 'untouchable' pig. Jabya's family lives on the periphery of the village 'proper' and is dependent on the villagers for survival. When the village headman tells Jabya's father to drive away the intrusive pigs from the village, Jabya is caught in a double bind: he does not want to be associated with the 'dirty' pigs, and certainly does not want to catch pigs near the school where Shalu would see him doing it. At the same time, the detested work could earn him some money, which the destitute Dalit family direly needs. After many attempts, when Jabya and his family are about to catch the pig, India's national anthem is played during the morning assembly in school. As Jabya and his family stand still to observe the national anthem, the pig slowly escapes from their reach.

The poignant scene strikes at the core of complacency, prompting the audiences to pause and reconsider the claims of the national anthem vis-à-vis Dalits in the Indian nation. Critiquing the romantic idea of love and consummated dénouement, *Fandry* deliberates on the meaning of adolescent desires in conjunction with their political underpinnings to argue that Dalit citizenship is incongruous with the caste – it remains postponed in the existing frame of the imagined Indian nation. In building this narrative, *Fandry* spectacularly employs the imageries and allegories of the pig and the black sparrow, which I explore below.

National Anthem and Dissonances

National anthem plays a pivotal role in the *performance* of the nation. In his influential book *Imagined Communities*, Benedict Anderson claims that 'no matter how banal the words and mediocre the tunes, there is in this singing an experience of simultaneity. At precisely such moments, people wholly unknown to each other utter the same verses to the same melody. The image [that occurs is]: unisonance.'[12] Even listening to or lip-syncing it effectuates a contemporaneous community, aurally and visually reifying the imagined community, Anderson emphasises. The above subheading engages with Anderson's musical formulation and highlights the discord between the promise and practice of the Indian nation community that *Fandry* unravels by weaving the national anthem into its narrative arc. The Indian national anthem, 'Jana Gana Mana', which spans approximately fifty-two seconds, chants the unity, grandeur and pluralism of India.[13] It is played on days of national prominence, such as Independence Day (15 August) and Republic

Day (26 January), or to mark important (inter)national sports events. The protocol demands that the national anthem be duly respected when played; it is one of the fundamental duties outlined in Article 51(A) of the Constitution. For instance, extolling it as the 'voice of the nation', and that of 'Bharat Mata' – the Mother India – Jawaharlal Nehru, India's first prime minister, urges that 'everyone must stand up when the national anthem is sung', and

> it must be sung in loud and clear voices, with eyes open. You must stand erect like soldiers and sing, not hum it under your breadth.... We must stand erect like soldiers and not shuffle around while it is being sung.[14]

Pandit Nehru's thoughts on the anthem are revealing, not least for the evocative abstraction of the nation community qua Mother India but also for his punctilious instructions regarding the protocols (Nehru also invokes the Hindu temple as the metaphor for the project of building 'modern' India). Manjule ingeniously improvises on the mandated observance to portray the Dalit family's predicaments against the avowed claims of the Indian nation in *Fandry*. The climactic scene, where Jabya and his parents and sisters are about to catch the pig after many vain attempts but stand still to observe the anthem, throws the Dalit family's utter otherness in the so-called imagined community into sharp relief. Far from resulting in a melodious unisonance echoing a shared sense of collective belonging in the contemporaneous nation community that Anderson explains, the observance of the anthem jarringly reveals what it means to be a Dalit in the caste-feudal village in post-Independence India. While projecting the Dalit life onto the screen in all its hues and pinprick of colours has been the hallmark of Manjule's cinematic oeuvre, *Fandry* stands out for its thought-provoking meditation on the meanings and praxis of democracy, fellow feeling and nation community from the Dalit standpoint.

What does the nation as a contemporaneous community mean for Jabya and his family, who are caught in the midst of doing a caste-based occupation? Conversely, what do they mean for the Indian nation? The anthem serves as a symbolic event during which the Dalit family's lived otherness in the village 'proper' in spatial, material and social terms is strikingly visibilised. The Dalit family lives in a dilapidated lean-to at the margins of the village, with no human dwellings in the surroundings. They have no land to cultivate or profitable profession to pursue. Jabya's father serves as an all-purpose village servant without any fixed monetary remuneration. He occasionally receives a paltry sum, subject to the village headman's whims. Jabya's mother, sisters and grandfather weave wicker baskets which Jabya sells in the nearby market. They must stealthily cut and fetch the wild shrubs for making baskets from the bush for fear of being chased away by the villagers; even discarded twigs are denied to them in the village. But Anderson contends that 'regardless of the actual inequality and exploitation that may prevail in each, the nation is always conceived as a deep, horizontal comradeship'.[15] It is the fraternity that ultimately makes a nation possible, insists Anderson.[16] Fraternity or 'the consciousness of kind' which connects people, overriding economic and social divisions, is central to B. R. Ambedkar's idea of the nation too.[17] Ambedkar[18] unequivocally states that the caste system prevents people, particularly the Hindus, from cultivating the consciousness of kind in India. He maintains that Hindu society suffers from an utter absence of consciousness of kind, and the Hindus harbour consciousness of their castes instead.[19] Ambedkar affirms that the 'Hindus cannot be said to form a society or a nation', and Indians, in general, are not a nation but 'only an amorphous mass of people'.[20] In the last Constitutional Assembly speech, which he delivered as the chairman of the Constitution drafting committee for independent India, he scathingly remarked that those who believed in India being a nation were 'cherishing a great delusion'.[21] Ambedkar asks, 'How can people divided into several thousands of castes be a nation?' and characterises castes as essentially anti-national because

> they bring about separation in social life. They are anti-national also because they generate jealousy and antipathy between caste and caste. But we must overcome all these difficulties if we wish to become a nation in reality. For fraternity can be a fact only when there is a nation. Without fraternity, equality and liberty will be no deeper than coats of paint.[22]

In contradistinction to Anderson, who disregards existing inequalities in the imagining of the nation, Ambedkar insists that inequalities borne of the caste system must be contended with so that the nation can be a possibility, and subsequently, fraternity can prevail in Indian society. He believes that liberty and equality are values that are established by the rule of law in the Indian Constitution and can be protected against violations through legal recourse. But the sense of fraternity, or the consciousness of kind, must be wilfully cultivated by the people if liberty, equality and fraternity were to be meaningful in India. Ambedkar instructs:

> The sooner we realize that we are not as yet a nation in the social and psychological sense of the word, the better for us. For then only we shall realize the necessity of becoming a nation and seriously think of ways and means of realizing the goal. The realization of this goal is going to be very difficult.[23]

The scene sequence on the anthem in *Fandry* captures Ambedkar's cautionary note and not only illuminates that India is not a nation yet but also highlights how Dalits continue to be denied membership – symbolic and substantial – in the Indian nation community.[24] Furthermore, Gopal Guru observes that Dalit dignity, self-respect and social justice, which Ambedkar prioritises over self-rule, continue to remain pivotal if the project of building the Indian nation were to be realised in the meaningful sense.[25] The following section will take up Jabya's insistence on dignity and self-respect beyond the frame of the Indian nation community.

The Pig and the Black Sparrow

As mentioned earlier, *Fandry* draws on the pig and the black sparrow as aesthetic, social and political allegories in weaving its narrative to striking effects. In the opening shot of the film, we hear twittering birds before we see any visuals. When Chankya tells Jabya that the black sparrow's feather ash could help Jabya in gaining Shalu's amorous attention, Jabya hunts for the elusive black sparrow in the sprawling rural landscape punctuated with sparse vegetation, until the decisive moment when Jabya's father irritably drags Jabya out of his hiding place in an alley into the plain sight of Shalu to catch pigs. This is the moment when Jabya's attempt to avoid being seen as a casteised 'untouchable' inevitably evaporates, clearing the illusion that he might take on a caste-less identity through the magic charm.

While Jabya does not want to be seen with the pig and runs after the black sparrow, the social allegories of the 'dirty' animal and the high-flying bird in the caste-feudal rural Maharashtra are unmistakable. When Jabya climbs a tree to check if there is a black sparrow nest on it, an old woman warns him: '[T]he bird is like a high caste Brahmin. If you touch it, the other birds will ban it from the flock and kill it with their beaks.'[26] In another instance, when a pig runs into the school playground brushing past Shalu and her friends, they go home to bathe and be 'purified' with cow urine. In the scene sequence, Shalu can be noticed affectionately touching the tethered goats. The treatment that the pig, the goat and the cow (with its urine) receive echoes Ambedkar's description of Indian society as a gradation of castes in which people are placed on an ascending scale of reverence and a descending scale of contempt in the gradational hierarchy.[27] The hierarchical gradation also besets the manner in which animals and birds are looked up to or looked down upon, because 'the upper caste establish continuity between the natural (animal) and the cultural life experience'.[28] On the one hand, the elusive black sparrow is 'compared' with the Brahmins; Jabya's predicaments, on the other, do not only resemble that of the detested pig. The pig stands as the metonymy for Jabya, dissolving any distance that the device of comparison or metaphorical allusion retains. Gopal Guru further remarks that the socially dominant castes reduce some people to the level of animals like pigs with their caste notion of purity–pollution.[29] The 'upper caste' villagers pejoratively address Jabya as *fandry*, which, Manjule explains, is a derogatory word used against outcaste communities.[30]. The metonymic linkage by the villagers otherises Jabya beyond the arc of simultaneity with the village 'proper' and he is reduced to and replaced by the animal.

The idea of simultaneity, fraternity and the consciousness of kind are entangled with the practice of seeing and the potential of desires. In *Ways of Seeing*, John Berger suggests that the way people see things is influenced by what they know or what they believe.[31] Our faculty for perception depends on our specific ways of seeing, Berger claims: '[W]e never look at just one thing; we are always looking at the relation between things and ourselves.'[32] From the beginning, Jabya strives to see himself in a positive light and wants to be seen by Shalu in this light. In a scene, when the village headman tells him to remove a piglet trapped in the drain, Jabya unequivocally refuses to do it, saying, 'I don't do this work.'[33] Informed by caste notions, the village headman assumes that it is fitting for Jabya to clean the drain by removing the piglet – an animal considered to be 'untouchable'.[34] Gopal Guru[35] contends that Dalits never grow up in the eyes of the 'upper caste' people. But in his analysis of *Fandry*, Prashant Ramprasad Ingole[36] insists that the reader or viewer needs an 'experiential eye' to see the anti-caste film. Jabya's lived experience allows him to perceptively understand the caste-reinforcing linkages between the pig and the detested labour that outcastes are forced to do in the caste system. Jabya refuses to conform to the caste dictates because he sees himself with his experiential eye, not as an 'untouchable' bearer of an ascribed identity, but as a defiant dreamer aspiring to live beyond the degrading web of caste.

Jabya's perception of himself in this light is a leitmotif that propels the cinematic narrative in *Fandry*. In another scene we find Jabya selling wicker baskets in the market, but when Shalu is about to walk past him, he promptly covers himself with the basket to hide underneath it. It is because he does not want to be *seen* selling baskets, which is another marker of (out)caste identity.[37] When catching the pigs turns out to be unavoidable for Jabya, he cajoles his parents to fix it on Sunday (that is, a holiday) so that he can avoid being seen at the degrading work.

Jabya's efforts at circumventing caste-based perception are complemented by his concomitant desires to be seen in the positive light of personhood. He craves to clothe himself in jeans and T-shirt, desires to be seen dancing impressively in the village fair and wants to be looked at as a virtuous person. Despite the limiting material existence which harshly constrains what he can afford, he grooms his hair and irons his old clothes with a vessel containing hot charcoals (which exemplifies his ingenuity) and desires to be seen as attractive; I argue elsewhere that bodily grooming for Dalits is a constitutive marker of their self-worth and humanity.[38] While Jabya adoringly glances at Shalu, seeing remains a one-way effort in the film. Aarti Wani[39] points out that Jabya is 'never quite certain if she [Shalu] is aware of him and whether her smiles, and the movements of her eyes and lips relate to him or not'. In the extended sequence where Jabya and his family are helplessly scampering after the pigs in the field, which is used for defecation by the villagers, they are looked on as spectacular objects of entertainment by the villagers. Shalu joins the onlookers in this sadist visual spectacle. She never *sees* Jabya.[40] In other words, the possibility of reciprocal gaze on equal footing remains precluded in *Fandry* because caste blurs Shalu's ways of seeing.

The ever-elusive black sparrow that deceptively offers the mirage of caste-less belonging in romantic love hovers as a political allegory for Jabya's postponed membership in the imagined Indian nation. Hugo Gorringe observes that the claim to nationhood is nothing more than a pretence in the presence of caste in India.[41] But refusing to remain enchanted by the illusory charm of romantic love and the nation, Jabya explores alternative routes and sites of dignified belonging. The *abhanga*s (lyrical poetry) by the fourteenth-century saint-poet Chokhamela offer him the possibility:

> [Sugar] cane is crooked, but its juice isn't crooked,
> Why be fooled by outward appearance?
> The bow is crooked, but the arrow isn't crooked,
> Why be fooled by outward appearance?
> The river is twisting, but its water isn't crooked,
> Why be fooled by outward appearance?
> Chokha is [outcaste], but his feelings aren't ugly,
> Why be fooled by outward appearance?[42]

Figure 1.1   Jabya, black sparrow and the pig

Chokhamela, known for his protest against untouchability and purity–pollution, affirms the virtue immanent in human beings in contrast to caste ascription in the *abhanga*s. When the *abhanga*s are sung and discussed in the class, Jabya finds himself reflected in the lyrical and philosophical depths of the *abhanga*s. He identifies himself with the uplifting message of the anti-caste literary tradition of the *abhanga*s with roots in the medieval Bhakti movement. Chokhamela's *abhanga*s provide the epistemic lens through which Jabya sees himself in life-affirming light, which sets him on the path of political consciousness. In the following and last section I analyse the politics of Jabya's desires.

Democracy and Dénouement

In conjunction with its critical examination of the nation community's claims, *Fandry* focuses on the meanings and practices of democracy in post-Independence India. The symbolic juxtaposition of India's anthem with the Dalit family's urgent concern for bare survival draws our attention to questions of material existence in contradistinction to the enchantment with abstract construction like the Mother India that Nehru – the 'secular-socialist' – invokes. In the scene sequence, when Jabya is buoyantly ruminating on Chokhamela's *abhanga*s in the class, he looks out the window and finds his mother and sisters collecting dry firewood near the school. When Jabya's mother comes near the window, an image of Mother India can be seen on the wall. When the teacher remarks, 'Jabya, your mother is here,'[43] Jabya walks to the entrance door, but by the time he reaches there, his mother had already walked away from the school. As Jabya stands beside the door, the camera lens captures the fading election notice scribbled in white chalk on the door. (Classrooms are temporarily used as voting booths during elections across India.) The extended sequence cast a light at the glaring difference between the bedecked image of Mother India in a flowering sari and the dishevelled Dalit mother labouring for daily survival. It brings to mind the cautionary note that Ambedkar spelled out in his last Constituent Assembly speech:

> On the 26th of January 1950, we are going to enter into a life of contradictions. In politics we will have equality and in social and economic life we will have inequality. In politics we will be recognizing

the principle of one man one vote and one vote one value. In our social and economic life, we shall, by reason of our social and economic structure, continue to deny the principle of one man one value. How long shall we continue to live this life of contradictions?[44]

Jabya and his family continue to live a life of contradictions. The 'accident of birth' traps them in a vicious cycle of material deprivation bound up with the denial of their social equivalence. The scene underscores that the promise of democracy cannot be reduced to episodic elections; it must encompass the practice of social equality and economic justice for the historically disenfranchised Dalits for democracy to be meaningful.

Jabya's insistence on attending school regularly is a determined attempt to break the caste-ascribed fate and refashion a better life through education – a rare resource to which the Dalit family had no access. He is the first person in his family to go to school. Jabya's yearnings are geared towards transgressing the limits imposed by caste. His adolescent desires imply the 'political' belief that he can be a dignified person: he writes letters in beautiful handwriting, dances to his heart's content, wants to dress in jeans and a T-shirt and dreams to be in love and be loved. And the very audacity to harbour these desires makes Jabya a subversive Dalit who stands up against the norms of caste propriety.

In this context, the motif of love acquires a deeply political meaning in *Fandry*. While the film delicately balances Jabya's love for Shalu with the obstacles that lay in his path in pursuit of love, it shatters the well-trodden dénouement of love that Indian cinema has dished out for ages. When Jabya's efforts to hide his outcaste identity from Shalu come to a poignant end while catching the pigs, the hard realisation dawns on him that there is no magical shortcut to becoming a caste-less dignified human being in a caste society. When the 'upper' caste villagers humiliate him with name-calling and taunts, he picks up a stone and hurls it with ferocious force at the tormentors. But the stone joltingly smacks at the camera lens, abruptly blacking out the screen. In this way, the closure of the film does not 'conclude' the narrative, inverting the perspective with which audiences have engaged with love stories in Indian cinema.[45] What follows afterwards remains the subject of speculations. However, the last scene is unequivocal on Jabya's character development: when he is about to unleash the stone, the black sparrow promptly appears in the background, but his aim has shifted to win back his dignity and self-respect through gritty confrontations.

The scene demonstrates his coming of age, not least in a political sense. Gopal Guru argues that 'developing an insight into humiliation is an epistemological act while communicating it to the tormentor is political'.[46] Although structural circumstances force him to catch and carry the pig, Jabya refuses to bear the caste humiliation any longer. His audacious action demarcates him from the pig with which he is conflated in the caste system. And in pursuit of his generic human identity, which constitutes the core of Dalit struggle,[47] Jambhuvant Kachru Mané is prepared to take a risk and throw the stone to confront the inhuman caste system.

Notes

1. Baby Kamble, *The Prisons We Broke*, trans. from Marathi *Jina Amucha* by Maya Pandit (Hyderabad: Orient Blackswan, 2008).
2. Gurram Jashuva, 'The Bat Messenger', in *The Oxford India Anthology of Telugu Dalit Writing*, ed. K. Purushotham, Gita Ramaswamy and Gogu Shyamala (New Delhi: Oxford University Press, 2016), 27–9.
3. Jashuva, 'The Bat Messenger' .
4. Cho. Dharman, *Koogai: The Owl*, trans. from Tamil by Vasantha Surya (New Delhi: Oxford University Press, 2015).
5. A library founded by Tamil Dalit filmmaker Pa. Ranjith in Chennai is also named 'Koogai'.
6. Y. S. Alone, 'Caste Life Narratives, Visual Representation, and Protected Ignorance', *Biography* 40, no. 1 (2017): 140–69.
7. Alone, 'Caste Life Narratives, Visual Representation, and Protected Ignorance'.
8. See https://www.instagram.com/malvikarajart/?utm_medium=copy_link (accessed on 5 December 2023).
9. Mari Selvaraj, for instance, remarkably employs animal allegory in his films. In *Periyerum Perumal* (Selvaraj 2018), a pet dog is portrayed as a 'member' of the Dalit family; a fettered donkey trotting away after being released raises thought-provoking questions about 'merit', competence and liberation in *Karnan* (Selvaraj 2021); pigs and dogs represent innocence, hubris and the abuse of power in *Maamannan* (Selvaraj 2023). A pet dog symbolises Dalit elan in Pa. Ranjith's *Kaala* (2018), while the presence of a pet dog punctuates and alleviates Dalit social alienation in *Geeli Pucchi* (2021) by Neeraj Ghaywan.

10. Nagraj Manjule (dir.), *Fandry* (Navalakha Arts and Holy Basil Productions, 2013).

11. Nagraj Manjule's oeuvre includes *Pistulya* (2009), *Fandry* (2013), *Sairat* (2016) and *Jhund* (2022).

12. Benedict Anderson, *Imagined Communities: Reflections on the Origin and Spread of Nationalism* (London and New York: Verso, 2016).

13. 'Jana Gana Mana' was penned by the Nobel laureate Rabindranath Tagore and was officially ordained as the national anthem of India by the Constituent Assembly on 24 January 1950.

14. H. Y. Sharada Prasad and A. K. Damodaran, *Selected Works of Jawaharlal Nehru*, Vol. 29 (New Delhi: Jawaharlal Nehru Memorial Fund, 2001).

15. Anderson, *Imagined Communities*.

16. Anderson, *Imagined Communities*.

17. Vasant Moon, *Dr. B. R. Ambedkar: Writings and Speeches*, Vol. VIII (New Delhi: Dr. Ambedkar Foundation, 2014).

18. Vasant Moon, *Dr. B. R. Ambedkar: Writings and Speeches*, Vol. I (New Delhi: Dr. Ambedkar Foundation, 2014).

19. Moon, *Dr. B. R. Ambedkar*, Vol. I.

20. Moon, *Dr. B. R. Ambedkar*, Vol. I .

21. Vasant Moon, *Dr. B. R. Ambedkar: Writings and Speeches*, Vol. XIII (New Delhi: Dr. Ambedkar Foundation, 2014).

22. Moon, *Dr. B. R. Ambedkar*, Vol. XIII.

23. Moon, *Dr. B. R. Ambedkar*, Vol. XIII.

24. I use 'Dalit' and 'outcaste' in the chapter depending on the context. While I want to underline agency and self-naming in 'Dalit', 'outcaste' refers to the Brahminical scriptural division whereby the group of people are placed 'outside' (that is, *antyaja*, *panchama*) the fourfold caste system.

25. Gopal Guru, 'Experience, Space, and Justice', in *The Cracked Mirror: An Indian Debate on Experience and Theory*, by Gopal Guru and Sundar Sarukkai (New Delhi: Oxford University Press, 2012), 71–106.

26. Manjule, *Fandry*.

27. Vasant Moon, *Dr. B. R. Ambedkar: Writings and Speeches*, Vol. II (New Delhi: Dr. Ambedkar Foundation, 2014).

28. Gopal Guru, 'Rejection of Rejection: Foregrounding Self-Respect', in *Humiliation: Claims and Context*, ed. Gopal Guru (New Delhi: Oxford University Press, 2009), 209–25.

29. Guru, 'Rejection of Rejection'.

30. Shalmali Jadhav, 'The Pig, the Black Sparrow and the Sheep: Human-Animal Entanglements in Fandry and Khwada', in *The Routledge Companion to Caste and Cinema in India,* ed. Joshil K. Abraham and Judith Misrahi-Barak (New York: Routledge, 2022), 249–59.

31. John Berger, *Ways of Seeing* (London: Penguin, 1972).

32. Berger, *Ways of Seeing.*

33. Manjule, *Fandry.*

34. Aarti Wani, 'Love in the Time of Pigs', *Economic and Political Weekly* 49, no. 12 (2014): 73–4.

35. Guru, 'Rejection of Rejection'.

36. Prashant Ramprasad Ingole, 'Inter (Caste) Love Stories: Experiential Eye (I) in *Fandry* and *Sairat*', *Economic and Political Weekly* 57, no. 9 (2022): 1–8.

37. For instance, Urmila Pawar dwells on basket-weaving work and Dalits in her memoirs *The Weave of My Life* (trans. from Marathi by Maya Pandit [Kolkata: Stree, 2009]).

38. Purnachandra Naik, 'Roars of Dalit Audacity', *Economic and Political Weekly* 56, no. 45–6 (2021): 72–3.

39. Wani, 'Love in the Time of Pigs'.

40. Wani, 'Love in the Time of Pigs'.

41. Hugo Gorringe, 'The Caste of the Nation: Untouchability and Citizenship in South India', *Contributions to Indian Sociology* 42, no. 1 (2008): 123–49.

42. Eleanor Zelliot, *From Untouchable to Dalit: Essays on the Ambedkar Movement* (New Delhi: Manohar, 2001).

43. Manjule, *Fandry.*

44. Moon, *Dr. B. R. Ambedkar*, Vol. XIII.

45. Hrishikesh Ingle, '*Fandry* and *Sairat*: Regional Cinema and Marginality', *Economic and Political Weekly* 53, no. 45 (2018): 46–53.

46. Guru, 'Rejection of Rejection'.

47. Guru, 'Rejection of Rejection'.

2

Speaking of Pain

Portrayal of Human–Animal Relations in Tamil Cinema

R. Samuel Gnanaraj

Introduction

… films were used as a source of information to understand society.[1]

Cinema is a democratic art that fundamentally expresses real-life experiences regardless of any differences. It has an indispensable role in presenting the heritage, culture and ethnicity of the people. Known as Kollywood, the Tamil film industry focuses primarily on the livelihoods of the Tamils, their culture and their social and political life. Films provide a platform to disseminate, express and communicate culture-based themes, political ideas and social realities, which are essential for building a better life for the people. Activists, politicians and ideologues use film as a medium of propaganda to spread their thoughts and ideologies and establish diverse political cultures. Since the 1950s, Tamil cinema has been dynamic in promoting the Dravidian movement and its ideas, aiming to promote self-respect, social justice, self-esteem and dignity among the indigenous Tamils. Vetrimaaran, a Tamil filmmaker, claims that 'Tamil cinema put forward the principles of Dravidian politics, and the new films lend strength to the ideals of Dravidian politics. Social realities and political circumstances provide themes to such movies'.[2] S. Theodore Baskaran, a Tamil film historian and wildlife conservationist, asserts the history of Tamil cinema along the same lines when he states that 'over the seventy-nine years of its existence, Tamil cinema has grown to become the most domineering influence in the cultural and political life in Tamil Nadu'.[3]

In this chapter, I analyse two films, Mari Selvaraj's *Pariyerum Perumal*[4] and Vetrimaaran's *Asuran*,[5] to examine notions of struggle, pain and suffering among the oppressed individuals and communities in Tamil society. Both these films expose their plight by showing the protagonists with their pet animal, a dog. The keeping of animals – that is, dogs – is a central part of both the films. Both can be seen as companion films associated with each other in various ways, including themes, storylines and narratives. They highlight the lives and livelihoods of the downtrodden people and the struggles confronted by them for decades. They allow us to identify the conditions of the deteriorating state of the marginalised people through the medium of films.

The chapter discusses the themes of social pain and political suffering, specifically delving into concerns like social injustice and political turmoil, which are deeply interwoven. The objectives of the chapter include understanding the portrayal of caste and its depiction in Tamil films, seeking to understand the relations between humans and animals and aiming to comprehend the social order through Tamil cinema. More specifically, the chapter aims to examine the prevailing discrimination against Dalits, who are treated as subhuman and placed at par with non-human animals – in this case dogs – a reality starkly captured by the films. The chapter is divided into three sections. The first section analyses the role of caste in Tamil films, emphasising pain and suffering and focusing on the human–animal relations. The second section concentrates on the sociological analysis of the presence of dogs, while the third section explores the interconnected nature of caste and human–animal relations.

Caste and Tamil Films

Popular films are very often fictional accounts where the audience is introduced to convenient narratives depicting a hero figure in a dominant role. The Tamil film industry also produces films for commercial and entertainment purposes, which tend to glorify these hero figures as demigods. Tamil fans are known to worship their film stars by installing giant cut-outs and offering milk just like at a place of worship, thus confirming their almost divine status. But Tamil films are also known to carry strong social and political messages of social justice. Here, fiction overlaps with the reality of socio-political issues. Many former chief ministers of Tamil

Nadu have played significant roles in the film industry in various capacities. C. N. Annadurai, with films like *Nalla Thambi* (Good Brother) in 1948 and *Velaikari* (Maid Servant) in 1949, M. G. Ramachandran's *Adimai Penn* (Slave Woman) in 1969, J. Jayalalithaa's *Vennira Aadai* (White Dress) in 1965 and M. Karunanidhi's *Parasakthi* (The Goddess) in 1952 are films that had significant social impact. These actors-turned-politicians used cinema as a medium to propagate their ideologies and share their concerns about social justice and discrimination. Following this route, the current crop of filmmakers also propagate political opinions and social messages of welfarism through their film scripts, dialogues, characterisation, landscapes and songs.

While there have been several films promoting social justice in the history of the Tamil film industry, a few have also showcased the dominance of the caste-based order, celebrating upper-caste figures who treat some humans as 'others'. As evident from the titles of films like *Chinna Gounder* (Junior Gounder) in 1992, *Thevarmagan* (Son of Thevar) in 1992, *Naatamai* (Village Chief) in 1994 and *Mappilai Gounder* (Gounder the Groom) in 1997, these films boastfully highlight the dominance of the upper caste and proudly carry in their titles their caste names such as Gounder and Thevar that glorify their identities. In many of these films, the central characters are upper castes who are shown treating the other characters, especially those from underprivileged castes, as subhuman. Such movies assert upper-caste pride through narratives of their social ascendance, violence and dominance. The oppressed are often dehumanised with deprecating language and frequently characterised as deviants. Antony Susairaj[6] argues,

> The representation of lower castes in films, especially in the way that they are dressed and the clothing that they wear is significant with regard to their identification in the social order. Dressing well or wearing white-coloured clothes has always been associated with the dominant caste. Indeed, until relatively recently, Dalits were prevented from wearing ironed shirts and sporting styled moustaches, and none of the characters portraying Dalits on screen are shown with twirled moustaches. In the majority of the movie scripts, they are seen as subservient, and Dalit men are denied a masculine identity in Tamil movies. The films have created an image that people from the slums belong to lower castes and are shown in a negative light, such as thieves, murderers, and the subject of most jokes.[7]

Similarly, Udhav Naig examines how Tamil cinema not only is biased towards the dominant caste but also justifies caste-based narratives. He writes,

> In the 1990s and 2000s, Tamil cinema was churning out movies that were centred around a dominant caste – a male with immense social power within the village. Films such as *Ejamaan, Nattamai, Chinna Gounder, Thevar Magan* and others justified the caste-Hindu male's glory and power derived from the remnants of the feudal system and the narratives would typically call the audience to imagine the past in the present. These films have had a deep social and political impact, particularly in the southern and western districts of Tamil Nadu, where each of the socially and politically dominant castes had their own on-screen heroes.[8]

In these films, the lives of ordinary people are often referred to as 'impure', 'polluted', 'untouchable' and 'unseeable'. The evidence of discrimination is readily discerned from the dialogue, especially when it is a conversation between upper-caste and lower-caste groups. The discriminatory mindset arising from the language creates a deepening division between the two groups. Exclusionary dialogue characterising people into 'us' and 'them' and 'ours' and 'theirs' is evident in these films. In many of them, only high-caste men are shown to be exclusively exercising social privileges. Films made in the last decade, however, have brought major changes in challenging the existing caste-based narratives. According to Antony Susairaj,

> The new wave films have dared to show the real situation of the misery of the Dalits on the screen and have given voice towards the liberty and equality of the Dalits. The new wave films have not only made the Dalits aware of the discrimination against them but also have made the higher castes aware that the suppression of the Dalits is inhumane. The portrayal of discrimination against Dalits in a realistic way in recent movies has brought a paradigm shift in the mindset of people of all castes from suppression of Dalits to liberation of Dalits.[9]

While the lives of the marginalised have remained unvalued for ages, of late, Tamil cinema has changed the orientation of films, often casting protagonists from the countryside in central roles, bringing more diversity and the voices of the marginalised castes into the mainstream. Films featuring anti-caste themes underpinned by an ideology of social justice have superseded films from the recent past that glorified dominant social groups and upper-caste consciousness. Inspired by the progressive ideology and movement of E. V. R. Periyar and Dr B. R. Ambedkar, in the last decade, films like *Madras* (2014), *Kabali* (2016), *Kaala* (2018), *Pariyerum Perumal* (2018), *Asuran* (2019), *Jai Bhim* (2021), *Karnan* (2021) and *Maamannan* (2023) serve as response and counter-narrative to the films that glorified the caste pride and honour of the upper castes in Tamil Nadu.

The stories of *Pariyerum Perumal* and *Asuran* orbit around the Tirunelveli and Thoothukudi districts, which are situated in the southern part of Tamil Nadu. In many Tamil films, these districts are shown as sites of anarchy, murders and conspiracies. Anand Pandian, in his article 'Cinema in the Countryside', claims, 'Caste clashes are an undeniable feature of public life in the southern Tamil countryside today, and they have been tackled quite successfully in numerous Tamil films.'[10] Films, therefore, became a powerful medium to sensitise people in Tamil Nadu. And an important part of this new wave of anti-caste films is the presence of animals, through which they etch powerful portrayals of the pain and struggles of the marginalised people.

The Portrayal of Pain within Human–Animal Relations

According to Seth Abrutyn, 'social pain is ubiquitous, it varies in important ways based on structural and cultural factors unevenly distributed in a community or society'.[11] The films *Pariyerum Perumal* and *Asuran* depict the struggle, pain and trauma of individuals and communities who belong to the oppressed castes. As Folkmarson[12] says, pain is the source of sorrow, suffering, hopelessness and frustration. In the absence of the articulation of pain that is inflicted, the animals present in their lives become metaphors to reflect the experiences of the Dalits.

These films also successfully highlight the protagonists' resistance against the social stigma imposed on them by the so-called higher castes. Such films not only show the pain but also the social lives, livelihoods, songs, food and culture of the oppressed, thus amounting to a paradigm shift in the history of Tamil cinema.

Pariyan, the protagonist in *Pariyerum Perumal*, is shown as sharing a strong emotional connection with his pet dog, named 'Karuppi' (a black female dog), while *Asuran* features the family of Sivasamy, who are struggling to protect their son, an endeavour in which their dog 'Sevala's' (Brown-shaded dog) role becomes central. Both films employ the imagery of animals to capture the pain of the lower-caste community. In both films, the death of a dog forms the turning point in the story. Karuppi is tied to a railway track and is killed by the approaching train, whereas Sevala is electrocuted by a fence set up by high-caste men. The two incidents can be categorised as murders, as it is the human perpetrators' actions that lead to the death of the dogs.

Pariyan and Sivasamy are shown as experiencing profound social and emotional pain when their dogs were killed. These transformative events of sorrow and hopelessness lead them to a deeper comprehension of the cruelty arising from rigid societal boundaries. The scenes where the dogs are killed are portrayed in a manner comparable to a grievous act of human loss. Their possessions, their rights, are taken by the oppressors, and the adversities they face are particularly agonising. The intense distress he feels is evident in Pariyan's grief-stricken words at the loss of Karuppi. He mourns, 'In the wilderness without you, how will I find my way? I told you a million times, why didn't you listen? Who called you that you went away? How many times have I told you, all humans are not the same. They pamper and kill. They choke you to death, they break your leg.'[13] The filmmakers metaphorically portray the protagonists' struggle and their miserable lives through the lives of their companion animals. In *Asuran,* the dog's death becomes a central point of pain for the protagonist and his family. At one point in the narrative, a member of Sivasamy's family says, 'Avanuku nai pochenu kavalai, enaku naaioda poichu nu aaruthalairuku' (He is upset about losing the dog, but I'm relieved that we only lost the dog). While Sivasamy's family is mourning, the upper caste show little remorse for their actions. One of them even says, 'Nobody can question us for electrifying the fence…. Who cares if your dog dies or your people die…?'[14]

Pariyan and Sivasamy experience pain through the destroyed bodies of their pet dogs. The bodies of the animals become a site for the upper caste to punish the lower caste, thereby likening the lower caste to animals. Animals become the subject for inflicting cruelty and violence. The filmmaker raises questions about existing inequalities by placing the lives of low-caste people alongside that of their dogs. In one of the scenes, Pariyan is invited by Jothi, a classmate, to a wedding function in her family, where he is humiliated by the upper-caste men. Refusing to treat him as even human, they beat him and urinate on his face, saying, 'Drink it, drink it, you came to *my* house.'

Pramod Nayar, in his book *Human Rights and Literature*, refers to Merleau-Ponty's argument, 'I can almost experience something of the other's embodiment … I can experience the movements of their body in the same way that I experience the movements of my own. More than this, I can feel their effervescence and fatigue.'[15] The film shows how such physical pain has become intrinsic to Dalit life. A kind of unerasable anguish that is felt by Pariyan is visualised with the imagery of a beaten-up dog.

A Sociological Analysis of Dogs

Domesticated dogs are social animals that live with human beings. There are working dogs, companion dogs, therapy dogs and hounds. In Tamil Nadu, there are unique indigenous breeds, namely 'Chippiparai', 'Rajapalayam' and 'Kombai', which can be found especially in Madurai, Tirunelveli, Thoothukudi and Virudhunagar districts.[16] These indigenous breeds are working dogs trained to guard farms and houses. The breeds are identified in the films by the filmmakers to show the bond between the protagonists and their dogs. By depicting the lives of the dogs, the social problems of Dalits can be visualised in societal spaces, which is evident in both the films. Both movies give prominence to the dog, a unique aesthetic intervention that metaphorically addresses the sensitive issue of caste atrocities prevalent in Tamil society. These are radical films that give space to what is otherwise 'absent' or 'invisible' in Tamil society and cinema by bringing them to the forefront, using animals, especially dogs, as their medium. To study the caste-based hierarchy or identify the issues related to caste is to expose the debased humanity of the caste order and, hopefully, transform it into a moral humankind. Films therefore serve as a powerful medium to disseminate social concerns that are otherwise hidden or disregarded by mainstream society.

The relationship between human beings and dogs portrayed in the films brings out a special message that emblematically captures the various unwritten social doctrines followed by different groups of people in Tamil Nadu. While some claim that 'dogs are faithful animals' and 'man's best friend', elsewhere dogs are considered 'dirty' and 'lowly' animals. Lisa Warden, a scholar of animal advocacy, in her article 'Jati Kutta: The Street dog, the Servant and Me', writes that the term 'pariah dog' has been used for over a century to refer to indigenous dogs. The use of the word 'pariah' is problematic as it derives from 'Paraiyar' – a Tamil word for landless agrarian slaves in south India who lived under a brutally oppressive feudal system.[17] Adding to this, Theodore Baskaran writes, 'Our canine culture was nurtured by farmers, hunters and tribal families. These are communities we now describe as Scheduled Castes or Scheduled Tribes. Many of the dog breeds were named after these communities.'[18] Likewise, the English word 'pariah' implies something dirty and lowly and therefore needs to be kept out, and the term is used as a slur. It has its roots in the Tamil word 'Paraiyar', which refers to a specific Dalit community in Tamil Nadu. Later, the word came to be associated with dogs, as in 'pariah dogs', which means free-ranging dogs or semi-feral dogs.

Similarly, in the hierarchical caste system, where some humans are considered superior and some inferior, in many cases, some animals, like dogs and pigs, are also seen as inferior and unclean animals. *Pariyerum Perumal* powerfully portrays the struggle of the marginalised community through the protagonist's strong bond with his pet dog Karuppi. The film *Asuran*[19] highlights a marginalised family struggling to protect themselves from upper-caste men, where the dog is shown as a vulnerable animal. The death of their dog is not a natural incident; rather, it is intentional. Electrified fences are erected to keep the lower-caste people away, as much as animals. Sevala, which is trained as a watchdog, fulfils its role when it attempts to protect the family's farmland from wild pigs, but gets stuck in the electrified fence and dies. Both films address the tension between the castes, and the figure of the dog is used to show the pain of the lower-caste community. In the films, one finds expressions of pride and valour about caste, which are a privilege available exclusively to the upper caste. Karuppi and Sevala are their innocent victims, who represent the oppressed people. The films are powerful and leave a mark in the long struggle against caste oppression in Tamil Nadu and act as a strong reminder of the effects of persistent caste-based violence on both Dalits and their animals. To mention one recent incident, in Virudhunagar district of Tamil Nadu, there was a report of a Dalit's dog biting an upper-caste Hindu man's dog. After learning about the dog owner's caste, the Hindu men allegedly killed the dog that belonged to the Dalit.[20]

Intersections of Caste and Human–Animal Relations

Pariyan hails from Puliyankulam, a settlement of low-caste families. The opening scenes of the film illustrate the hardships and trials that define

his life, which in turn is a reflection of the lives of his entire village of
outcastes. When Pariyan boards the bus, an old man offers him a place to
sit. Immediately after hearing that Pariyan is from Puliyankulam, the old
man leaves the seat, preferring to stand for the rest of the journey than sit
next to a low-caste man. This shows the discriminatory attitude of the elderly
man towards Pariyan and his community. At the beginning of the film, a
significant note is displayed, which unambiguously states, 'Caste and religion
are against humanity.'

Even though the dog Karuppi dies early in the film, till the end, her
imagery appears whenever Pariyan faces oppression from high-caste people.
Suraj Yengde, in his article 'Relying on the Constitution Is Not Enough',
comments:

> As much as Dalits feel empowered in a constitutionally mandated
> democratic republic, any hope of their issues being redressed withers
> away when reality comes knocking. After every gruesome atrocity or
> everyday humiliation they undergo at the workplace or in their shared
> housing, the promise of constitutionalism shatters into pieces. Dalits
> are often accorded second-class citizenship.[21]

In many scenes, Karuppi shows herself as a metaphorical image which
symbolises the oppressed humans and their innocence. Though she dies
early in the film, she continues to be present as a source of emotional support
and strength to those who are discriminated against and victimised. As the
audience get a close look at the inequality rooted in the societal structures
through the protagonist's life and struggles, they quickly realise that in the
eyes of the high-caste men, Pariyan is subhuman, being equivalent to the
status of a dog. His hopes for a dignified life are blocked by the biases and
prejudice that he encounters at every step. In the film, an old man is hired
by the upper castes to kill young men and women who transgress caste
norms when they fall in love outside their castes. The filmmaker shows the
old man as a 'watchdog', who is always on alert to guard the caste pride of
upper castes and to torture or even exterminate those who dare to disregard
caste boundaries or challenge the injustices of the caste order. In the film, the
old man is shown to be committing acts of violence against the oppressed
on three different occasions: when he forcibly pushes a young man from a
moving bus, when he kills a girl by choking her and then hangs her body to

destroy the evidence, and when he kills a schoolboy by drowning him in a pond. All these actions can be considered to be acts of honour killing. On every such occasion, the old man exclaims, 'I murder for the honour of our women; it is my offering to god!' His words illustrate the fact that protecting the honour of women and caste pride has always been a common pretext to attack or kill Dalits and other backward castes who dare to challenge the caste order.

Therefore, the upper-caste treatment of Dalits as the equivalent of dogs in both films highlights the nature of inequality and discrimination against marginalised peoples. Pariyan, a young man, is not aware of the social structure and the reality of the world around him; at the same time,

Figure 2.1   Pariyan and Karuppi

Pariyan's classmate Sankaralingam is aware that Pariyan is from the low-caste settlement of Puliyankulam. Even Sivasamy is unaware of the discrimination existing around him and believes that his high-caste landlord treats him as an equal. The film *Asuran* recounts the 'Kilvenmani massacre' that happened decades ago, where forty-four Dalits were murdered and the houses of the Dalits burned by the men of the landlords. The provocation was that the Dalit villagers dared to ask for the land given to them by the British government as part of a welfare scheme for depressed communities. The incident was an organised crime, and later, it turned out that the police had tried to cover it up. *Asuran* is a reminder of the extreme nature of the existing forms of oppression and injustice against Dalits. Despite the similarity in metaphors and imagery, both films follow distinctive narrative styles as they tell us about the pain, sorrow and trauma embedded in caste society as well as in human–animal relations.

Concluding Remarks

The films intricately intertwine the themes of pain and the human–animal relations, emphasising the mistreatment of Dalits and their dogs. The portrayals reveal the dehumanising nature of discrimination which profoundly impacts the social structure. The protagonists Pariyan and Sivasamy from the films *Pariyerum Perumal* and *Asuran* are both shown as being discriminated against by the landlords, who see them as dogs, ill-treating them and subjecting them to unbearable pain. The vehemence and contempt of the oppressed towards the Dalits are sharply displayed in both films. The existence of untouchability and discrimination is institutionalised by the upper castes, and these oppressive structures are closely examined in the films through the lives of low-caste communities and through their relations with non-human animals. Both films reveal the prevailing casteism in Tamil society, and highlight the agony of its victims through the emotional connection they are shown to be sharing with their dogs. To conclude, films always revisit the past. In the hope of change, one must look to learn and relearn from the past to establish fairness in society. The lived experiences of the marginalised are deeply connected with non-human animals, who provide them with a sense of dignity that their fellow humans in society deprive them of.

Notes

1. Selvaraj Velayutham (ed.), *Tamil Cinema: The Cultural Politics of India's Other Film Industry* (London and New York: Routledge, 2008).
2. TNN, 'New Tamil Films Are Political Tools for Social Transformation', *Times of India*, 22 March 2022, https://timesofindia.indiatimes.com/city/thiruvananthapuram/new-tamil-films-are-political-tools-for-social-transformation/articleshow/90385021.cms, accessed 7 September 2022.
3. S. Theodore Baskaran, *The Eye of the Serpent: An Introduction to Tamil Cinema* (Madras: East-West Books, 1996).
4. Mari Selvaraj (dir.), *Pariyerum Perumal* [Film] (Neelam Productions, 2018).
5. Vetrimaaran (dir.), *Asuran* [Film] (V Creations, 2019).
6. Antony Susairaj, 'The Paradigm Shifts in the Portrayal of Caste in Tamil Cinema and Its Impact on the Tamil Society', *Journal of the Nanzan Academic Society Humanities and Natural Sciences* 20 (June 2020): 121–38.
7. Susairaj, 'The Paradigm Shifts in the Portrayal of Caste in Tamil Cinema and Its Impact on the Tamil Society'.
8. Udhav Naig, 'Pa. Ranjith: The Game Changer of Tamil Cinema', *The Hindu*, 1 September 2022, https://www.thehindu.com/entertainment/movies/pa-ranjith-the-game-changer-of-tamil-cinema/article65836578.ece, accessed 23 October 2022.
9. Susairaj, 'The Paradigm Shifts in the Portrayal of Caste in Tamil Cinema and Its Impact on the Tamil Society'.
10. Anand Pandian, 'Cinema in the Countryside: Popular Tamil Film and the Remaking of Rural Life', in *Tamil Cinema: The Cultural Politics of India's Other Film Industry*, ed. Selvaray Velayutham (Abingdon: Routledge, 2008), 124–38, 124.
11. Seth Abrutyn, 'The Roots of Social Trauma: Collective, Cultural Pain and Its Consequences', *Society and Mental Health* (November 2023), DOI:10.1177/21568693231213088.
12. Lisa Folkmarson Kall (ed.), *Dimensions of Pain: Humanities and Social Science Perspectives* (London and New York: Routledge, 2012).
13. Selvaraj, *Pariyerum Perumal*.
14. Vetrimaaran, *Asuran*.
15. Pramod K. Nayar, *Human Rights and Literature: Writing Rights* (Basingstoke: Springer, 2016).
16. S. Theodore Baskaran, *The Book of Indian Dogs* (Aleph Book Company, 2017).

17. Lisa Warden, 'Jati Kutta: The Street Dog, the Servant, and Me', *Between the Species: A Journal for the Study of Philosophy and Animals* 25, no. 1 (2022), 125–67.

18. Express News Service, 'Indian Dog Breeds Named After SC/ST Communities: Writer', *The New Indian Express*, 13 May 2017, https://www.newindianexpress.com/cities/chennai/2017/may/13/indian-dog-breeds-named-after-scst-communities-writer-1604319.html, accessed 5 September 2022.

19. Vetrimaaran, *Asuran*.

20. Express News Service, 'Virudhunagar Dog-Biting Dog Leaves Shadow on Nasty Caste Politics', *The New Indian Express*, 25 August 2021, https://www.newindianexpress.com/states/tamil-nadu/2021/Aug/25/virudhunagar-dog-biting-dog-leaves-shadow-on-nasty-caste-politics-2349308.html, accessed 26 January 2022.

21. Suraj Yengde, 'Relying on the Constitution Is Not Enough', *The Hindu*, 14 July 2019, https://www.thehindu.com/opinion/op-ed/relying-on-the-constitution-is-not-enough/article28429664.ece, accessed 9 September 2022.

3

Cast(e)ing Animals in Cinema

Exploring Human–Animal Relations through *Fandry* and *Pariyerum Perumal*

Akshay Sawant

Bangladeshi migrants are like termites

— Amit Shah, Home Minister of India, addressing a rally in
Kota, Rajasthan, 22 September 2018

There are only five animals with which I am deeply familiar. Of them,
dogs and cats are meant for poetry. It is forbidden to write about cows or
pigs. That leaves only goats and sheep. Goats are problem-free, harmless
and, above all, energetic.

— Perumal Murugan, *Poonachi, or The Story of a Black Goat* (2018)

What Do Animals Have to Do with Caste?

In Indian social geographical context, animals have been both the means
and the effects of the production and reproduction of caste. Society may be
seen as a multispecies ecosystem where animals hold a significant position in
everyday life, rituals and human life events. They appear in people's lives in
multiple ways: social, economic or political. The association between humans
and animals may result in doubly reinforcing oppressions or privileges
through association with each other.[1] While human–animal relations
remain under-theorised in caste studies and caste remains the least discussed
in animal studies, they are instrumentalised to maintain the typologies of
caste.[2] To consider broadly, in a caste society like ours, the cow becomes holy
and a subject of protection, whereas the pig is considered polluting; at times,

its sight is also deemed filthy and avoidable. These two animals, in particular, denote the contradictions between pure and impure. Notably, in the Hindu imagination, animals have an assigned caste identity. They are considered to inherently possess social qualities associated with their particular caste assignation.[3] Doniger contends that the Hindu mythological texts use horse, dog and cow as 'symbols of power, pollution and purity' respectively, wherein the Kshatriyas or rulers are associated with horses, lower castes with dogs and Brahmins with cows.[4] At the same time, Perumal Murugan laments, quoted at the beginning of the chapter, that writing about certain animals becomes a 'forbidden' act.[5] In such a condition, it is vital to engage with human and animal relationships to understand their connectedness and the complex problem of caste.

This chapter is a step towards analysing caste as an order that affects human–animal relatedness and shapes them differently according to the status of humans and animals. Paying attention to these relationships helps us understand the continuity of caste practices even under changing political-economic conditions. Analysing human–animal relatedness can also help uncover the masked ideological premises of caste practice. Being attentive to human–animal relatedness can reveal hidden dimensions of hierarchy and power in intra-human relations.

Given these premises, I locate this chapter in human–animal studies scholarship, where the focus is on the symbolic meaning of animals that are used in the discourse about humans, their caste, class, gender, nationality and emotions. In other words, this work does not concern animals and their material reality. However, the chapter focuses on the meaning that humans make out of them. Various scholars have argued for the limits of such an approach in animal studies and rightly ask us to focus on animals in their fullness.[6] Notwithstanding the benefits of such a framework, the chapter contends that studying the symbolic meanings of animals in relationships can yield a variety of conceptual and epistemological challenges in understanding caste.

In what follows, the chapter analyses two films[7] of recent times that speak to the centrality of the human–animal relationship considering typologies of caste. The first is a Marathi film, *Fandry* (2013), directed by Nagraj Manjule.[8] The story of *Fandry* is interwoven with two animals: one, a black sparrow that is impossible to touch, the other, *fandry* (Marathi word for pig), whose touch is impossible to avoid for the Dalits[9] portrayed in the film. The second is a Tamil film, *Pariyerum Perumal* (2018), directed by Mari Selvaraj.[10] The film narrates the story of the oppressed-caste youth Pariyan, hailing from Puliyankulam village near Tirunelveli, and his companion dog Karuppi (Tamil word for black). The dog gets killed by some oppressor-caste members early in the film, yet remains as a companion to Pariyan in his struggle against caste-based violence. In doing so, the chapter probes the concepts of untouchability, disgust and forced labour, which is also manifested in the film *Fandry* through animals such as sparrows and pigs, and contrasts that with the concept of fraternity.

The recent success of Nagraj Manjule and Mari Selvaraj – two prominent filmmakers, the former in Marathi and Hindi[11] and the latter in Tamil cinema – and their filming experiments enable a debate on caste and demand the audiences rethink their caste practices. Manjule's films focus on the lives of Dalits in rural Maharashtra and urban slums. At the same time, Selvaraj focuses on assertion among Dalits in Tamil Nadu. Both filmmakers highlight the nuances of everyday life, the everyday culture of Dalits and the discrimination they face at the hands of upper castes. Their films have become testimonies to the mainstreaming of marginal everyday experiences.[12]

The discourse on caste and cinema in India has recently attracted due academic attention, resulting in diverse research from various perspectives. While some studies have focused on marginal narratives and subjectivities as forms of resistance which brings into question the various tropes used in mainstream cinema,[13] others focus on the issue of Dalit representation.[14] They also question the absence and presence of Dalit filmmakers themselves.[15] These films are seen as cinematic interventions to disturb the 'unconscious of caste' and produce an anti-caste aesthetic through emotive and expressive archives.[16] Therefore, this scholarship helps us understand the politics of the art form and its social and cultural significance. However, the question of caste in cinema – or in other literary forms – has been the least discussed through the lens of human–animal relations.[17]

(Im)possibility of (Un)touch: Tales of Sparrow and Pig

Set in Akolner village in Maharashtra, *Fandry* is the life story of school-going Kaikadi[18] boy Jambuvant's (Jabya, played by Somnath Awaghade) impossible crush on Shalu (played by Rajeshwari Kharat), an upper-caste girl. The film opens with a sequence of Jabya, with a catapult in hand, set in a rural landscape, taking unsuccessful shots at a *kali chimani* (black sparrow). Later, the film confirms that the desire to overcome caste boundaries and have a romantic relationship with Shalu is manifested through the black sparrow. Time and again, we see Jabya, accompanied by his friend Pirya (played by Suraj Pawar), roaming around in the fields to pursue a black sparrow. Manjule uses the elusive nature of the sparrow to suggest Jabya's difficulty in getting hold of Shalu. According to a local myth, an upper-caste girl could be attracted by sprinkling the ashes of a black sparrow on her. In this way, Jabya's life is intimately connected with the sparrow. Throughout the story Manjule has interwoven the real and the illusionary: Jabya's imposiblity of attracting an upper caste girl and catching a black sparrow. Both the narratives are interwoven together that is expressive and striking.

Black colour has been used throughout the film to showcase the impact of Brahminical notions. Jabya is anxious about being dark-skinned and routinely applies face powder in an attempt to lighten his complexion. In several situations, upper-caste people from the village demean him, terming him a *kaalya* (blackie). However, the black colour of the sparrow is associated with a desire to transgress the caste boundaries.

Jabya and Pirya anxiously search for the black sparrow every day. During their search, once they climb a tree to check if a nest located on it is of a black sparrow or a white one. An old lady (played by Jyoti Subhash) laments, 'Get down. It does not matter if the sparrow is black or white. Sparrow is Brahmin, and if anyone touches her, others do not take her into their folk.' In order to preserve the caste boundaries, the Brahminical principles make it impossible for Dalits to transgress their own caste and enter into a higher caste and make re-entry impossible for those higher castes who once cross the (caste) boundary. Manjule rightly portrays Brahminhood as a no-entry zone for the lower castes. Anything that breaks the caste codes – here portrayed as touch by others – will lead to one being ousted. The notion of the polluting touch and the ostracism by the community are used to establish an analogy between the Brahmins and the sparrow. It reminds us of B. R. Ambedkar's remark, made in *Annihilation of Caste*, where he contends that caste 'embodies the arrogance and selfishness of a perverse section of the Hindus who were superior enough in social status to set it in fashion, and who had the authority to force it on their inferiors'.[19]

Manjule, in a remarkable juxtaposition, places this impossibility of touch with the impossibility of untouch. He uses the pig, which is considered filthy, disgusting and radically polluting in the Brahminical points of view as well as in that of orthodox Muslims. Pigs are considered 'untouchable', and even an accidental touch of a pig needs to be purified with a bath. In one scene, we find Jabya, who, in his continuous gazing, is about to make the first move on Shalu with the excuse of borrowing a notebook. A pig runs wildly and brushes against a girl, one of Shalu's friends, generating a burst of collective laughter. Shalu immediately alerts her friend not to touch her, as the pig has come into contact with her. The notion of untouchability of the pig is transferred to the 'touchable' girl. This is reason enough for Shalu to get a half-day holiday from school. While explaining it to the teachers, Shalu finds it hard to control her amusement, and so do her teachers.

Later, Shalu takes the girl home for a cleansing bath. The girl's mother asks her to take a bath and sprinkles cow urine (considered pure by Brahmins) on her. As per the Brahminical codes, the impurity caused by the touch of an impure pig has been purified by the 'holy' and 'pure' cow's urine.

The impossibility of untouch is figured again in the sequence of events in the film. For example, Patil[20] (played by Suresh Vishwakarma) asks Jabya to free a piglet trapped in a water tank. That night, he has a terrifying nightmare of drowning in the well. In the nightmare, finding himself trapped in a deep well full of darkness and impossible to climb out of, his vision gets blurred, and the world around him is shaky and unstable. The dream of a touchable sparrow he had days back becomes a nightmare of the untouchable pig. At that very moment, two conversations ring continuously in his head: Shalu screaming, 'Don't touch her! A pig touched her!', and Patil asking him to release the trapped piglet. In the nightmare, it is Jabya himself who is trapped, and not the piglet, collapsing the divide between Jabya and piglet.

Another scene that highlights this impossibility of untouch is shown during the procession of an annual religious festival. A pig runs through the procession touching the *palkhi* (the deity's palanquin). On the following day, Patil insists that Kachru[21] (played by Kishor Kadam), Jabya's father, take care of the troublesome pigs. Unable to decline, their entire family has to be deployed to prevent pigs from touching the *palkhi*.

These incidents in the film reveal how Manjule marks the practice of untouchability as a no-exit zone for Dalits. This practice does not contend with whether one touches the pig or not. Instead, it goes beyond to mark these bodies as ontologically polluted. The scene in which Jabya returns to school after an absence of four days is a good example. Pirya, in the absence of Jabya, has to sit with a classmate from the dominant caste, who keeps bullying him. Pirya, distressed with the bench mate, informs the teacher that 'he complains even if my hand touches him'. The teacher, understanding the issue, asks Pirya to move to the back bench. The scene showcases that Dalits' corporeal existence is considered evidence of low-ness, and they are considered disgusting and not worthy of touching and being touched.[22]

Pig Cuts His Way: Spiral Web of Defilement

'Dalit literature' has long been alluding to inter-species relationships. Many have portrayed the nature of these relationships and the castedness it foregrounds in their autobiographical narratives or through poems and stories. For example, Omprakash Valmiki in his autobiography, *Joothan* (2003), writes,

> Pigs were an important part of our lives. In sickness or in health, in life or in death, in wedding ceremonies – pigs played an important role in all of them. Even our religious ceremonies were incomplete without the pigs. The pigs rooting in the compound were not symbols of dirt to us but of prosperity, and so they are today.[23]

Therefore, pigs have been linked with everyday forms of Dalit labour, food and ritual culture.

A Kaikadi respondent from Marathwada argues in a similar line as Valmiki. He contends, 'We were primarily associated with three trades: rearing pigs, weaving baskets, and excavating sand from the river bed with the help of donkeys' (interview, 3 April 2022). He further mentions that the latter two have stopped because of technological advancements and changing market conditions. People use plastic or metal baskets, whereas sand is excavated using mechanical excavators and trucks. However, their dependency on rearing pigs has continued (interview, 3 April 2022).

The pig has a significant role in the lives of Dalits, both materially and culturally. In the Brahminical tradition, a value system gets built around the pig and those associated with any work related to them. This value system has psychological as well as material consequences. Many do not want to be associated with the work, yet they repeatedly get forced into it. As the film showcases, stigma is attached to the work related to pigs. Jabya and his family are forced into doing the caste-based occupation of rearing pigs. Jabya's refusal to remove the piglet from Patil's tank resulted in a reprimand to Kachru by Patil, who reminds him to teach his son their traditional caste-based work. Public humiliation becomes a mechanism for forcing the next generation into the caste-based occupation. Similarly, in the procession scene mentioned earlier, Jabya's father is reluctant to catch pigs as his daughter's marriage is nearing. However, they end up performing the task against their own will because of the limitations of earning opportunities in a caste society or for fear of retaliation from the dominant caste.

In the final pig-catching sequence, Jabya runs away and hides behind a stone structure, avoiding being seen by his classmates, especially Shalu. While hiding, he accidentally comes close to catching the black sparrow. The means to achieve Shalu is just in front of his eye. But, when he is about to catch the bird, a pig cuts across the way of his desires, suggesting that hiding or concealing one's caste identity will not be possible permanently, though it might provide a temporary relief.

Throughout the film, the association with certain animals becomes the organising principle for caste norms. The Brahminical ideological apparatus creates a particular value system in the human–animal relatedness, decreeing a lowly status to the animals attached to Dalits' everyday lives. The animals related to Dalits get associated with impurity, and the Dalits in contact with those animals, by implication, become impure. Therefore, this hegemonised value system of the discourse created by the upper caste and restrictions on access to work coerce Dalits into a spiral web of defilement.[24]

So, we see Jabya and his family mocked and ridiculed by others who see their predicament as a matter of amusement. This association with animals is more mundane, intimate and bodily. Caste ideologies draw on metaphors of stigma and defilement to enable differentiated conceptions of subjectivity and to render the body a culturally legible surface.[25] Jabya's anxieties become manifestations of this impossibility of touch and untouch. In order to get out of this spiral web of defilement, Jabya attempts to conceal his caste identity. This is seen in a series of telling moments, such as Jabya hiding behind the basket or trying to slip away to avoid being seen by his classmates while performing the task of catching pigs or getting angry at his mother for coming to school. For Jabya, both concealing and revealing his caste identity become a problem. The association with animals throws the attempts at caste concealment into crisis.

The Dalit as Pig: Politics of Animalistic Metaphors

Jabya's father, being old and suffering from a leg injury, is not up to the ordeal of catching the slippery pigs, so he beats a reluctant Jabya into assisting him with the task. The spectacle of Jabya's thrashing and his distraught family's frantic scramble to catch the squealing, filthy pigs draws an audience; upper-caste villagers shout caste insults at them while posting pictures of the 'fandry match' on their phones. Many students, including Jabya's classmates and his love interest Shalu, join in. The catching of pigs becomes a stage where village caste dynamics play out. When his father brings the hiding Jabya out in public, the Nhavi caste[26] boy jokingly says that a different *fandry* has been found instead of a pig. He starts shouting 'ye fandry', instigating a burst of collective laughter. The Patil classmate of Jabya joins the chorus of calling him *fandry*.

We find a similar instance of collective reaction in Valmiki's autobiography, *Joothan* (2003). He writes about his experience in school. Instead of thrashing him for the mistakes he made, his teacher in the school used to grab his shirt and ask, 'How many pieces of pork did you eat?' The whole class would laugh, just like in the scene in *Fandry*. 'The boys would torment me about it. Abey, chuhre ke, you eat pork.'[27]

The pig, alive or dead, becomes an animalistic metaphor for demeaning and dehumanising Dalits. This animalistic metaphor, to use Ghassan Hage's argument in the race context, reveals the nature of casteist classifications.[28] It opens up an important question. What does the imagery of the Dalit as a pig tell us about how Dalits are treated by upper castes? What kind of power do they hold, and what are their practical dispositions towards Dalits?

By locating our intellectual query on human–animal relations, we are in a position to see the hidden dimensions of power relations, which may remain masked in intra-human interactions. These animalistic characteristics are not banal or spontaneous. They are rigorous categories with a 'practical orientation'.[29] As shown in the pig-catching sequence in *Fandry* or the school experience of Valmiki, everybody readily joined in the collective activity of dehumanising Dalits. Animalistic metaphors act as a 'manual' with complete 'what to do instructions'.[30] When using such a metaphor of the pig for Dalits, the upper castes know what they want to do. It is a declaration of the intent to maintain the power dynamics. At times, using the metaphors of animals, as Amit Shah's address to the rally quoted at the beginning of the chapter conveys, violence is instigated.[31] When Shah mentions that Bangladeshis are like termites, everyone understands they must get rid of termites by a collective cleansing act. Animalistic metaphors thus serve as calls to participate in the action, violent as well as casual ways of dehumanisation. It invites people to participate in spreading hate or ridiculing and eliminating the disgusting object, and the intent here is to make the target group feel inferior and insecure.

It is this inferiority complex that Jabya and the educated people mentioned in *Joothan* internalise. Valmiki writes, 'Yes, the educated among us, who are still a minute percentage, have abandoned these conventions. It is not because of a reformist perspective but because of the inferiority complex that they have done so. The educated ones suffer more from this inferiority complex, which is caused by social pressures.'[32]

We now know that one aspect of this social pressure is manifested by the use of animalistic metaphors. It is significant for the studies then to look closely at these animalistic metaphors to understand their use in maintaining the complex problem of caste and caste hierarchies.

In a telling ultimate sequence of the film, Jabya, dropping the pig from his shoulders, inhabits an assertive Dalit identity. Shaking off his inferiority complex, and using the same now as a weapon, he hurls a stone at the upper-caste Patil. In a manner of unburdening himself from the negative association with the pig, Jabya liberates himself to acquire a confrontational subjectivity.

Disgust and Untouchability: Spatial Connotations

In an informal conversation,[33] Santosh Sankhad, the national award-winning art director of *Fandry*, discussed the behind-the-scenes details of the *palkhi* procession sequence. For that scene, the villagers had given the *palkhi* for the shooting. However, as news got around that a pig would come into contact with the *palkhi* during the shoot, the villagers withdrew permission to use the *palkhi*. The film crew duly told them that the pig would not be a real pig. Instead, it would be a digital one created later on a computer. Nevertheless, the villagers insisted and refused the use of the *palkhi*, leaving the crew to build a new one overnight.

What do we understand from the reactions of the villagers who refused to give the *palkhi*? Joel Lee shows how caste as an order of affect could be useful to understand the emotional force it exerts in everyday life.[34] He argues that 'the caste order structures emotions in a particular way, and in turn depends on emotions, thus structured, for its reproduction over time'.[35] In other words, Lee suggests that caste shapes emotions and those emotions also shape caste and reproduce it. Based on two north Indian vernacular sources from the early twentieth century, he attempts to throw light on the inculcation of disgust. With the focus on disgust, Lee claims, the scholarly investigation has shifted from 'the victims of the untouchability to its perpetrators'.[36] He contends that *grihna* (Hindi word for disgust) is employed as the ground for practising untouchability and should not be thought of as 'a "natural" and essential reactive emotion'; instead, the notion of disgust operates both as an individual internalisation and 'as a social affect'.[37] Therefore, the display of disgust should be understood as a feeling of group socialising rather than merely located as an individual psyche.

From the reaction of villagers, it is evident that disgust has a collective manifestation and plays out differently in the public sphere. The scenes in *Fandry* and Valmiki's narrative from the school open up further nuances of this concept. As mentioned, animalistic metaphors generate intent and invites others to join in oppressive actions. In some sense, the notion of disgust does the same. While some people seem to have a sense of disgust against the pig, the same people enjoy a feeling of amusement when they see someone else touch the pig. Disgust about some object or a thing also becomes a point for mocking others connected with those disgusting objects. Moreover, mocking could be for the 'caste other' or a member of their own caste.

In the film, the captured pig is carried by Jabya and his sisters using a long stick with the animal hanging upside down against the backdrop of the great social reformers Babasaheb Ambedkar, Savitribai Phule, Shahu Maharaj and Sant Gadge Baba painted on the school wall. The spectators again mock the family, saying, 'Brace yourselves, Kachru's army has arrived.' Dada Patil, who was at the forefront in the mocking, covers his nose and comments in disgust, 'Kasla vaas sutlay sagla' (How stinky it is!). These were the same people who enjoyed the 'fandry match', putting its status on social media and terming themselves the 'cheerleaders'. The moment they come into the vicinity of the pig, in the space where smell reaches their nostrils, it creates disgust.

Lee argues that spatial practices informed by caste ideology are 'a correspondence among castes, spaces, and sensorially charged forms of labor'.[38] Smell, therefore, he argues, becomes, in varying degrees, the organising principle of space in caste society. In the example stated here, the smell not only creates disgust but also has spatial connotations. Though smell has a transgressive potential that touch might not possess, knowing this fully, caste society organises the space. This could be seen in residential areas where meat-eaters are not allowed to buy flats, or fish markets and meat shops either are not given permission or are asked to relocate as people feel disgusted by the sight or smell of non-vegetarian food.[39] This is also seen in the example mentioned earlier of villagers denying the *palkhi* to be used for shooting. Disgust, therefore, becomes an organising principle, in varying degrees, of the space where untouchability is practised, as emphasised by Lee.[40]

Your Paw Scrapes/Are My Trails: Fraternity (Re)defined

Through the analysis of *Fandry* with a focus on human–animal relationships, we have mainly discussed untouchability, disgust and forced labour and foregrounded how inferiority complex and humiliation occur. However, the humiliation or inferiority complex could be inverted to invoke the meaning of emancipation. It could be used to make a claim against the very power that caused this humiliation.[41] In some way, Mari Selvaraj's film *Pariyerum Perumal* (The God Who Mounts the Horse) uses this humiliation as a claim against the oppressors. Selvaraj attempts to portray this through human–animal relatedness. It is to analyse this human–animal relatedness that we shift.

Pariyerum Perumal, released in 2018, narrates the story of oppressed-caste youth Pariyan (played by Kathir), hailing from Puliyankulam village near Tirunelveli, Tamil Nadu. The film takes us through the emotionally intense struggles of the law college student Pariyan, who aspires to become like his role model, Dr B. R. Ambedkar, hoping his education will help him fight for the rights of his community. It presents a compelling narrative of Pariyan's fight for dignity and respect, displaying the existent caste practices, prohibitions and atrocities.

The film begins with the credits featuring background music of chirping birds, the panting of a dog, buzzing flies and the echoes of dry grass swaying in the breeze. Mari Selvaraj, the director, uses the sounds to introduce us to the landscape and the non-humans inhabiting it. In the following scene, Pariyan and his friends are seen relaxing in a pond, humming a local song and bathing their respective dogs in the scroching heat, when Pariyan realises that his pet dog Karuppi is missing. In what follows, some upper-caste people are seen tying Karuppi to the rail track, where the beloved dog gets brutally crushed by a fast-moving train.

In the subsequent scenes, we get insights into the shared life of Pariyan and Karuppi. Pariyan is devastated by the death of Karuppi. A heart-wrenching funeral song titled 'Karuppi' also serves as a haunting evocation of the experience of marginalisation faced by Pariyan and his community. The mourning and the last rites for Karuppi show that she is respected and emotionally integrated into the lives of the community. A portion of the song in Tamil and its translation are as follows.

Ippa udane naan unna pakkanum
Mookkil mugam vachi orasanum
Un naakkil nakki en azhukka kazhuvi poghanum
Enga vandha unna paakkalam
Yaar andha kaattil odanji kedappadu neeya illa naana
Naana ille neeya
Neeya ... Naana ... Naana ... Neeya ...
Karuppi
Irandhadhu neeya iruppadhu naana
Iruppadhu neeya irandhadhu naana

I need to see you now
I want to cuddle you now
I want your tongue to lick my dirt clean
Where do I see you now!
Who is it lying broken in the forest?
Is it you or me!
Is it me or you!
You... Me... Me... You...
Karuppi
You are dead; Am I alive!
Are you alive; Am I dead![42]

With the death of Karuppi, Pariyan feels some inseparable part of him has died and his agony is expressed in the song. Selvaraj blurs the human–animal binary by evoking Pariyan and Karuppi's subjectivities as inseparable and synthesised together.[43] The old and the young join in mourning the dog's

death and the life she has lived. The collective mourning marks the shared
life with the nature they inhabit and a way to negotiate the pain inflicted
by Karuppi's death. A culture, this film showcases, where life is valued, love
is shared, and care is extended to non-humans. It also contrasted with the
upper-castes' behaviour towards fellow humans and non-humans.

The song describes the relatedness between Pariyan and Karuppi in the
following, powerfully imaginative words.

> Adi Karuppi
> Enn Karuppi
> Nagathadame en paadha
> Nee illaadha kaattil
> Naan eppadithaan thiriveno

> Dear Karuppi
> My Karuppi
> Your paw scrapes
> Are my trails
> In the wilderness without you
> How will I find my way![44]

In the caste-ridden society where feelings for fellow beings are fractured
along caste lines, the lower-caste people are not treated with compassion,
love or care. Pariyan relates himself with Karuppi as his companion, a fellow
being with whom his world is entangled, with whom he shares the joys and
pains of life. She becomes a guiding companion for Pariyan, even after her
death.

Karuppi, killed by dominant-caste members, returns time and again
whenever Pariyan faces challenges in his life. Her traces permeate his
entire life. In the latter part of the film, the song 'Naan Yaar' (Who Am
I?) stands out distinctly for its metaphors questioning caste discrimination
and reflecting the trauma and mental agony of Pariyan, who faces severe
humiliation because of his caste identity. The lyrics of the song are as follows.

> Rayil thedi vandhu kollum, naan yaar?
> Pookkum maramengum thookkil thongum, naan yaar?
> Nadhiyil sethu meenaai mithakkum, naan yaar?
> Kudisaikkul kathari yerindha, naan yaar?

Ther eradha saamyingu, naan yaar?
Unkai padaamal thanneer parugum, naan yaar?
Oor suvarkatti dhooram vaikka, naan yaar?
Malakkuzhikkul moochaiyadakkum, naan yaar?

Who am I that trains chase to mow down?
Who am I that hangs dead from blossoming trees?
Who am I that floats up as dead fish in rivers?
Who am I that died burning inside my hut?
The God your chariots refuse, who am I?
I drink water without touching you, who am I?
A village keeps me away with a wall, who am I?
I breathe my last in a shithole, who am I?[45]

Along with showcasing the trauma, mental agony, and humiliation of Pariyan in a metaphorical sense, the song also shows images of venomous animals, such as snakes and scorpions, as Pariyan was tied to a chair in a claustrophobic dark room. The physical violence against Dalits is portrayed here through the imagery of these animals. It resonates with many of the real-life caste-based killings that happened in the past, reminding us of the rampant brutality and subjugation Dalits have to face at the hands of upper castes. Confined in a room and tied to a chair, the scene portrays the impossibility of his relationship with Jo (played by Anandhi) due to their caste backgrounds. It also reminds us of the darkness of an inescapable and terrifying nightmare of drowning in the well that Jabya in *Fandry* goes through.

In such a vulnerable position, yet again, Karuppi's image appears to rescue Pariyan from the bite of the venomous animals that metaphorically represent upper castes. Now, the wounded dog appears in a vision, coloured blue, and provides him with hope and the strength to fight. The deployment of the blue colour, which is considered to be the symbol of Ambedkarite assertion, indicates the transformation of Pariyan's life seeking social justice and equality. The blue-coloured Karuppi with a confident and relaxed yet alert posture stands for Ambedkarite politics, gesturing assuredness, hope, and assertion. The reappearance of Karuppi shows that Pariyan is missing her companionship. Her presence fulfils him and rescues him from the deepest of the problems.

Pariyan needs that fraternal relationship with the others that can help him fight the problem of caste. In a graded social order, there is the impossibility of fraternity. In the words of Ambedkar, 'Virtue has become caste-ridden, and morality has become caste-bound. There is no sympathy for the deserving'.[46] However, *Pariyerum Perumal* seeks to achieve that ideal. The message it attempts to convey is that in a fraternal fellowship, one treats other humans and non-humans as the objects of love and desire. Towards the end of the film, Pariyan, badly injured by the professional 'honour killer',[47] is left on the train track to die a similar death as Karuppi. Karuppi, once again, is shown to come to awaken Pariyan, thereby saving his life. Karuppi's death on a train track and Pariyan's plotted murder merge their lives. Metaphysically, their lives are intertwined, reminding us of their relatedness shown in the mourning song.

Figure 3.1   Associated living

Mari Selvaraj emphasises the value and importance of fraternity against caste by redefining human kinship and multispecies relatedness. The film showcases how his emotional affinity with Karuppi becomes a source of Pariyan's demand for fraternity. Pariyan, faced with violence and oppression at the hands of his lover Jo's fellow caste members and her father (played by G. Marimuthu), insistently demands to be treated equally and fraternally. In the film, Pariyan demands fraternity as an ethical and philosophical response to the caste-bound moral order that is deformed and results in alienated selves. It demands a fellowship that does not tolerate difference as an aspect of hierarchy and inequality,[48] goes beyond human relations and extends to the non-humans, while the casteist discourse continues to do animalisation of the oppressed.

Concluding Remarks

This chapter locates itself in the scholarship on human–animal relations, focusing on the symbolic meaning of animals. Based on the existing scholarship, the chapter comments on the relations between animals and caste practices and highlights the significance of the framework of human–animal relatedness in caste studies. By juxtaposing the narratives around a sparrow and a pig, as shown in the film *Fandry*, the chapter comments on the impossibility and possibility of (un)touch. This juxtaposition shows Brahminhood as a no-entry zone and untouchability as a no-exit zone.

As per the Brahminical tradition, a value system is built around various animals attaching stigma and impurity to Dalits and the animals associated with them. This value system, coupled with forced labour, puts Dalits in a spiral web of defilement, where they become untouchables because they touch pigs, and pigs become untouchable because Dalits touch them – making both Dalits and pigs disgusting. I argued that this disgust has a collective manifestation and generates intent, and invites others to join in mocking those considered disgusting. I further demonstrated, using Lee,[49] that disgust is an organising principle, in varying degrees, of the space where untouchability is practised.

This chapter highlights how the caste issue is discussed using animalistic metaphors. Using the framework of analysing human–animal relations, hidden dimensions of instrumentality and power in intra-human relations could be revealed. It pushes us to rethink the category of human. Examples of

Fandry and *Pariyerum Perumal* also show that human subjectivity, in general, is crucially formed in relation to the non-human world. The subjective position of Dalits, in particular, is marked by the value attached to the animals they are (dis)associated with. The human–animal relatedness at the margins, as portrayed in the film *Pariyerum Perumal*, emphasises the significance of fraternity against caste by redefining both human kinship and multispecies relatedness. This relationship with animals, along with other things, contains and contests their marginality and shapes their subjectivity.

Notes

1. Yamini Narayanan, 'Animating Caste: Visceral Geographies of Pigs, Caste, and Violent Nationalisms in Chennai City', *Urban Geography* 44, no. 10 (2023): 2185–205.

2. Yamini Narayanan, 'Cow Protection as "Casteised Speciesism": Sacralisation, Commercialisation and Politicisation', *South Asia: Journal of South Asian Studies* 41, no. 2 (2018): 331–51.

3. Wendy Doniger, *The Hindus: An Alternative History* (New York: Penguin Press, 2009).

4. Doniger, *The Hindus.*

5. Perumal Murugan, *Poonachi or the Story of a Black Goat,* trans. N. Kalyan Raman (Chennai: Context Publishing House, 2018).

6. Erika Cudworth, *Social Lives with Other Animals: Tales of Sex, Death and Love* (Basingstoke: Palgrave Macmillan, 2011); Richard York and Stefano B. Longo, 'Animals in the World: A Materialist Approach to Sociological Animal Studies', *Journal of Sociology* 53, no. 1 (2017): 32–46.

7. The analysis of the films is done with the understanding that films are viewed as reservoirs of cultural meaning and feelings that audiences may use for a variety of purposes. However, the reactions of audiences are not considered here for analysis. Instead, it presents an analysis of scenes of interest.

8. Nagraj Manjule (dir.), *Fandry* (Mumbai: Navalakha Arts and Holy Basil Productions, 2013).

9. I am using the word 'Dalit' to imply castes considered 'untouchables' and notified and denotified tribes.

10. Mari Selvaraj (dir.), *Pariyerum Perumal* (Madras: Neelam Productions, 2018).

11. Manjule recently directed his first Hindi film, *Jhund* (Mumbai: T-Series, Tandav Films Entertainment Pvt. Ltd and Aatpat Films, 2022).

12. Hrishikesh Ingle, 'Fandry and Sairat: Regional Cinema and Marginality', *Economic and Political Weekly* 53, no. 45 (2018): 46–53.

13. Ingle, 'Fandry and Sairat'

14. Sowjanya Tamalapakula, '"C/O Kancharapalem"' and the Politics of Unspeakability of Caste', *The Wire*, 14 October 2018, https://thewire.in/film/c-o-kancharapalem-and-the-politics-of-unspeakability-of-caste, accessed 20 May 2022.

15. Suraj Yengde, 'Dalit Cinema', *South Asia: Journal of South Asian Studies* 41, no. 3 (2018): 503–18.

16. Manju Edachira, 'Anti-caste Aesthetics and Dalit Interventions in Indian Cinema', *Economic and Political Weekly* 55, no. 38 (2020): 47–53.

17. In a recent article, Shamali Jadhav engages with human–animal entanglements in the films *Fandry* and *Khwada* and demonstrates how categories of 'human' and 'animal' are constituted in a caste society, and further contends that these films open up possibilities to (re)imagine 'interspecies alliances' and the categories of 'human' and 'animal'. S. Jadhav, 'The Pig, the Black Sparrow, and the Sheep: Human–Animal Entanglements in Fandry and Khwada', in *The Routledge Companion to Caste and Cinema in India*, ed. J Abraham and J. Misrahi-Barak, 249–60 (London: Routledge India).

18. Kaikadi comes under denotified tribes. Many communities were 'notified' as being 'criminals by birth' by the colonial state under the Criminal Tribes Act 1871. The post-colonial government 'denotified' them in 1952.

19. Bhimrao Ramji Ambedkar, *Annihilation of Caste: The Annotated Critical Edition*, edited and annotated by S. Anand (New Delhi: Navayana, 2014).

20. 'Patil' is a surname belonging to the Maratha caste, a dominant caste in Maharashtra.

21. *Kachra* literally means garbage. In the Brahminical tradition, demeaning names are assigned to Dalits.

22. Bhimrao Ramji Ambedkar, *Dr. Babasaheb Ambedkar: Writings and Speeches Vol. 7* (Bombay: Government of Maharashtra, 1990)

23. Omprakash Valmiki, *Joothan: An Untouchable's Life*, trans. A. P. Mukherjee (New York: Columbia University Press, 2003)

24. V. Geetha, 'Bereft of Being: The Humiliations of Untouchability' in *Humiliation: Claims and Context* ed. Gopal Guru (New Delhi: Oxford University Press, 2009), 95–108.

25. Anupama Rao, 'Stigma and labour: Remembering Dalit Marxism', *Seminar* 633 (May 2012): 23–7.

26. Nhavi is a middle caste traditionally occupied as barbers. They come under the Other Backward Classes category.

27. Valmiki, *Joothan*.

28. Ghassan Hage, *Is Racism an Environmental Threat?* (Cambridge: Polity Press, 2017).

29. Hage, *Is Racism an Environmental Threat?*

30. Hage, *Is Racism an Environmental Threat?*

31. The Hindu Correspondant, 'Bangladeshi Migrants are like Termites: Amit Shah', *The Hindu*, 22 September 2018, https://www.thehindu.com/news/national/bangladeshi-migrants-are-like-termites-amit-shah/article25017064.ece, accessed 19 March 2022.

32. Valmiki, *Joothan*.

33. This informal conversation with Santosh Sankhad happened during my friend Anurup Khillare's MPhil thesis work.

34. Joel Lee, 'Disgust and Untouchability: Towards an Affective Theory of Caste', *South Asian History and Culture* 12, nos. 2–3 (2021): 310–27.

35. Lee, 'Disgust and Untouchability'.

36. Lee, 'Disgust and Untouchability'.

37. Lee, 'Disgust and Untouchability'.

38. Joel Lee, 'Odor and Order: How Caste Is Inscribed in Space and Sensoria', *Comparative Studies of South Asia, Africa and the Middle East* 37, no. 3 (2017): 470–90.

39. Haima Deshpande, 'Food Apartheid: Non-vegetarians Not Allowed', *Outlook,* 29 April 2022, https://www.outlookindia.com/magazine/national/food-apartheid-non-vegetarians-not-allowed--magazine-192445, accessed 20 May 2022; DNA Correspondant, 'Dadar Fish Market to Be Shifted', *DNA*, Mumbai edition, 16 April 2016, https://www.dnaindia.com/mumbai/report-dadar-fish-market-to-be-shifted-2202185, accessed 17 May 2022.

40. Lee, 'Odor and Order'.

41. Sanjay Palshikar, 'Understanding Humiliation', *Economic and Political Weekly* 40, no. 51 (2005): 5428–32.

42. Lyrics and translation of the song retrieved from https://popnable.com/india/songs/128185-santhosh-narayanan-karuppi/lyrics-and-translations, accessed 28 June 2022.

43. B. Geetha, 'Ella Manusanum Inga Onnu Illa: Imag(in)ing the Claustrophobia of Caste in *Pariyerum Perumal*', in *The Routledge Companion to Caste and*

Cinema in India, ed. Joshil K. Abraham and Judith Misrahi-Barak (London: Routledge India, 2022), 387–401.

44. Lyrics and translation of the song retrieved from https://popnable.com/india/songs/128185-santhosh-narayanan-karuppi/lyrics-and-translations, accessed 28 June 2022.

45. Lyrics and translation of the song retrieved from https://ck2.blogspot.com/2018/10/naan-yaar.html, accessed 28 June 2022.

46. Ambedkar, *Annihilation of Caste*.

47. Throughout the film, an old dominant-caste man is shown killing people who have tried to transgress the boundaries of caste to maintain the 'honour' of caste.

48. V. Geetha, 'Caritas and Maithri', *Seminar* 662 (2014): 14–17.

49. Lee, 'Odor and Order'.

DALIT IMAGERIES AND TEXTUAL NARRATIVES

4

The Changing Iconography of the Owl in Dalit Narratives

A Study of Cho. Dharman's *Koogai*

Shibangi Dash

Since the inception of literature, animals have always been speaking, even if they may not have always been audible. Especially in Dalit writings, the constant presence of animals and birds such as dogs, buffaloes, cows, pigs, vultures and many more cannot be disregarded. The Tamil writer Cho. Dharman uses the figure of the *koogai* (the Tamil word for owl) in his narrative to raise some pertinent questions on how the state deals with caste atrocities in India. Dalit lives are often marked by a degree of liminality, rendering them non-human. 'Owl' is commonly used as a term of abuse, similar to how caste names such as *chamar*[1] and *bhangi*[2] themselves are used as swear words. In Tamil, another word for the owl colloquially is *aandai*, which is, again, often used to ridicule or to insult someone. The Hindi word for owl is *ulloo*, a slur that implies stupidity. So, by placing owl as a central figure in the narrative, is Dharman reclaiming an expletive or is he creating an alternative meaning to the word?

One of the major objectives of this chapter is to question the construction of animalities. Animalities or animal-ness is often posited in contrast to a conventional understanding of basic human nature (such as possessing autonomy or self-awareness) and underlining the human–animal distinction by relegating animals to an instinctive bestiality.

Besides the physical presence of the owl in *Koogai*, it also serves as a vehicle for the need to raise Dalit consciousness, subjected to dehumanisation, by embracing the Ambedkarite ideals of self-dignity, liberty and equality. *Koogai* interrogates and addresses the overlapping binary construction of the marginalised Dalit, often rendered as the other, and the animal.

The positioning of animal imageries in a narrative adds an urgency to the struggle for Dalit dignity. Aniruddha Mukhopadhyay[3] in his paper interrogates the rhetorical deployment of animal tropes for the realisation of Dalit consciousness and in understanding the Dalit subject, particularly in autobiographies. This chapter extends Mukhopadhyay's work by drawing upon a fictional piece focusing on one creature – that is, the owl, a bird often considered ominous in South Asian folk narratives.[4]

How did animal tropes come to be an integral part of Dalit writings? Historically, Dalits have tended to animals either as herders or as those responsible for disposing animal carcasses. Bama[5] in her autobiographical work, *Karukku*, discusses how the activity of hunting reflected their community life, wherein the meat of the hunted prey would be shared with everyone.[6] Hindu scriptures see dogs as *achhut* (Hindi word for untouchables), as discussed by Wendy Doniger,[7] where she mentions the story of an ascetic who transforms his pet dog into a powerful animal to protect it from the attacks of predators. But when the pet dog, presently in the form of a powerful lion, attacks its 'master' the ascetic, it is turned back to its original form. The didactic element of this story implies that dogs were not to strive to be above their social station in life, finding a semiotic resonance with the Dalits.[8]

There are different ways in which animal analogies can be used. The dominant castes use it to dehumanise Dalits, and Dalits use it not only to document their trauma but also to showcase their revolutionary resistance to Brahminical hegemony. Dalit narratives reflect a complex relationship between Dalit subjects, their communities and animals. Often, they share an intricate cultural relationship with animals. As Mukul Sharma[9] notes in his essay, the idea of bestiality is symbolised in the context of caste by referring to Dalits as 'being not-human, to be a commodified entity'.[10] Dalit narratives have compared the plight of Dalits to the treatment meted out to animals, describing how they are often whipped, humiliated and subjected to torture.

While discussing liberal humanism and the abstractness that lies therein, Cary Wolfe[11] points out how the 'question of the animal' or the non-human other is sacrificed. Barring fables like the *Panchatantra* or *Aesop's Fables*, where there is a constant presence of animals in the narratives, they are accorded a marginalised position. This creates a categorical distinction between humans and animals. But this distinction becomes suspended in the allegorical nature of language in the realm of literature. Literature serves to distinguish humans from animals by its pedanticism, but it also confuses and juxtaposes them.

The constant abject presence of animals in literature suggests that literature is a discourse wherein humans simultaneously declare their divergence from animals and take the measure of their suggestive similarities as well. Dalit autobiographies often talk about the non-human plight of their narrators. For example, Manohar Mouli Biswas[12] in his autobiography compares the lives of his community with 'the common chunoputi fish, stayed back in our motherland, primarily because of sheer helplessness'. This construction of a human–animal divide might be imagined as a space of contestation where the marginalisation enforced by the state relegates them to the status of exploited species. But *Koogai* as a narrative questions if there is much of a difference between the condition of owls and Dalits and the violence perpetrated on both of them. Analysing *Koogai* through the lens of the owl takes on the central question of representation. It also explores the agency that lies with Dalits, revisiting the notion of subject and object.

Owls spend the day concealing themselves in hollow tree trunks or deserted and ruined houses away from the human gaze. They are heavily dotted and freckled with brown markings, which help them camouflage and perfectly merge with their surroundings. By focusing on the figure of the owl, Dharman forces readers to reflect upon the extent to which contemporary city life has helped to camouflage Dalit identity. The more significant question that arises out of this debate is why there is still a need for concealment of identities.

Despite the abolition of untouchability in 1950, caste discrimination is still rampant in India. Gopal Guru[13] in his essay argues how Dalits have been marginalised after being dominated and suppressed since ages. When it is a matter of access to basic resources like housing, clean drinking water and education, there is still marked caste discrimination in rural as well as urban areas.[14]

It is only since the 1990s that Tamil Dalit literature has emerged actively and grown into an important and vocal expression of Dalit strife and assertion.[15] The publication of *Koogai* in 2005 created a stir in the Tamil literary world because of its radical experimentation in form and the grounded realities it depicted. In fact, A. R. Venkatachalapathy, in his introduction to the translation of *Koogai* to English, compares the novel to Imayam's *Koveru Kazudhigal*, translated as *Beasts of Burden*, owing to its portrayal of Dalit lives using similar tropes of 'Dalit oral lore and traditions, which have found no chroniclers'.[16] *Koogai* was seen as a confluence of social realism and magical realism.[17] Cho. Dharman's *Koogai*[18] is a genuine creative evolution of both the literary modes, well acclimatised to the existential reality of contemporary Tamil Nadu and to the *karisal* region (area of the black cotton soil) in particular. Through a wide array of complex characters, with the owl at the centre, Dharman is reacting to a dominant narrative that portrays Dalits as victims who are without any cultural or material resources. The unique narrative, presented almost as an ethnographic document, highlights the significance of the problems faced by Pallars[19] in this region of Chitthiraikudi village and their near exodus to the slums of Kovilpatti in Tamil Nadu.

In one of his interviews, Cho. Dharman says, 'I do not use my work to propagandise. I write what I see. There is no room for imagination and embellishment.'[20] But it is not entirely possible to separate Dalit literary works from the Dalit movement because Dalit literature is intrinsically protest literature. As with every radical literary piece where non-linear narratives seem to be the standard form, *Koogai* too sticks to it. The plenitude of spoken rhythms, the rhetoric of performative poetry or ritual, the colloquial register and the poetic descriptions of the landscape paint the storyline of *Koogai*.

In an act of subversion, after Mookkan and Muthukkaruppan enjoy a hearty meal and take a nap under the village banyan tree, in a wonderful play of words Dharman merges the blissful landscape with elements of magical realism. He writes,

> ... *Suddenly a whirlwind blows in, turning the hanging roots into monstrous gnarled trees and the tendrils into enormous pythons, their snarling mouths split open. And suddenly overhead there's a star-burst, like a shower of fragrant blossoms from the World of the Gods.* (Italics in original)[21]

But amidst this idyllic scene lies the oppression that is meted out by not only the Brahmins but the dominant middle caste groups as well. The *owl* and the *state*, signified by the Dalits, mostly those from the Pallar community to which the central characters belong, and the police respectively, territorialise the novel. They are the two major protagonists and antagonists in the narrative.

The hierarchy of caste in all its manifestations is ever-present in the novel. The vibrancy of characters gives a gloss to the narrative. There is Seeni, the elderly, tenacious farmer who insists that the Pallars' contribution in funeral rites be treated with reverence and dignity and not as menial tasks. There are the spirited Muthukkaruppan and Mookkan, who defy reviled traditions and try and gulp down a meal at the 'club house' (nothing more than a shack where intermediate castes assemble for a meal). The father–son duo, Appusubban and Ayyanar, are remarkable for their fortitude and their doggedness in trying to escape from the clutches of the police because they have been falsely implicated by the upper castes. Peichi, an intelligent woman who is also Kaali Thevar's wife, is notable for her courage and fierceness. She is a spectator to the rapid changes that move her people to new areas, newer forms of oppression and religious conversions. A new greedy political class that needs the numbers of her people for elections is actually an offshoot of the *jameen* (also known as the *zamindar*) who had exploited them in the village and now continues to take advantage of them in the town. A divide-and-rule stratagem has been employed by the *jameen* to create a rift among the Dalit communities. The Chakkiliyars[22] remain on the fringe, ill-treated by the dominant forces, including the Pallars. Muthaiya Pandiyan, belonging to the dominant caste, almost behaves like a dictator in the village and decides the fate of the Dalits. He exploits the couple Shanmugam and Karuppi. When Muthaiya Pandiyan takes advantage of Shanmugam's daughter, Shanmugam no longer tolerates it but burns him down in his hut. The social and sexual exploitation reaches its apogee and pushes the oppressed to protest and break the bondages. The novel hints at the tragedy of progress and migration that propels Dalit communities to wander. When they are cheated of their rights to the land, they migrate by the truckload from villages to neighbouring towns to work in matchbox and ginning factories and as stone-breakers in quarries.

Within these episodes of defiance and resistance rhetoric, what role does the *koogai* play? Biologist Edward Wilson[23] wrote that animals are 'agents of nature translated into symbols of culture'. But how humans portray animals is not simply a figurative question. Margo DeMello[24] in his critical study on human–animal relations says,

> The ways in which we paint, worship, and tell our stories about animals also shape how we treat them in turn. In addition, for many people, the real relationships that humans once had with animals have been largely supplanted by symbolic representations, with important implications for people and animals alike.

In an attempt to revive the glorious past of the Dalits, Cho. Dharman comes to signify the exploited Dalits and their resplendent history. When Seeni adopts the owl as a revered guardian deity in an act of faith and self-affirmation, fortune changes for the Pallar community and good things begin to happen. Before leaving for the city, a Brahmin allocates his lands to Pallars, bestowing on outcastes a means of agency. Previously, this community was not even allowed to share the waters of the common well they themselves had dug. But now the status quo is disturbed. For the first time, Dalits are not at the mercy of the upper castes. They refuse to handle the latter's corpses or to build the bier and the funeral car. There comes a day when even Gengiya Naicker, an upper-caste man, begins to respect the bird after his family starts to have more than a single child after receiving the blessings of Koogai-Saami (the owl god). In another episode, Seedevi, the goddess of wealth, takes the shape of Koogai-Saami and blesses Seeni. It is Seeni who brings a new life to the Pallars by acquiring the land for cultivation from Nataraj Iyer. But soon his people start to revile him because of their newly upgraded lifestyle. They also gradually lose faith in the *koogai* god. They plan to demolish the Koogai-Saami temple and build a Kaali temple in its place. Seeni takes the Koogai statue and starts his journey into the magical land. At the end of the novel, we witness a gang of boys dragging the now-powerless Koogai statue along the road.

What makes animals so suitable to be used as symbols? In his work on totemism,[25] anthropologist Claude Lévi-Strauss stresses that animals are chosen as totems not because they are good to eat, but because they are 'good to think [with]'. Lévi-Strauss finds animals to be emblematic, and because they have lived closely and intimately with humans, they have been assimilated into 'human' society. They also represent social hierarchies and classifications like clans and other aspects of kinship systems; in India, we can associate them with the caste system as well. DeMello further says that animals aptly 'represent human behaviours, desires, and dreams, and in this case stand for humans themselves'.[26] Some animals in India are politicised as being 'sacred'. This results in 'casteised speciesism', which refers to a socio-ecological phenomenon wherein certain animals are empowered by humans by associating them with the dominant castes while some others are undervalued by associating them with the oppressed castes. In India, cows are identified with Brahmins, horses become symbolic of the Kshatriyas while animals like pigs and dogs are associated with the lower castes.[27]

Before delving into the human–animal analogy of this narrative, we also need to understand what an analogy is. Derrida[28] clarifies that 'an analogy is always a reason, a logos, a reasoning … that moves back up toward a relation of production, or resemblance, or comparability in which identity and difference coexist'. With this we address a fundamental question: by implying that humans are non-animals or that animals are non-humans, are we reinvigorating the notion of reason and its otherness? Simultaneously, by creating the dichotomous structure of human–animal, are we emphasising that it resides at the core of the human itself? Do humans create non-human animals to cure their own existential malaise? So, instead of viewing animals as infrahumans, as primitive compared to the rationality of humans, they may be understood not with respect to any otherness or difference but as a continuation to humans. How is this relevant to our discussion of *Koogai*? The analogy becomes obvious when we observe how the dominant castes view the oppressed castes as 'undignified', 'barbaric' and 'primitive'.

It is almost customary to use animal tropes in political rhetoric. Perpetrators and victims are often qualified as 'beasts' or 'animals', which suggests that animals play an important symbolic role in politics. The discourse of animal studies believes the role of animals in human society has been downplayed. When we talk about treating a human like an animal, it amounts to calling them an animal, and becomes a way to degrade and dehumanise them. Throughout history, Dalits have been subjected to the systemic violence perpetrated on them by the upper castes. They have been beaten like animals, branded like animals and bought and sold like animals; they had their humanity and individuality ignored, just as humans do with animals. So, what are the implications of calling people by animal names, especially when those names are used as pejoratives? Animal pejoratives thus reinforce discriminatory attitudes towards marginalised humans by comparing them with another marginalised group: that is, animals. It is also notable that negative animal imagery is most often used to malign women and minorities.

Classical Tamil literature evokes *koogai* as an ominous bird, the carrier of bad news. The eerie hoot of the owl is considered particularly inauspicious, and in popular parlance, the bird is also called *sakkuruvi,* the sparrow of death, with a hoot that is said to foretell death. Attempting to elaborate the various meanings associated with the hoot of the owl, Dharman says,

The owl's call, once heard
Foretells a death. Twice heard,
A dire fate. Three throaty moans

Will bring a temptress to your bed.
Four hoots announce
A dreadful stirring in the land.
Five screeches send you forth upon
A long journey.
When the owl emits six
Staccato shrieks
It means the next in line
Has arrived to take your place.
Seven times it calls to restore to you
The things you've lost.
Eight times it hoots, and quite suddenly
You die.
A call repeated nine times or ten
Is by far the best. But by then
You are already dead.[29]

A similar hooting of the owl is heard before a riot ensues between the Pallars and the Paraiyars (a Dalit community, most of whom converted to Christianity). The crack between the Pallars and the Paraiyars was also palpable in the riot that allegedly resulted after a chariot was driven across the Pallar street by the Paraiyars. But as the narrative further interrogates the incident, it is revealed that sacrificing calves and the consumption of beef by the Paraiyars was the bone of contention between the two communities. It is interesting to note here the upper castes do not appear in the scene objecting to the consumption of beef; rather, it is the Pallars who objected, which further problematises the discourse around beef politics.

The neglected and submerged voices of the Dalits are expressed through the hoot of the owl. Dharman says his writings are a plea to allow the *koogai*s, or Dalits, to emerge from their areas of segregation into open spaces. The *koogai* knows the secret to the art of the ambush. It waits for the right moment to rebel and fight back. The *koogai* once reigned in the night with its nocturnal power, but now during the day its powerlessness prompts even insignificant birds to attack the *koogai*, which is effectively excluded from open spaces during the day time. It is similar to the fact of the public sphere being inaccessible to Dalits as it has been encroached upon by the upper castes. The *koogai* uses its strength only to find food. Darkness and exclusion are integral parts of its life. Despite Cho. Dharman's analogy of Dalit lives to that of the forlorn *koogai*, he also presents the resplendent life of the Dalits and their joys, sorrow, angst and hope in all its hues and shades. He also puts forth the resilience of Dalits in more than just existing; they are presented as being full of hope and life. This elevates Dharman's narrative to a position where it is reflective of the Ambedkarite vision of a life of dignity, equality and liberty.

Thus, Dharman symbolises the *koogai* as a bird of peace which shuns greed and whose life is like a meditation. He calls on each *koogai* to be a *yogi* (the Sanskrit word for ascetic or monk). John Berger[30] in his seminal essay 'Why Look at Animals?' suggests that the first human metaphor was animal and that the relation between humans and animals was from the very beginning conceived of as a metaphoric relation. This relationship has also evolved over time, from being muses to being captive objects. To talk of the human–animal relation signifies neither the abstract nor the non-existent; rather, it is to remark that such tropes mediate our understanding of what we have in common with animals and what we do *not* have in common with them. Such tropes allow us to mark differences as well as make associations with animals. There exists a sort of symbiotic relation between humans and animals. In *Koogai*, the owl and Appusubban protect each other from their respective predators. Appusubban protects the owl while it is being attacked by other birds, and the owl protects the man from evil spirits.

It will be myopic to view only the emblem of the owl in *Koogai*. Besides the owl imagery, a plethora of animal images have also been used abundantly throughout the narrative. The presence of a chimerical creature which had the face of an owl and a lion's mane is used to denote the local deity Chenga Madaiya, who is the saviour of sheep, wherein the sheep stand for Dalits. When the police reach Peichi's home in search of Appusubban, the crows, with their rigorous cawing, shield him from them. In an act of protection when the land is inflicted with pests and worms, Koogai-Saami releases a flock of cranes to devour the pests, illustrating Dharman's wonderful play of magical realism. The police-state has continuously been identified with lions, who are experts in devouring goats and other cattle (Dalits). Appusubban, Ayyannar and other Dalits are identified with sparrows. The other sparrows from the nearby trees provided them refuge in their hiding from the police-lion. This concealed their human appearance, and they became masters of disguise. The lions in turn forgot how to rage.

Seeni laments the plight of owls in contemporary India. Indians who practise black magic kill owls during Diwali, the festival of lights, to ward off evil or to gain magical powers. Villagers kill owls for their meat, firmly believing that it would cure their illnesses. The need for the owl arises when humans want to appease their desires, and so do the marginalised Dalits' lives matter only when it suits the purpose of the oppressor. In *Koogai*, the dominant castes are also termed 'birds of prey' while Dalits are depicted as a flock of birds taking confused flight when a stone is flung at them, revealing their fragility, meekness and victimisation. Kali Thevar's act of enticing Peichi is compared to a spider weaving its web to catch a cicada. Muthaiya Pandian's sexual assault on Karuppi is compared to a hawk attacking a chick. A vivid image of a falcon (an upper caste) attacking a parrot (the lower caste) has also been employed by Dharman. Eventually, the parrots unite and fight off the falcon. But in episodes like those of Mookkan and Muthukaruppan, after they dine at the club house, the two justify it by saying if an elephant is having his day, the cat should also have one. They compare caste divisions by relating those to not only the physical strength of the animals but also their agility. These remarks hint at the rising power of the oppressed castes.

These instances in *Koogai* throw light on the theory of dominance hierarchy, a system of ranking animals. Just like the caste system stipulates a social hierarchy of human beings in India, the non-human animal world is also seen as following an ecological hierarchical system. This has been emulated by Dharman in *Koogai*. The lions, the elephants, the mighty creatures are associated with the dominant castes, while the relatively physically weaker animals such as goats, sheep, lambs and sparrows are related to Dalits. By following this analogy, Dharman's narrative is in a way subsumed by the same social order which the *koogai* challenges in the first place. It is not often that the bravery of Dalits is compared to that of a tiger or a lion, or any other predator for that matter, in Dalit writings. The binary and the subsequently employed imagery of predator and prey is very much present in the literary world as well. *Koogai*, rather, presents a holistic imagery of who is the predator and the prey.

The comparison of Dalits with the owl and other animal imageries show anthropomorphism at play here. Anthropomorphism is attributing human emotions and traits to non-human entities (like animals in this study). Lorraine Daston and Gregg Mitman's collected volume[31] argues something similar – that anthropomorphism may have its place for reassessing human difference. Daston and Mitman write in their introduction, 'Before either animal individuality or subjectivity can be imagined, an animal must be singled out as a promising prospect for anthropomorphism';[32] they believe the animal must be seen as someone capable of pain and pleasure, as having his or her own affects and capacities. Before the figure of the owl is deconstructed, the narrative of the Pallars in *Koogai* should be seen as a vibrant tapestry of their plight, but it is the internal conflict and hierarchy among Dalit castes that makes Dharman's work distinctive.

But with the impulse to anthropomorphise, there is a tendency to erase the boundaries of difference. This 'difference' is crucial even in our understanding of *Koogai,* so that we see Dalits as fellow beings or subjects and their pain and pleasure may also be conceived of. Hence, as Kari Weil[33] argues, there is a need for 'critical anthropomorphism' so that the difference is acknowledged and the 'animal' is very much present inside the non-animal human as well. As their identity gets inserted into the national discourse from the fringes of society, Dalits are also reclaiming their humanity, as more-than-animal, with the assertion of the Dalit discourse. *Koogai* comes across as a socio-historical novel set in the middle decades of the twentieth century, when the entire country was caught up in sweeping agrarian and industrial changes. How did these reforms affect Dalit lives? *Koogai* enables us to notice that many of them still subsist as bonded labourers. Yet, despite the portrayal of Dalits as bonded labourers, they are not confined solely to these watertight compartments.

A. R. Venkatachalapathy, in his introduction to the translation of *Koogai,* argues that in adapting the fertile *karisal* land storytelling tradition, the novel form has moved beyond a simplistic realism to reach a culturally rooted realism accommodating modern tendencies in the narrative.[34] In this landscape Dharman records the minor tectonic changes that result in major shifts when a village is confronted with migration, urbanisation and an increasingly assertive Dalit population. Using the figure of an owl, Cho. Dharman juxtaposes social realism and magical realism to create a neo-cultural Dalit realism[35] to focus on the plight of Dalits and revive their self-respect and dignity.

Literature is that discourse which provides an avenue for the silenced animals to speak. Rancière had spoken of 'mute speech', which has come to be associated with the language of Dalits as well. But, slowly, with the emergence of neo-critical realism[36] in Dalit narratives, more and more new voices are being heard. Age-old beliefs, unfortunately, are not obliterated over time; instead, they sometimes get enhanced and amplified, thereby giving certain creatures like owls a bad name.

Figure 4.1   Koogai, the Owl deity

Animals have been portrayed in the art, literature, folklore, religion and language of human cultures for millennia. As such, they are important symbols that humans use to make sense of the world. Animal collectives usually bear the figurative burden of social movements. For instance, in India, *Panchatantra* has a long story of a fight between the crows and owls. At the end, the owls are burnt along with their nests by the clever crows. The life story of Dalits and the *koogai* almost run parallel. Koogai-Saami is a god who does not talk, who keeps his pain, suffering and sorrow inside himself. But as the situation arises, he offers protection to the ones he represents – the Dalits.

The Dalit identity is a political identity. It is not just crushed or broken, but also signifies a category that radicalises the consciousness of the oppressed. A new phase of Dalit assertion is articulated by writers such as Cho. Dharman who exemplify strategies of coping, negotiation and resistance in Dalit writings, where the use of animal metaphors, imageries and symbols strengthen their writing in impactful ways.

Notes

1. *Chamar*: They are considered as an 'untouchable' caste in India. The term literally means skin. Historically, they were relegated to the task of curing hides and making shoes.
2. *Bhangi*: Another 'untouchable' caste in India. They are forced into the role of scavengers and thus compelled to do sweeping, waste removal and cleaning toilets.
3. Aniruddha Mukhopadhyay, 'From Worse than Dogs to Heroic Tigers: Situating the Animal in Dalit Autobiographies', *South Asia: Journal of South Asian Studies* 44, no. 4 (2021): 756–71, DOI:10.1080/00856401.2021.1946642.
4. Owls are nocturnal creatures that prefer to live in solitude; they fly silently and their mournful cry is often believed to symbolise evil and death. The hooting of owls was regarded as an ill omen. Sanskrit literature and Sangam Tamil literature associate owls with death. *Panchatantra*, the famous Indian fable book, has a story of a fight between crows and owls. In the end, the clever crows burn the owls along with their nests. During Diwali, the festival of lights, owls are killed by the practitioners of black magic to ward off evil or to gain magical powers. For more, see Bruce Marcot and David H. Johnson, 'Owls in Mythology and Culture', in *Owls of the World: Their Lives, Behaviour and Survival*, ed. James R. Duncan (Toronto: Key Porter Books, 2003), 88–105.
5. Bama, *Karukku*, trans. Lakshmi Holmstrom (New Delhi: Oxford University Press, 2000).
6. Bama, *Karukku*, 63.
7. Wendy Doniger, *On Hinduism* (New York: Oxford University Press, 2014).
8. Doniger, *On Hinduism*, 493–94.
9. Mukul Sharma, 'My World Is a Different World: Caste and Dalit Eco-Literary Traditions', *South Asia: Journal of South Asian Studies* 42, no. 6 (2019): 1013–30, DOI:10.1080/00856401.2019.1667057.
10. Sharma, 'My World Is a Different World', 1027–28.

11. Carry Wolfe, *Animal Rites: Animal Culture, the Discourse of Species, and Posthumanist Theory* (Chicago: The University of Chicago Press, 2003), 9.

12. Manoharamauli Biśvāsa, *Surviving in My World: Growing Up Dalit in Bengal*, trans. and ed. Angana Dutta and Jaydeep Sarangi (Kolkata: Samya, 2015), 84.

13. Gopal Guru, 'Dalits from Margin to Margin', *India International Centre Quarterly* 27, no. 2 (2000): 111–16, 111.

14. An empirical study by Sukhdeo Thorat reveals how caste determines the urban rental housing market. Also see the International Dalit Solidarity Network's 'Manual Scavenging' webpage (idsn.org/key-issues/manual-scavenging/, accessed 28 November 2023) and the Human Rights Watch report on manual scavenging at www.hrw.org/report/2014/08/25/cleaning-human-waste/manual-scavenging-caste-and-discrimination-india, accessed 28 November 2023.

15. Some of the Tamil Dalit writings are Bama's *Karukku* (1992) and *Sangati* (1994), Imayam's *Beasts of Burden* (1994), K. A. Gunasekara's *The Scapegoats* (1999), Abimani's *Tettam* (2001) and P. Sivakami's *Grip of Change* (2006).

16. A. R. Venkatachalapathy, introduction to Cho. Dharman, *Koogai the Owl*, trans. Surya Vasantha (New Delhi: Oxford University Press, 2015), xxxiv.

17. Social realism: A literary form which presents an explicit picture of society in the form of a reportage-like narrative which portrays its hierarchical structure, poverty and social injustice. Premchand, Mulk Raj Anand and Raja Rao created socially realist novels to present a realistic picture of society, while adding certain magical elements to comment on the contemporary social reality.

18. Dharman, *Koogai the Owl*.

19. The Pallar, who prefer to be called now as Devendrakula Vellalar, are an agricultural community from Tamil Nadu. The traditional occupation of the Pallars is ill-defined. They could be gravediggers. However, most Pallars are agricultural labourers but conditions such as poverty and drought have forced them to take up other menial jobs.

20. 'Cho Dharman: Alone in Shadowland', interview by V. Shoba, *Open The Magazine*, 24 January 2019, https://openthemagazine.com/lounge/books/cho-dharman-alone-in-shadowland/, accessed 22 November 2023.

21. Dharman, *Koogai the Owl*, 10.

22. Chakkiliyar: They are traditionally involved in leather work and are considered 'untouchable' in the village caste system.

23. Edward O. Wilson, *Biophilia: The Human Bond with Other Species* (Cambridge: Harvard University Press, 1984), 97.

24. Margo DeMello, *Animals and Society: An Introduction to Human–Animal Studies* (New York: Columbia University Press, 2012), 238.
25. Claude Lévi-Strauss, *Totemism*, trans. Rodney Needham (London: Merlin Press, 1964).
26. DeMello, *Animals and Society*, 288.
27. For a more detailed study on casteised speciesism, refer to Yamini Narayanan, 'Cow Protection as "Casteised Speciesism": Sacralisation, Commercialisation and Politicisation', *South Asia: Journal of South Asian Studies* 41, no. 2 (2018): 331–51, DOI:10.1080/00856401.2018.1419794.
28. Jacques Derrida, *The Beast and the Sovereign*, Vol. 1, trans. Geoffrey Bennington (Chicago and London: University of Chicago Press, 2009), 14.
29. Dharman, *Koogai the Owl*.
30. John Berger (ed.), *Why Look at Animals?* (New York: Vintage, 1992).
31. Lorraine Daston and Gregg Mitman, 'Introduction: The How and Why of Thinking with Animals', in *Thinking with Animals: New Perspectives on Anthropomorphism,* ed. Lorraine Daston and Gregg Mitman (New York: Columbia University Press, 2005), 1–14.
32. Daston and Mitman, 'Introduction', 11.
33. Kari Weil, *Thinking Animals: Why Animal Studies Now?* (New York: Columbia University Press, 2012), 20.
34. Venkatachalapathy, introduction to Dharman, *Koogai the Owl*, xxvi.
35. I use this term to draw attention to the newer genres of Dalit writings (such as Devanoora Mahadeva's *Kusumabale*, G. Kalyan Rao's *Untouchable Spring*) which employ Dalit cultural motifs to reinvent their identity and establish an alternative historiography.
36. Neo-critical realism is an expansion of Aijaz Ahmed's use of critical realism which he refers to as 'a critique of others … in the perspective of an even more comprehensive, multifaceted critique of ourselves'; Aijaz Ahmed, *In Theory: Classes, Nations, Literatures* (London: Verso, 1992), 118. Neo-critical realism, therefore, could be used to deconstruct Dalit writings further.

5

'Dhed and Bhedh'

Caste and Animals in Select Short Stories of Ratan Kumar Sambharia

Deepak

C. S. Lewis, the British theologian and novelist, once proclaimed: 'The tame animal is in the deepest sense the only natural animal.'[1] It prompted a passionate protest from Evelyn Underhill, another theologian who had an aversion for the introduction of modern artifice to nature's pristine being, who said, '... if we ever get a sideway glimpse of the animal-in-itself ... we don't owe it to the Persian cat or the canary, but to some wild free creature living in completeness of adjustment to Nature a life that is utterly independent of man'.[2]

Both these strands of thought symbolise an age-old tussle among thinkers to define essential animal subjectivity. Lewis eulogised the 'tameness' of animals that has played a crucial role in human civilisational projects ever since the first agricultural settlers used bullocks to plough the land. Underhill, on the other hand, is concerned about the primal essence of life, uninfringed upon by motives of human progress. These concerns for nature preservation with utilitarian logic gained potency as human civilisation progressed. But as we shall see in this chapter, human–animal interactions in frontier spaces display a complex dynamism beyond such binary arguments.

As the distance between wilderness and civilisation grew, human–animal relations diversified into various spheres of proximity where they interacted in distinct ways. Irrespective of these differences, every sphere continuously created cultures populated by ideas and representations of other species to deal with their relative distancing.[3] Modern zoos, anthropomorphic fables, constellations, zodiacs and religious symbols are some examples of such relative degrees of substitution. These substitutions were gradually embedded with pedagogic and moralistic functions whose objectives turned more didactic than representative. Such symbolic representations of animals witness a receding animality with a growing extent of human agency. This testifies to the Baudrillardean horror at the potential of simulacra in human–animal interactions, as anticipated by Underhill.

Human exceptionalism, seen as a definitive feature of modern human social structures, is another marker of this fracturing relationship. Its stressing of man's dominion over natural resources and sanctioning disproportionate profiteering echo economies of racial theory, caste system and gender hierarchisation in its legitimisation of a discriminatory structure of labour exploitation in favour of an exclusive privileged group. It has received serious contestations from scientific theories like evolution, which propose animalistic origins of humanity and question the superimposition of sacrosanct Godliness over the human form. Notably, in tribal societies, the human form is not held supreme. Their lineages are drawn from animal ancestors, and the worshipping of totems and adopting animalistic attributes illustrate how animals are mythologised.[4]

As tribal cultures are assimilated into larger societies, totemic deities are gradually replaced with anthropomorphic figures. Indian theology features the worship of animals as rides or symbolic companions for divinities, making for an evident hierarchisation between totemic deities and hegemonic cultural icons. Further, the development of Brahminical cosmologies that regard human birth as superior to other organic forms and maintain that a soul needs to reincarnate countless times to attain a human form has strengthened human exceptionalism in Indian society.

Sanctifying the worship of animal divinities, on the one hand, and demonising communities working with or close to real animals, on the other, form a complex social reality in India. The basis for the extended arrangement of familial ties under the caste system, *gotra* (literally translates to 'related to cow'), hails the drawing of lineage from animal herds belonging to particular personalities. However, the cultural expressions and lifestyles of Dalit communities based around the animal economy are devalued in the Brahminical structure of society. This chapter attempts to examine this complex cultural economy and the interdependent lives of Dalit individuals and animals, both demographics that exist on the margins of Indian society, through an analysis of Ratan Kumar Sambharia's four short stories 'The

Goat's Two Kids', 'The Buffalo', 'The Famine' and 'Salvation'. This chapter will also argue for the possibility of a non-binary (between natural and artificial) space for human–animal interactions offered by marginal frontier cultures like Dalit cultures.

Literary Analysis

Ratan. K. Sambharia is a Hindi Dalit writer whose stories are based around his small native village, Bharawas, on the borders of Haryana and Rajasthan. His short stories fictionalise rural Dalit lives where animals command considerable linguistic, financial and emotional space. His language is replete with animal symbolism, and he constantly employs animal features to describe his characters' appearances, actions and motives. Ramdulare, in the short story 'The Goat's Two Kids', 'claws at his own body like a bear'.[5] Later, in the same short story, a casteist Dan Singh becomes 'as pitiable as a sacrificial goat' after being handcuffed, which makes Dalpat feel as if he 'had vanquished a mighty elephant'.[6] In the short story 'The Buffalo', Mangla dreams 'like a fish swimming in water'.[7] The linguistic atmosphere is so heavily ingrained with animal names and their symbolisms that even the short stories that do not have animal characters feel like they are being narrated in an environment with animal presence. In the short story 'A Chance Meeting', the old man follows Saanwali 'like the tamed monkey of an itinerant juggler'.[8] In another short story, 'The Old Woman', the protagonist's disappointment is referred to as '…if a rogue elephant had trampled on all her hopes'.[9] Even inanimate objects like a flame in the short story 'The New Masseur' 'flicker[s] like a serpent's tongue',[10] and Surti's dreadful memories in the short story 'Word of Honour' 'hiss like a snake'.[11]

Although animals in these narratives shoulder the descriptive purposes of the writer, the conscious use of abundant animal symbolism by Sambharia signals the centrality of animals in the day-to-day lives of rural Dalit communities whose domestic spheres remain incomplete without the presence of animals. For instance, the image of an empty animal pen is repeatedly featured in his stories. Both Dharamkali and Mangla, in the short stories 'The Goat's Two Kids' and 'The Buffalo', respectively, reiterate the cultural wisdom of not keeping the animal-pen empty as it remains a haunting symbol of financial dilapidation.[12] The gradual transformation of an empty pen into one bustling with animal activity forms a central motif that carries the storylines forward. In his writings, animals also function as supplements to fissures in Dalit individuals' lives with whom they cohabit. For example, in the story about a goat and its two kids, Dalpat and Dharamkali attempt to deal with their children's physical absence by adopting a pregnant goat and later her kids as a subconscious emotional substitution. A robustly built and fertile animal in the story 'The Buffalo' supplements Mangla and Sonwa's modest physical attributes, which have been preventing them from getting a suitable match.

On a financial level, the animals in Dalit households also serve as a means of survival and social standing. Chandu's prosperity in the short story 'Salvation' is referred to in terms of his livestock, 'a dozen goats and a pair of cows'.[13] Similarly, the narrator in the short story 'The Famine' recounts, 'He [Surdas, the blind bull] had helped them [Minkhu's family] come out of penury and saved them from starvation. He had earned Minkhu a certain status in the village.'[14] Such newfound financial prosperity by Dalit households kindles jealousy in casteist elements, motivating caste conflicts where the bodies of animals are rendered as sites of violence. This jealousy leads Dharampal to murder Dalpat's goats in 'The Goat's Two Kids'. Lambardar's malign intention of usurping Mangla's buffalo for money and honour in 'The Buffalo' is another example of this phenomenon.

The need to derive nutritional resources from livestock in Dalit households that lack access to multidimensional dietary options also cannot be overlooked. Sambharia's characters consume dairy products like milk and buttermilk as staple foods. Mangla stresses the heavy udders of his buffalo while describing her. The narrator in the short story 'The Goat's Two Kids' qualifies the excellent milk-bearing capacities of Dalpat's goat as worthy of more affection from her master. But there are stark differences between such resource derivation for sustenance and blind, insensitive profiteering by industrial capitalism. Industrial capitalism dislocates bodily sufferings or possible individuality from the end product, conclusively receding the animal and invisiblising it to the full. Dalit communities serving as manufacturing units for animal-derived products and their dislocation away from the main village settlement in India historically extended this deindividuation and invisiblisation to them. In both cases, the structure distances the subject affected from the immediate personal presence of its benefactor.

The Bull versus the Bullocks

In 'Salvation', Sambharia berates the loss of animality of domesticated animals. Contrasting images of 'hennaed ... garlanded' bullocks drawing the idol chariot and the 'ferocious ... mountainous' bull mark the moral failing of tame-domesticated animals standing in direct contrast to wild animals.[15] For Gilles Deleuze and David Guattari, this wildness constitutes the essence of animality. They maintain that animality is defined as 'the power to be wild and unsocialised, to be deindividuated and multiple – a power of which', they claim, 'pets have been stripped'[16] – such an essence stations animal subjectivity beyond human discursive structures and is inherently unfettered.

Sambharia goes further to highlight the physical incompetence and sexual emasculation of bullocks, drawing the religious procession in front of a lonesome, raging bull in the street. This situation foregrounds Nanak's character arc, where he goes from a man subservient to a religious order that treats him as an untouchable but extracts the labour required for its benefit, to him chasing after the *mahant* (the head priest) in anger, finally freeing himself of social barricades. Nanak's transformation bridges the difference between the bullocks and the bull, domestication and wildness, unrecompensed labour and self-determination.

The bullocks' encounter with the bull also familiarises them with a lost part of their primal animality as they wonder: 'We too were born of a cow. Had we not been castrated, we would have been bulls too!'[17] Sambharia, here, criticises human control over animal sexuality, which includes the heightened reproductivity of female animals and the castration of male members. Both of these actions are inspired by utilitarian motives, directed towards maximising productivity from animals for human gains and removal of hindrances to the process of labour extraction. According to John Berger, this gross utilitarian conduct of humans with animals, as livestock or as trophy pets, is tantamount to their deanimalisation. He maintains that moulding them into 'creatures of their owner's way of life' and convenience should be considered an unnatural and violent reconstruction of an artificiality.[18]

The utility principle also enforces a hierarchy of valuation for animal lives. Sambharia's short stories recount multiple instances of reductive behaviour from upper-caste characters who dismiss the emotive content of human–animal relations forged in Dalit households, hoping to buy their derelictions off. Dan Singh's pleading to compensate Dalpat for his dead goats with two buffaloes to evade arrest in 'The Buffalo' exemplifies such hierarchisation, where buffaloes seem more deserving of living than goats based on their higher market value. This process also strips some animals of their right to live when they are not outright beneficial to human prosperity and well-being. For example, Sambharia's resolution of communal tensions in the short story 'Lathi' is affected by the scene of Harman Chacha and Chand Mohammad nonchalantly killing a snake to save their cattle.[19]

Edibility is another criterion of a utilitarian hierarchy for humans, wherein animals are preferred or tabooed based on cultural constructs of deification, domestication and culinary preferences. These constructs are multifaceted and complex. They involve the individualisation or humanisation of select animals. Cultures differ significantly in their choices of animals that can enter private domestic spaces and thus qualify for their pity, while other animals are condemned to suffer deaths that remain invisiblised to cultural imagination. This is why we often see political clashes between cultural schemes to project social power on what is served on the platter. An animal accorded with humanistic individuality by its human companions would accrue intense emotive affections from them, making them ethically inedible as contrasted with the deindividuated invisibility of animals processed through the modern industrial complex. Sambharia's short stories feature narratives of domesticated animals acquiring humanistic individuality in Dalit households in return for serving as means of survival over the years. In the short story 'The Buffalo', Mangla smears the buffalo with *dithona*, a mark to ward off evil eyes in Dharamkali. In the short story of the goat and its kids, the narrator watches the steps of her pregnant goat like she would of a daughter. In the short story 'The Famine', Surdas is described as 'no mere animal, but the life of the entire family'.[20] Sambharia's aesthetic choice to use non-neuter pronouns like 'him' and 'her' instead of 'it' also symbolises this humanisation process. He also recognises the limits to the individualisation of domesticated animals by stopping short of providing human nomenclature to his animal characters (Surdas being an exception). He does not endorse his animal characters as categorically liberated or Dalit households as idealised havens. He recognises that these domesticated animals lie carefully positioned between their state of wilderness, free of human subjection and their life as tame humanised pet animals. His aesthetic commitment is to bring to light the empathetic interdependence of human–animal relations in Dalit cultures.

'Untouchability' of the Holy

Sambharia also exposes the hypocrisy inherent in the caste system that calls upon Dalits to handle unsavoury interactions with the animality of even holy animals and, in turn, marks them polluted for this act of 'handling'. In 'Salvation', the *mahant* calls upon Nanakram and his son, Chand Singh, to chase a bull away and protect the dignity of religion while upper-caste individuals hide their cowardice behind comfortable religious dictates, saying, 'It was Ramnavami. Would they commit the sacrilege of harming the animal … the progeny of a sacred animal like the cow … and risk going to hell?'[21] Nanakram and Chand Singh valiantly fight off a hostile bull from the path of the chariot carrying the idol. The bull had been defending its territory and mating rights while remaining oblivious to being marked as an evil intervention into religious sanctity.[22] Sambharia's insistence on portraying this superimposition of humanistic meaning bares the forcible anthropomorphising of animal sensibilities that declines animals their subjectivity.

Bruce Bagemihl, a Canadian biologist-linguist, writes of such anthropomorphisation similarly:

> For most people, animals are symbolic: their significance lies not in what they are, but in what we think they are. We ascribe meanings and values to their existence and behaviours in ways that usually have little to do with their biological and social realities, treating them as emblems of nature's purity or bestiality to justify, ultimately, our views of other human beings.[23]

The *mahant* demonises the bull as a religious obstacle to be stepped over in the spiritual journey of Nanakram, whose orthodox upbringing receives this superimposition passively before it is shunned towards the end of the story.

It is important to highlight that literary representations of animal existence need not be limited to anthropomorphised projections. The tendency to imagine animals as being indefensibly trapped in human dominion appears ideological in the light of Sambharia's short stories and animal presences like the bull in 'Salvation', which serves as a counterexample of animal assertion.

Spectacle of Pain and the Scope of Justice

It is notable that in 'Salvation', upper-caste individuals lay the responsibility of saving the sanctity of a religious code at Nanakram's feet, but later prohibit him from touching the same idol he saved on account of him being an untouchable. Nonetheless, the story portrays the Dalit individual's mastery over natural elements. Under the caste system, such mastery has ironically positioned Dalit communities as frontiers between Indian society and the wilderness – literally, occupationally and figuratively. The location of their settlements along the peripheral lane, facing topographical features of the region, insulates upper-caste houses, thus forming a literal defensive frontier for the village. Occupations undertaken by these communities that involve handling animals (even those considered divinities) are declared unclean, along with their practitioners. Like in 'Salvation', their essential services are devalued and demonised by a society that would not function in their absence. The most discriminatory aspect of this process is the derecognition of their social contract participation, which excludes them from the scope of social justice and consequently strips their humanity and rights. According to the relational theory of the scope of justice, 'principles of social justice apply among people who are engaged together in a co-operative practice'.[24] Despite such co-operative services provided by Dalit communities, which remain indispensable for Indian society, they were made to occupy a highly unfair arrangement of staying within the social contract but outside any scope of social justice. Devaluing their experiences of emotional violence also pushes popular perceptions about Dalit communities towards animality, placing them as a symbolic frontier between society and the wilderness.

Sensations of pain and loss serve as defining features of inclusion into the scope of justice and are considered humane. In 1789, Jeremy Bentham wrote regarding the moral basis on which to ground our treatment of animals: 'The question is not, can they reason, nor can they talk? But can they suffer?'[25] The constant stress on scientific findings (like those of Jagdish Chandra Bose) that prove that sensations of pain occur in plants as a rebuttal to ecological violence ironically strengthens the pain-hence-alive hypothesis. But to feel pain internally is not enough. It is equally important that a spectacle of suffering is produced that incites pity in a perceptive audience. As mentioned earlier, the extension of deindividuation and invisiblisation to communities working in proximity to animals, along with the inherent alienation induced by the caste structure, reduces the willingness of inter-caste public perception of pain and suffering. Casteist elements like Dan Singh in the short story 'The Goat's Two Kids' symbolise such unwillingness and refusal to acknowledge the emotional violence perpetrated on Dalpat and his chattel, which is evident from his remark, 'You know we do not count dedh and bhedh – cobblers and goats – as living beings, right?'[26] Such proclamations conflate the twin concerns of this chapter together – animalisation of humans and the anthropomorphisation of animals – which shall be perused in the following section.

Sambharia's short stories also point to increasing human encroachment as a source of human–animal conflicts. The wild-animal-state-of-nature

Figure 5.1   Animal–human interconnectedness

subjectivity romanticised by Deleuze, Guattari and Underhill is thus rendered incompatible with the complexities of human social structures like property rights and land enclosures. Dharampal, in the short story 'The Goat's Two Kids', does not recognise any ethical failing in his brutal killing of two young goats for trespassing on his property. He says, 'What atrocity? They kept coming over to our house at any time of the day. So, I have killed the wretches.'[27] The urinating habits of Chand Mohammad's cow, in the short story 'Lathi', also cause an altercation with Harman Chacha that sets the narrative and its exploration of psychological vulnerability. Its resolution also culminates in the killing of a snake from 'their property' to safeguard the livestock. In sum, proximity to human settlements moulds the lived experiences of animals categorically.

Concluding Remarks

> My dog. – I have given a name to my pain and call it 'dog': it is just as faithful, just as obtrusive and shameless, just as entertaining, just as clever as any other dog – and I can scold it and vent my bad moods on it, as others do with their dogs, servants and wives.
>
> – Friedrich Nietzsche, *The Gay Science*[28]

There is a generalised distinction between the three modes of animal being today – wild animals, domesticated livestock and tamed pets. Like the bull in 'Salvation', the wild animal is incontrovertibly immune to human structures. The position of pets in human–animal relations has been a relatively recent philosophical conundrum of animal studies. Culturally specific parameters demarcate companionship between animals that can be livestock or pets for a particular community, with the pet gaining more mobility and access into private human spheres than livestock. Nonetheless, pets, like livestock, go through cycles of natural selection affected by human preferences for selective physiological or behavioural attributes. A culminating product of this process, as with an urban pet, is a reproduction of lifelike toys and aesthetic animal imagery. It works as a supplement for an idealised human that says what we want it to say and sees what we want it to see. A brief reference to a similar supplementation by Dharamkali and Dalpat in adopting a pregnant goat in the story of 'The Goat's Two Kids' has already been made. However, it is relevant to this discussion that

Sambharia's Dalit households do not own pets but have primarily livestock. Livestock could indulge in its animality without appearing uncharacteristic, unlike pets whose training is aimed at amusingly mirroring human behaviour. This resemblance is, by design, supposed to fall just short so as not to stroke the existential anxieties of boundaries for both the pet and the owner. The unnatural nature of a perfectly conversant pet would seem a borderline caricature and has been a recurrent popular literary trope, such as in Art Spiegelman's *Maus* or George Orwell's *Animal Farm*.

The lack of a linguistic function is characteristic of the complexity inherent in human–animal relations. This absence of conversational space is what Berger calls an abyss of non-comprehension that defines human–animal relationships whose essence lies in its unbridgeable gap.[29] Peter Beatson visualises this gap through an anthropocentric conceptual cartographical field where human interaction with wilderness is modulated through lenses like culture, politics, economy, demography, and so on.[30] The animal being is non-cognisant of these structures and thus non-conversant. But time and again, fascination around a structural inversion has been quite popular. The literary trope of a jungle boy is found across cultures worldwide. There have been curious cases of young children living away from settlements, deep in the wilderness and unbeknownst to human structures, like Peter the wild boy, discovered in Germany in 1725.[31] Zoo animals are the other end of the inverted spectrum, whose existence Philip Armstrong calls 'a simulacrum, a sign of the absence of an authentic human–animal relationship'.[32] These animals are stripped of their natural industry and expression, only to be ingrained with tropes of human amusement and entertainment.[33]

Sambharia's short stories portray Dalit cultures where the human–animal relationship is more dynamic than these spectrums and does not fit an exploiter–saviour binary. Sharamchand's 'leather-shod shoes' and his supposed role as the harbinger of justice for the dead goats encapsulate this complexity.[34] This complexity is referred to by John Berger when he points out, 'A peasant becomes fond of his pig and is glad to salt away its pork. What is significant and difficult for the urban stranger to understand is that the two statements in that sentence are connected with an "and" and not by a "but".'[35] Such complexities caution against the romanticisation of rural societies as havens of human–animal co-existence, as lived experiences, and the animality of non-humans remains disproportionately dominated by humans here as well. But Sambharia's short stories show that despite the onslaught of industrial capitalism, Dalit cultures maintain an economy based on animals that offers scope for their individualisation and development of emotional bonds.

Notes

1. Andrew Linzey, 'C.S. Lewis's Theology of Animals', *Anglican Theological Review* 80, no. 1 (1998): 60–81.
2. Linzey, 'C.S. Lewis's Theology of Animals'.
3. Peter Beatson, 'Mapping Human Animal Relations', in *Theorising Animals: Re-thinking Humananimal Relations*, ed. Nik Taylor and Tania Signal (Boston: Brill, 2011), 21–58.
4. Manash Pratim Goswami, 'Totemism and Tribes: A Study of the Concept and Practice', Research Gate (July 2018), https://www.researchgate.net/publication/326655380_Totemism_and_Tribes_A_Study_of_the_Concept_and_Practice, accessed 12 January 2022.
5. Ratan Kumar Sambharia, 'The Goat's Two Kids', in *Thunderstorm: Dalit Stories,* trans. Mridul Bhasin (Gurgaon: Hachette, 2015), 19–35.
6. Ratan Kumar Sambharia, 'A Chance Meeting', in *Thunderstorm: Dalit Stories,* trans. Mridul Bhasin (Gurgaon: Hachette, 2015), 36–56.
7. Ratan Kumar Sambharia, 'The Buffalo', in *Thunderstorm: Dalit Stories,* trans. Mridul Bhasin (Gurgaon: Hachette, 2015), 65–82.
8. Sambharia, 'A Chance Meeting'.
9. Ratan Kumar Sambharia, 'The Old Woman', in *Thunderstorm: Dalit Stories,* trans. Mridul Bhasin (Gurgaon: Hachette, 2015), 83–96.
10. Ratan Kumar Sambharia, 'The New Masseur', in *Thunderstorm: Dalit Stories,* trans. Mridul Bhasin (Gurgaon: Hachette, 2015), 193–211.
11. Ratan Kumar Sambharia, 'Word of Honour', in *Thunderstorm: Dalit Stories,* trans. Mridul Bhasin (Gurgaon: Hachette, 2015), 143–64.
12. Sambharia, 'The Goat's Two Kids'; Sambharia, 'The Buffalo'
13. Ratan Kumar Sambharia, 'Salvation', in *Thunderstorm: Dalit Stories,* trans. Mridul Bhasin (Gurgaon: Hachette, 2015), 164–78.
14. Ratan Kumar Sambharia, 'The Famine', in *Thunderstorm: Dalit Stories,* trans. Mridul Bhasin (Gurgaon: Hachette, 2015), 97–109.
15. Sambharia, 'Word of Honour'.
16. Kari Weil, 'Is a Pet an Animal? Domestication and Animal Agency', in *Thinking Animals: Why Animal Studies Now?* (New York: Columbia University Press, 2012), 53–62.

17. Sambharia, 'Salvation'.

18. John Berger, 'Why Look at Animals?', in *About Looking,* ed. John Berger (New York: Vintage Books, 1992), 3–28.

19. Ratan Kumar Sambharia, 'Lathi', in *Thunderstorm: Dalit Stories,* trans. Mridul Bhasin (Gurgaon: Hachette, 2015), 179–92.

20. Sambharia, 'The Famine'.

21. Sambharia, 'Salvation'.

22. Sambharia, 'Salvation'.

23. Bruce Bagemihl, *Biological Exuberance: Animal Homosexuality and Natural Diversity* (London: Profile Books, 1999).

24. David Miller, 'Justice', *The Stanford Encyclopedia of Philosophy* (Fall 2023), ed. Edward N. Zalta and Uri Nodelman, https://plato.stanford.edu/archives/fall2023/entries/justice/, accessed 24 October 2021.

25. Jeremy Bentham, 'A Utilitarian View', in *Bioethics: An Anthology,* ed. Udo Schüklenk and Peter Singer Helga Kuhse (Sussex: John Wiley and Blackwell, 2016), 529.

26. Sambharia, 'The Goat's Two Kids'.

27. Sambharia, 'The Goat's Two Kids'.

28. Friedrich Nietzsche, *The Gay Science* (New York: Vintage Books, 1974).

29. Berger, 'Why Look at Animals?'

30. Beatson, 'Mapping Human Animal Relations'.

31. Michael Newton, 'Bodies Without Souls: The Case of Peter the Wild Boy', in *At the Borders: Beasts, Bodies and Natural Philosophy in the Early Modern Period*, ed. Erica Fudge and Susan Wiseman Erica Fudge (London: Macmillan Press, 1999), 196–214.

32. Philip Armstrong, 'The Gaze of Animals', in *Theorising Animals: Re-thinking Humanimal Relations,* ed. Nik Taylor and Tania Signal (Boston: Brill, 2011), 175–99.

33. Berger, 'Why Look at Animals?'

34. Sambharia, 'The Goat's Two Kids'.

35. Berger, 'Why Look at Animals?'

6

Holy Cow, Unholy Meat

Food Ecologies, Affective Communities and Violence in *The Revenge of the Non-Vegetarian*

Greeshma Mohan

The Indian writer Upamanyu Chatterjee, whose debut novel *English, August*, published in 1988, examined the coming of age of Agastya Sen, a disenchanted junior civil servant in a moffusil Indian town, returns to examine bureaucratic power in his recent novella titled *The Revenge of the Non-Vegetarian*.[1] Published in 2018, the novella features Agastya's father, Madhusudan Sen, as a budding officer of the Indian Civil Services posted in the fictional north Indian state of Narmada Pradesh in newly independent India. Sen's proclivity for beef and his difficulty in sourcing meat in a predominantly Hindu town serve as a fertile ground for debates around the politics of food choices – who gets to choose, who bears the burden to service that choice, the cost of consuming meat in a geographically 'vegetarian' region and the larger ethics of a non-vegetarian diet. While Sen clandestinely ropes in a Muslim subordinate, Nadeem Dahlvi, to replenish his appetite for beef, in particular, this secret contract is sundered when Dahlvi and his family are murdered. This crime echoes the escalating violence of 'gau rakshaks', or self-styled cow protectors, mostly male and always Hindu, who assault and sometimes lynch those who belong to historically marginalised religious and caste communities, especially Muslims and Dalits, for consuming or simply possessing beef. The lynching of Mohammed Akhlaq by upper-caste Hindu Thakurs in Dadri, a village in Uttar Pradesh, in 2015 is one of the few cases of lynching that has garnered attention, with the perpetrators still left free.[2] The novella exposes the slow judicial process in postcolonial India, the impossibility of an equitable punishment for crime, and the idea of revenge as a stand-in and an instantaneous substitute for justice.

My chapter takes off from Arjun Appadurai's observation that food as 'a powerful semiotic device' not only signifies certain meanings in social transactions but also has an affective power of evoking strong emotions.[3] In fact, vegetarianism is often defended through recourse to the affective: the pain and suffering undergone by animals, the disgust and repulsion inherent in the slaughter of meat, the absolute state of abjection of factory-farmed animals, and so on. Leela Gandhi refers to Gandhi's alimentary disaffection, wherein his discomfiture is largely centred on having to subsist on 'bread, porridge, and potatoes',[4] a diet that only heightens his homesickness and leads him to discover a subculture of English vegetarianism in fin de siècle London. The societies and clubs that made up this subculture were, to Gandhi, exemplars of hospitality to colonial subjects such as himself. A shared ethics centred on abjuring meat allows Gandhi to imagine such a subculture as premised on generosity, kindness, openness, friendship and sociality, or, as Leela Gandhi identifies it, 'vegetarian xenophilia'.[5] That food can generate affective communities which include social others is worth noting.

Yet the current discourse around vegetarianism in India creates sociality not through friendship but through violence towards religious minorities. The anxiety of the impure, meat-eating other can be managed only through repeated performative acts of lynching in the name of protecting the cow. The phenomenon of 'cow protectors' patrolling Muslim-majority districts on the lookout for 'trafficking' of cows exemplifies an existing undercurrent to establish a Hindu majoritarian state. Parvis Ghassem-Fachandi excavated precisely this disavowal of Muslims during his fieldwork in Gujarat in the early 2000s. The admixture of fear and hatred of meat and its mostly Muslim consumer is expressed in corporeal ways, such as vomiting and fainting, and enables the identity formation of the contemporary Hindu subject. Ghassem-Fachandi is interested in how religious belonging and nationalism are viscerally experienced by Hindus as strong feelings, sentiments and as affect, or what he calls forms of 'cultivated digestive disinvestment' solely premised on repulsion for meat and meat-eating minorities.[6] Yet, for the 'gau rakshaks', aversion for meat is coupled with violence towards its consumer, as though meat-eaters and those in professions who come in contact with cattle (butchers, tanners) embody threat and contagion. The 'gau rakshak' is not merely, as Ghassem-Fachandi puts it, 'a hyperbolic vegetarian' but a militant one who uses violence to alleviate his disgust and fear of the Muslim.

In *The Revenge of the Non-Vegetarian* the protagonist Madhusudan Sen is fastidious about having some amount of meat in every meal; he is accustomed to 'eggs and sausages, liver, toast, fruit'. Sen lives on Temple Road in the Civil Lines area of Batia, an area informally designated as vegetarian due to its proximity to the Dayasagar Adinath temple. When thwarted by his upper-caste Brahmin cook, Murari, who refuses to depart from upper-caste dietary laws that prohibit alliums and meat, Sen comes up with an ingenious plan to source his meat. He arranges for his junior officer, Nadeem Dahlvi, to provide him with two home-cooked non-vegetarian meals on a daily basis. Sen is particular about the kind of meat he enjoys, indicating that chicken is to be avoided, as it was 'so tasteless that it made him feel vegetarian', and that he preferred eggs, river fish and red meat, specifically beef.[7] Although Sen tries to couch this pact as a mere financial transaction, the element of subterfuge is apparent since Dahlvi, a Muslim, ensures that his most trustworthy peon, also a Muslim, would deliver the food to Sen's house.

However, this secret arrangement is revealed when Sen's 'principal protein and cholesterol supplier', Dahlvi, is murdered and burnt along with his family at his house. When asked about the Dahlvis, the servant, presumably a lower-caste Dalit, Basant Kumar Bal, characterises them as a family that always ate well while he would be expected to survive on their leftovers. His angry exhortation about the Dahlvis literally starving those who labour for them is the only instance in the entire novel of Bal as a speaking subject, demonstrating what can be understood as agency, volition and emotion.

However, when Bal is found missing and later located in the Dahlvis' well along with their jewels and, significantly, the cooking vessel – now smelling of putrefaction – used to store the beef curry, it is revealed that he is the murderer. The murder is revealed to have been committed by a hungry Bal, as an act of defiance against routine deprivation and humiliation at the hands of the Dahlvis, as borne out by the events leading up to the murder: Bal is portrayed ferrying aromatic beef stew to Dahlvi's house, acutely aware that he would not be allowed to taste even a morsel – it is the proximity, the invasive smell of beef, that makes him experience his deprivation keenly – when he decides to consume a portion of it clandestinely in a field. This act of transgression is framed as an idyllic, heavenly, pleasurable experience for Bal, not only because he satiates his desire for beef but also because he is removed from the social order of a small town, wherein he is only visible as a servant, in servitude:

> When he can't be seen by any passerby he ... sits down cross-legged himself and, with the kulchas, eats about a third of the meat. For twenty minutes, the only sounds around him are the hoot of a distant train approaching the level crossing, the clamour of birds returning to roost in their favourite trees, the tinkling of bells of passing bicycles, the rustle of a bandicoot amongst the stalks of sugarcane and his own methodical, noisy chewing. The meat is soft, well-stewed. He masticates even the bones to powder, swallows them. He burps. It will soon begin to get dark. He burps again. He is sated, for five minutes, he cannot move or think.[8]

Satiety is portrayed as a vegetative state of inaction, and opposed to volition. Bal's response to the beef stew is anything but calculated; it is the impulsive, instinctual and immediate response of a hungry man, and is similar in nature to the murder he is about to undertake. When Bal returns to the Dahlvi household, he is told off for eating the stew by the sister-in-law, who is described as 'a fleshless, despondent thing' – malnourished, yet an insider, and thus able to exercise authority over Bal. Only when the family dog paws the vat of stew does Bal understand it as 'an insult to his sense of self', that there could be continuities between his appetite and the animal's, that both are similarly deprived, abject subjects, and the recognition of their coincidence enrages him so much that he kills the dog and the rest of the family.[9] Here, it would be apt to quote Elspeth Probyn, who understands that eating is a visceral reminder of our immediacy and coincidence with the animate other, 'it is something we all have to do, and it is a powerful mode of mediation – it joins us with others'.[10] The murders are presented as crimes of passion, as unthinking, instinctual and belonging to the realm of immediacy than pre-meditation. Therefore, Bal's revenge must be understood as that of the deprived servant, who has, for years, survived on the leftovers of non-vegetarian meals consumed on a daily basis in the Dahlvi household.

The Limits of Hospitality

Hospitality and its limits, its reflection in the apportioning of food to guests and superiors at the cost, deprivation and hunger of others within the household, are continuing themes in the novella. Appadurai notes that, in the South Asian context, food 'can serve diametrically opposed functions' of constructing 'social relations characterized by equality, intimacy, or solidarity' or 'rank, distance or segmentation', and these invisible hierarchies guide rules of hospitality in the Indian household. The Dahlvi household can be seen as situated within a form of hospitality centred on Appadurai's idea of gastropolitics, which he defines as 'the conflict or competition over specific cultural or economic resources as it emerges in social transactions around food'.[11] Nadeem Dahlvi provides shelter to his sister-in-law and her daughter only insofar as they bear the burden of preparing meals along with housekeeping, and eat last – only after the family has been served. Appadurai enumerates the norm as – 'if the kinsman who is a long-term and economically dependent "guest" is a woman ... she can either put up with the overdetermined negative status of being a dependent, but peripheral, female or she can slide into the role of "servant", which is also encoded largely in gastropolitical terms, such as the receipt of leftovers'.[12] Notably, a woman in such a position can gain centrality and eke for herself power in the household by claiming the role of servant or housekeeper.

Among the Dahlvis, unsurprisingly, the men would have precedence over the women when it came to food consumption, even as they remained completely disengaged with the process of preparing meals. Bal, however, exists beyond the familial hierarchy; as an outcaste, he is defined solely by his proximity to their leftovers – both as edible food for himself and as an unfinished meal to be discarded – which is an acute form of exclusion and 'gastronomic humiliation' similar to the historical exclusion of lower castes and Dalits.[13] The consigning of leftovers signifies Bal's total abjection, and becomes a possible motive for the murder. Bal's characteristic muteness should be read in terms of his continued humiliation at the hands of the Dahlvis, as a daily experience wherein he is 'rendered inferior or deficient in some respect by others in a deliberate and destructive way' through 'a constant threat to his sense of self-worth'. For Palshikar, humiliation is a form of communication, made possible by a shared language of governing social norms.[14] The shared language in the text is food cooked in the Dahlvi hearth, which works as a threshold to exclude those like Bal.

Sen's relationship with the Dahlvi household, in comparison, is of intimate hospitality, as a long-standing guest whose meals come directly from the Dahlvi hearth. In a sense, he is both hosted by and held hostage by the Dahlvis, since his appetite is chained to their whims, and he can never know in advance what he will be eating – hospitality, therefore, is conceived as an index of 'entanglement, precarity and collective transformation'. Sen is reminded of his alimentary dependence on the Dahlvi household in less than a day of the family's passing. Here it would be apt to reiterate Julietta Singh's conception of hospitality as 'an interplay among multiple agents: it is a relation, a dynamic, a volley', a negotiation of identities that goes beyond the mere passive ingestion of the offerings of the host.[15]

Derrida theorises that at the heart of hospitality lies an aporia, an antinomy that makes absolute openness to the other in all iterations, 'who or what turns up before any determination, before any anticipation, before any identification whether or not it has to do with a foreigner, an immigrant, an uninvited guest, or an unexpected visitor, whether or not the new arrival is the citizen of another country, a human, animal, or divine creature, a living or dead thing, male or female', impossible; this openness for Derrida is unconditional hospitality, hospitality in its ideal form. However, this law of unconditional hospitality is threatened and undermined by prevailing laws. As Derrida explains,

> there would an antinomy, a non-dialectizable antinomy, between, on the one hand, The law of unlimited hospitality (to give to the new arrival all of one's home and oneself, to give him or her one's own, our own, without asking a name, or compensation, or fulfilment of even the smallest condition), and on the other hand, laws (in the plural), those rights and duties that are always conditioned and conditional ... in particular across the family, civil society, and the State.... The antinomy of hospitality irreconcilably opposes The law, in its universal singularity, to a plurality that is not only a dispersal (laws in plural), but a structured multiplicity, determined by a process of division and differentiation.[16]

I will be looking at the particular tension between hospitality in its ideal form sans all conditions and hospitality as it is played out in Chatterjee's novella. I propose that the various forms of hospitality – for instance, Dahlvi's sister-in-law's position as a long-standing guest, the transactional relationship between Sen and Dahlvi, or Sen's singular act of generosity towards Bal by allowing him one non-vegetarian meal while in prison – must be viewed as springing from the host's need to be seen as a benevolent, liberal master.

In fact, Judith Still reads the encounter as less of an invitation than as a visitation, an arrival that the host must be open to, yet notably she adds a caveat regarding the impossibility of such a utopian state. She is less invested in proving the 'failure' of the universal law of hospitality, especially when it cannot pass muster in practical situations, than in using the impossible law to etch out certain qualities inherent to hospitality. She formulates hospitality as a 'material structure that regulates relations between inside and outside' which also has 'crucial affective elements: the emotional relations associated with hospitality such as heartfelt generosity or sincere gratitude'.[17] More importantly, she draws our attention to two aspects of hospitality, specifically its peculiar invasiveness and its temporality; as she puts it, 'hospitality is a particular form of the gift that involves *temporary* sharing of space, sometimes also time, bodies, food and other consumables'.[18] This formulation is premised on the idea that hospitality, akin to gifting, involves both giving and expecting something in return: in other words, the promise of reciprocity that is underwritten into gift exchange. Gifting, which is a sign of hospitality, is invasive: it is presumed that a person would enjoy or find pleasure in the given gift; while arising out of generosity, it also evokes feelings of obligation, gratitude and expectation of something of equal or greater value to be given back to a previous state of equality before the exchange. For instance, this exchange in Chatterjee's novel: after Nadeem Dahlvi's death, his brother Arif steps in to provide the magistrate with his daily intake of non-vegetarian food, and Sen is 'both annoyed – "Really, how could you think of food in the middle of such a tragedy!" – and touched – "But thoughtful of you to remember the needs of others at a time like this."'[19] Arif Dahlvi's continued hospitality towards Sen is contingent upon the expectation that the murderer will be brought to justice. Sen's visible annoyance can be attributed to him wanting to appear as a liberal figurehead and even-tempered guardian of law, but he is reminded of the primacy of his appetite, and relief on finding that his digestive needs will be met, and ultimately his continued dependency on the Dahlvis, one that he is beholden to return. In recasting hospitality as a temporary, albeit long-drawn arrangement, Chatterjee exposes its affective dimension, its transactional nature, wherein the guest feels grateful, even indebted to his host, years after the extension of hospitality.

Alternately, Derrida tries to locate the beginnings of exclusion in the very act of hospitality; the very moment of inviting the other into one's home – the crossing of the threshold of the public into the private – encompasses both inclusion and exclusion.[20] Chatterjee's novel imagines thresholds both as porous boundaries for some and as impenetrable walls for others and encapsulates Still's argument that hospitality fundamentally involves the crossing of boundaries and thresholds between 'the self and the other, private and public, inside and outside, individual and collective, personal and political, emotional and rational, generous and economic'.[21] In the South Asian context, caste and religious codes underwrite the limits of hospitality, where often religious others are allowed to enter the home but not consume from the hearth. Similarly, in Indian households, the maintenance of caste boundaries is transferred onto inanimate objects such as utensils, insofar as separate plates and tumblers are used to serve visitors, whose caste cannot be known beforehand, hence avoiding the host of pollution.

Mastering Disgust

Mastery is crucial to both hospitality and humiliation, in that it is always the master of the house who invites the guest in – enacts the conditions and limits of hospitality – to partake of whatever is on offer, and is premised on transforming the object through total control. As Julietta Singh reminds us:

> As a pursuit, mastery invariably and relentlessly reaches toward the indiscriminate control over something—whether human or inhuman, animate or inanimate. It aims for the full submission of the object—or something *objectified*—whether it be external or internal to oneself. In doing so, mastery requires a rupturing of the object being mastered, because to be mastered means to be weakened to the point of fracture. Mastery in this sense is a splitting of the object that is mastered from itself, a way of estranging the mastered object from its previous state of being.[22]

Given this, Bal's murder of the Dahlvi family and their dog can be seen as stemming from such 'a desire or demand for recognition' as human and equal.[23] Bal experiences mastery as physical strength, and soon turns to rage, resulting in the murders carried out in quick succession, followed by relief at having 'one free evening' to himself.[24] Bal soon realises the irony of the situation, that his 'free' evening will be spent in cleaning up the scene of the crime. Therefore, the murders, which are a result of class and caste rage, allow Bal to see himself not as the mastered object but as the master.

Singh draws our attention to how submission makes extraordinary demands of the object – including objectification, reduction to an inanimate, unthinking 'thing', ruptured to the point of being fragile and weak – resulting in a departure, an estrangement 'of the mastered object from the previous state of being'.[25] Since Bal is afforded no interiority by the author, his exact motive for the murders cannot be ascertained but only conjectured. His progressive dehumanisation over the years to a state of being worse off than the Dahlvi family dog ruptures his sense of being human, superior in rank to an animal. Bal is solely defined by his appetite for meat, which is seen as an abnormal, uncontrollable urge that could drive him to murder. While investigating the murder of the entire Dahlvi family, even the police attempt to entice Bal with a non-vegetarian meal, in order to get the confession of murder from him.

However, Chatterjee's text is as much invested in beef eating as a pleasurable experience as it is in animal slaughter, which makes such consumption possible. Midway through the novel, after Bal has been imprisoned, the author presents us with the pitiful image of a calf being led to slaughter. The horrors of the slaughterhouse are indicated through the repulsive smell it emanates, so much that Sen, who is coincidentally in the vicinity, is assaulted by, and drawn to, the stench 'of carrion, of rotten flesh and hot glue – that his stomach, for the first time in his life, had actually heaved'.[26] At this stage in the novel, Chatterjee undertakes an extensive description of a frightened buffalo calf being slaughtered sans anaesthesia – this primal scene is aimed at an affective transformation of Sen and the reader by creating a sense of shock, disgust and sympathy – which importantly changes the tone of the novel and introduces the idea of the ethics of meat consumption:

> The cement floor of the shed was slippery with excrement, blood, offal and gore. Inside, it hit them like a hard slap on the head, the din of the animal world giving voice to its terror—the mooing of cattle sensing slaughter, the bleating of goats about to have their limbs broken and their blood drained out of gashes in their throats, hens in cages, clucking in frenzy seconds before being pulled out and beheaded. Sen himself, gazing about him, felt totally unmanned at all that carnage,

those bits of skin and hair and clumps of crimson flesh scattered all over
the floor. And the stench was frightful; the terrible fetor from the vicinal
boiling house for the button factory mingled with the permanent smell
of fresh, raw meat, of animal excrement, blood and fear and the sweat
of the butchers.[27]

The scene establishes the political economy of a meat-centric diet, the
obscuring of the (now industrialised) production of meat and its tenuous
journey from factory to the dinner table. Sen is blissfully unaware of how
his meal is put together and, more importantly, that a non-vegetarian
diet is contingent on killing, centred on the enslavement and slaughter of
animals, which essentially causes animals pain and suffering and violates
their freedom. It is only in the slaughterhouse that Sen is forced to confront
the fact that the meat he consumes in so cleaned, processed a form as to
make its visceral source unrecognisable is derived from living beings akin to
himself. The slaughterhouse scene is particularly gory since it carries traces of
guts, viscera, blood, flesh, skin, and fetor of formerly living beings, the stark
opposite of the neat meat cutlets Sen consumes. Witnessing animal slaughter
disgusts meat eaters such as Sen since it 'violates the comfortable assumption
of morality and transcendence that underwrites our sense as autonomous
beings'. Animal slaughter hollows out the liberal discourse premised on man's
rationality that makes him superior to the rest of species, of which Sen is an
exemplar: 'in the killing and eating of animals we appear not as transcendent
and rational creatures, but as mortal beasts subject to all the vulnerability
and more of the brutality characteristic of other animals'.[28] Confronted by
the slaughter, Sen's transformation is both affective and corporeal: his spine
tingles and teeth twinge, and his conversion to vegetarianism is assured:
'this is for the likes of me, this unspeakable savagery and torture; this blood
sport with sacred life is but to create some cutlet or curry or kebab for the
dinner tables of carnivores'.[29] It is the labour behind transforming dead
animal flesh into a cutlet or sausage – divested of its animal origins – that
shocks Sen since he has probably never handled or cooked his own meat.
This episode is noteworthy since it reminds Sen, the figurehead of liberalism
and sovereignty, of his dependency on animal slaughter, making him aware
of his vulnerability, even mortality, much like the animal that forms part of
his diet.

When Sen is made aware of the cost of his dependency, he immediately
shuts down the slaughterhouse and abjures meat for an extended period, since

Figure 6.1 'Holy' cow

both are acts of mastery. This is significant because it represents the liberal master's attempt at managing his disgust in the realm of personal food choice, which, in the words of Lavin, indicates 'retreat from public life, indulging in longing for a purity, a privacy or a transcendence that is unavailable in the messy realm of collective living but can at least be fantastically established within the confines of the home'.[30]

Therefore, it is the politics of purity that creates a through line between vegetarianism as an ethical, reformative choice (as atonement undertaken by Sen) and the militant vegetarianism of the cow protectionist militias. The nostalgic desire to restore a muscular, vegetarian Hindu nation, unsullied by Muslim 'invaders' and the colonial encounter, is itself a part of an elaborate mythography endorsed by right-wing Hindutva groups; yet such mythographies become, as Appadurai puts it, 'charters for new social projects' such as anti-cow-slaughter laws, the disenfranchisement of minorities (through laws like the Citizenship Amendment Act) and the incarceration of dissenting voices, as seen in India.[31] The ability to demarcate certain communities as dirty and contaminating due to their food choices and proximity to cattle and mark them as worthy targets of vigilante violence in order to shore up a pure, masculine Hindu nation is made possible only through the creation and perpetuation of affective states of fear, disgust and anxiety. To conclude, we need to imagine ethical choices that are not underwritten by a politics of purity.

Notes

1. Upamanyu Chatterjee, *The Revenge of the Non-Vegetarian* (New Delhi: Speaking Tiger, 2018).
2. Although cow vigilantism has been around, it has become increasingly frequent since 2014. Of the numerous cases of Muslims being lynched by cow protection armies for slaughter, possession or transport of cows, the most well known is Mohammed Akhlaq's lynching in Dadri, Uttar Pradesh, in 2015, which set a template for future attacks on unarmed Muslims.
3. Arjun Appadurai, 'Gastro-Politics in Hindu South Asia', *American Ethnologist* 8, no. 2 (1981): 494–506.
4. Leela Gandhi, *Affective Communities: Anticolonial Thought and the Politics of Friendship* (New Delhi: Permanent Black, 2006).
5. Gandhi, *Affective Communities*.
6. Parvis Ghassem-Fachandi, 'The Hyperbolic Vegetarian: Notes on a Fragile Subject in Gujarat', in *Being There: The Fieldwork Encounter and the Making of Truth*, ed. John Borneman and Abdellah Hammoudi, 77–112 (Berkeley: University of California Press, 2009).
7. Chatterjee, *The Revenge of the Non-Vegetarian*.
8. Chatterjee, *The Revenge of the Non-Vegetarian*, 52.
9. Chatterjee, *The Revenge of the Non-Vegetarian*.
10. Elspeth Probyn, *Carnal Appetites: Food Sex Identities* (London: Routledge, 2000).
11. Appadurai, 'Gastro-Politics in Hindu South Asia'.
12. Appadurai, 'Gastro-Politics in Hindu South Asia'.
13. Appadurai, 'Gastro-Politics in Hindu South Asia'.
14. Sanjay Palshikar, 'Understanding Humiliation', *Economic and Political Weekly* 40, no. 51 (2005): 5428–31.

15. Julietta Singh, 'Future Hospitalities', *Cultural Critique* 95 (2017): 198–206.

16. Jacques Derrida, 'Step of Hospitality/No Hospitality', in *Of Hospitality*, ed. Anne Dofourmantlle and Jacques Derrida, trans. Rachel Bowlby, 4–14 (California: Stanford University Press, 2000).

17. Judith Still, *Derrida and Hospitality: Theory and Practice* (Edinburgh: Edinburgh University Press, 2010).

18. Still, *Derrida and Hospitality*.

19. Chatterjee, *The Revenge of the Non-Vegetarian*.

20. Derrida, 'Step of Hospitality/No Hospitality'.

21. Still, *Derrida and Hospitality*.

22. Singh, *Unthinking Mastery: Dehumanism and Decolonial Entanglements* (Durham and London: Duke University Press, 2018).

23. Singh, *Unthinking Mastery*.

24. Chatterjee, *The Revenge of the Non-Vegetarian*.

25. Singh, *Unthinking Mastery*.

26. Upamanyu Chatterjee, *The Revenge of the Non-Vegetarian*.

27. Chatterjee, *The Revenge of the Non-Vegetarian*, 84.

28. Chad Lavin, *Eating Anxiety: The Perils of Food Politics* (Minneapolis: University of Minnesota Press, 2013).

29. Chatterjee, *The Revenge of the Non-Vegetarian*.

30. Lavin, *Eating Anxiety*.

31. Arjun Appadurai, *Modernity At Large: Cultural Dimensions of Globalization* (Minneapolis: University of Minnesota Press, 1996).

HUMAN–ANIMALS RELATIONS IN THE NORTHEAST

7

Without a Pig, a Bodo
Life Is Incomplete

Rachan Daimary

Introduction

There are various ways to view tribal communities and their relations with animals, both domesticated and wild animals. The worldview of tribal communities is incomplete without the presence of animals. This chapter discusses the exceptional human–animal relations of a tribe, the Bodo,[1] from northeast India. Among all the tribal societies, the Bodo are known as the largest tribe in the plains of the northeast region. However, this community has a few characteristics that make them different from others. For example, pigs, known as *oma* in Bodo language, are an important part of the Bodo community, reflecting a strong human–animal bond, which is the focus of the chapter. The relationship between humans and animals in Bodo society has its own value for defining the community as an inimitable tribal group in the world. In this chapter, I look at the Bodoland Territorial Region (BTR) and examine (*a*) the everyday lives of the Bodo with respect to pigs, (*b*) the importance of pigs in the sociocultural milieu, (*c*) pigs as an economy and livelihood and (*d*) the transformation in Bodo–pig relations.

The BTR is an autonomous area in Assam, India, and a proposed state in northeast India. It consists of five districts situated on the northern bank of the Brahmaputra river, at the foothills of Bhutan and Arunachal Pradesh.[2] It is a subdivision of the government established in accordance with the Sixth Schedule of the Indian Constitution. It was formerly known as the Bodoland Territorial Council (BTC) when it was a separate region. Traditionally, the

Bodo community lived, and many still live, in forested landscapes adjoining the foothills and near streams or rivers. Their lives continue to be intricately connected to flora and fauna. As animists who see the world of plants and other beings as part of their social lives, the Bodo belief system and their daily lives are informed by their relations with the surrounding environment. The existence of pluralistic gods and goddesses is central to the religion that the Bodo follows. One example of their linkages with nature is the *sijou* plant (*Euphorbia splendens*), a member of the Euphorbiaceae family. This plant is worshipped and plays a major role in Bodo daily practices, with religious significance linking it to folk narratives. The Bodo believe this plant is a living embodiment of the Bwrai Bathou, or Supreme Soul. The Bodo follow a belief system centred on Bathou Bwrai or Sijou (a name derived from the plant). *Ba* denotes five, while *thou* denotes in-depth thought, literally referring to the five supernatural elements – land, water, air, fire and the sky – and signifying 'deep five thoughts'. The animistic religion followed by the Bodo connects the community with various natural elements. Several animals, besides pigs, are considered significant – for example, ducks, fowl, goats, cattle and dogs. Pigs, in particular, are central to the lives of Bodo economically, socially and culturally.

Oma in Bodo Lives

In the Bodo language, pigs are referred to as *oma*. With multifaceted relations with the Bodo, the role of *oma* ranges from utilitarianism to cultural symbolism and sociocultural relevance. Women mainly look after *oma* by feeding, rearing and selling them during financial need. Considered as 'fixed deposits', they are a form of economic security. More importantly, they are important sacrificial animals during religious ceremonies, which relates to the social status of the Bodo. Previously, those who were considered rich, or *mahajan*, in the Bodo language, tended to carry out more pig sacrifices than others. Unlike the caste-based Hindu societies of the rest of the country, among the Bodo, it is a matter of pride to be associated with pigs.

I belong to the Bodo community, and I consider *oma* as my favourite animal. I can even vouch for this for many others in our society. It is not only about pork consumption as a preferred meat, but pigs also become an important marker of our identity as Bodo. It is the community's symbol of pride to consume pork as a food. This was not the case earlier; the Bodo community was hated for consuming pork in Assam. Upper-class Assamese called us *suwar khowa* (pork eaters in Assamese) in a derogatory way. Not long ago, Bodos were not permitted to enter hotels. If they did, after eating in the hotels, they had to wash the utensils after paying the bill. Further, if a Bodo visited an upper-class person's home as a guest, the Bodo would wash the entire house before leaving. Eating pork is an identity for the community which was, I feel, forced upon or given to us by Assamese society. But with the flow of time, the educated section of people in Assam tried to eradicate this stigma from society. Conversion to Christianity and Brahminic religions is known for reducing such stigma in Bodo society and for achieving social equality. Consumption of pork (*oma bedor*), however, has increased now in most of the Assamese society.

It is said that without a pig, a Bodo's life is incomplete. The significance of the pig begins with the birth of a new child in the Bodo family. A week after the child's birth, *oma khaji* is prepared and offered to the ancestral deity to welcome the newborn. *Oma khaji* comes from *khaja janai*, which means having a feast with food and beverages, especially pork, chicken and local wine (*jou bidwi*). I grew up in a village and have participated in these rituals where *Oma khaji* was distributed. Rice wine and *Oma khaji* together are important for making offerings to ancestors and for the family or the village feast. A special hut, called *oma gondra*, is built for the pig, and the plate from which the pig consumes its food is called *naodra*.

Another interesting aspect is that people believe that a Bodo's home is where wild boars (*hagrani oma*) turn into domesticated pigs as they attain adulthood. This depicts how the domestic worlds and the forest worlds of the Bodo are linked through the hunting of wild boars and the collection of herbs and other forest produce. With indigenous knowledge of their surroundings, especially animals, Bodo's lives are deeply connected with the forested landscape. People and animals are part of larger social networks, taboos and animal and spiritual worlds.

Wild boars were hunted for food in the past, and this continues in some Bodo habitats at present. Bodos, before the hunting trip, would pay respects to the mighty nature by offering *goi jora-fathwi jora* (betel nut and betel leaf) for their safety and success. Hunters would often bring the young boars when the mother was killed and raise them. This, people say, led to the domestication of the pig, which eventually became an essential component of their indigenous sociocultural milieu. While the Bodo can hunt wild boars, there is a restriction on hunting several animals. The earliest Bodo customary law book, *Boroni Fisa O Aain* (Son of Bodo and Their Laws), published in 1915, discusses several species that in Bodo society is prohibited from being killed or eaten. Squirrels (*mandaab*), pangolins (*kheothai*), wild cats (*jinar mwsa*), snakes (*jibou*), leopards (*mwsa lokra*), jackals (*siyaal*), vultures (*sigwn*) and crocodiles (*guler*) are examples of tabooed species. It is considered a sin in the community to kill them. There is a fine, or those who kill them are shunned by society. This is an example of an inbuilt mechanism to prevent overhunting and ways to conserve species.

The importance of pigs in Bodo society becomes evident during social events and ceremonies. For example, the Kherai festival, the most important festival among the Bodo, is celebrated in the month of April to promote fertility in crop production and to protect the community from any misfortune. Offering animals is a common practice. Mainao Garja is one among the several rituals observed in the paddy field by the landowner. Known for its pig sacrifices, a virgin sow (*oma bundi*), seen as a sign of purity, is sacrificed. The head of the pig becomes an important offering to the deity Mainao, and the rest of the body parts are cooked in the paddy field and distributed to others in the village, along with *jou bidwi* (local wine). When they return home, the pig head is stored in the *bakhri* (granary). The owner cannot eat the pig's head on that day, but the following day, it can be consumed.

Pigs are essential, especially during weddings, picnics, funerals and other Bodo social gatherings. The traditional ceremony of *saori janai* is performed by individual families towards the end of the agricultural season. Neighbours offer their help to families in completing farming. Owners arrange various foods, wine, fruits, rice cakes and tea for those who contribute labour. Pork forms a special item on the menu (see Table 7.1). At least three items, or sometimes more, are cooked. Some of them are *oma onla, oma khaji, bibw bithwi, oma bhaji, oma saonai, oma hangnai* and *oma gwran aeonai*. All these items have pork as the main meat. On this day, the owner of a paddy field offers a six-month- to one-year-old pig for this special occasion. It is an occasion of gathering and it also helps complete farming duties on time.

Similarly, in marriage ceremonies, when the groom goes to bring his bride with his relatives, *barlamfa* and *bwirathi*, a male and a female relative, accompany the groom. It is an honour to take up this role for these relatives and to entertain the guests on their way to the bride's home. The specially appointed relatives distribute beetle nuts and beetle leaves while performing a dance by carrying the head and legs of the pig that had been sacrificed

Table 7.1 Important terms with *oma* attached to it and their meaning

Bodo language	Meaning
Oma khopthaang	Half of the pig's torso gifted to the bride's family
Oma khaji	Special pork prepared during a ceremony or ritual
Oma lanjai	Tail of a pig
Oma gondra	Pig shelter made from bamboo strips
Oma naodra	Wooden pod that is used for fodder.
Oma bundi	Female pig
Oma bonda	Male pig
Oma bedor	Pork meat
Uphri	A special food for pigs
Oma thaokri	A special pig sacrificed for rituals

Source: Author.

for the occasion. Another pig is offered, after the marriage, at the maternal uncle's house to offer their respects. Pork, therefore, is an important element of the marriage ceremonies as part of the special feast and is also offered as a gift. In the customary traditions of the marriage, half of the pig's torso (*oma khopthaang*) is gifted to the bride's family from the groom's side. When the bride takes the surname of her husband, the day is observed with a ritual called Nerid Dannai or Nerid Bosonai, and *oma khaji* is offered to commemorate the significance of conversion of surname. Traditionally, members of both families sit together, along with a few guests, and celebrate the ritual by offering *oma khaji* to the supreme soul, Bwrai Bathou. Many songs and folktales are part of Bodo everyday lives and are also performed during special occasions.

Folk Tales, Songs and Mythology

Pigs appear prominently in the folk songs and folk tales of the Bodo. These songs and their taglines indicate the significance of pigs in the community.

… *Oma lanjaya dolor thaya be songsara bw dolor thaya* …

This life is very dynamic and not static like the tail of a pig.

There is another song which defines the significance of the pig during marriage. There was a king named Daolaraja who had a daughter. He had been rearing a pig for her marriage ceremony since her childhood. One day, the pig escaped to the forest, and they could not bring it back. The king ordered his soldiers to capture the pig, but everyone failed. It was a special animal for the princess's marriage, and if it was not caught, the king feared a delay in the princess's marriage. Heavily disappointed, the princess tried to find the pig near the Sonashree River on a boat and sang this song filled with deep sorrow, which is still sung during weddings to acknowledge the feelings of a young lady before their marriage.

> … *Thou khathi aw thou, thou, thou, thou* …
> *Jainw homnu hagwn Omakhw bejwngnw jagwn ang jiw aw juli* …

> … Let us go nearer, let us go, let us go, let us go …
> Whoever will catch my pig I will get married to him …

Earlier, most of the village families reared pigs for their son's or daughter's wedding. Such a practice can still be seen in Bodo villages, where it has long been a community practice. The pig has to be ready for the celebration day regardless of the family condition. The pig always gets first priority for any kind of celebration in the community, especially *oma thaokri*.

The following is another song related to paddy cultivation and crop raiding by birds and animals. Pigs are also known for raiding crops and destroying farms. The song is about such a situation when a farmer shares his sorrow.

> *Ha ladwngmwn agini khona*
> *Mosow ladwngmwn gong mena mena*
> *Jamphwi daria daria mai gainaya*
> *Dao zalangbai Oma zalagmai*
> *Makhou zabaonu aang lwi*[3]

> … Bought a land aside
> Bought a cow with strong horned
> Cultivated paddy by harvesting waterside
> But chicken and pig ate all of them
> What should I eat now!…

Pigs as an Economy and Livelihood

The majority of the Bodo are dependent on the informal economy, such as subsistence farming, exchanging homegrown vegetables or goods with neighbours, and vending small shops in the roadside markets. The community also used cowries[4] as a form of currency for exchange in the past.[5] Consequently, the community domesticated pigs, and these animals became part of the Bodo's informal economy, maintaining self-sustenance. Earlier, the community depended on hunting and gathering, agriculture, animal husbandry and handicrafts. Later, they slowly shifted to agriculture and a nature-based economy. Since ancient times, *mwihur* (hunting) has been a popular activity among villagers. During the Bwisagu festival, community hunting is common; at this time, the village surrounds itself with large nets (*mwihur ni je*) in forest patches. By driving deer and wild pigs into the nets and by shouting and playing drums, the animals are trapped. The animals are also stabbed with spears (*jong*) and bludgeons (*gondrai/dongfangni dangai*) when they run into the nets. In the community, hunting with bows and arrows (*bwrla-theer*) and spears was a common practice.

Hunting is a complex issue that is a matter of concern in conservation forums. Unsustainable hunting, according to ecologists, has resulted in the local extinction of species and the creation of 'empty' woods.[6] When human populations were low and traditional hunting tactics were in isolated settlements, older hunting practices were considered sustainable.[7] However, it is important to remember that hunting among the Bodo is not just practised for trade or profit; it is also carried out to prevent crop raiding by wildlife. Certain taboos are followed that reflect indigenous conservation strategies. For example, the Bodo never hunted more than they needed and avoided overhunting during the seasonal hunting period in the month of April. Mostly males take part in this community hunting practice. Hunting is also seen as a leisure activity and a way to preserve tradition.

The role of gender in rearing pigs is an important part of understanding human–pig relations among the Bodo. Women take the sole responsibility for collecting fodder for pigs, cooking, feeding and rearing pigs. This is carried out as an economic investment, and later, pigs, when they become adults, are sold for cash. Pigs are also exchanged and bartered during ceremonies between relatives. Women purchase gold jewellery once a year by selling a pig. They also economically support the family with their earnings.

It is ensured that the pigs are raised with care so that they earn a profit in the market. The byproduct obtained from winemaking, *uphri,* is fed to pigs. Bodo women are known for making rice beer, traditional liquor and indigenous wine. Adding *uphri* to pig food is believed to increase the fat and weight of the pig within a short period of time. Usually, the pig takes one to two years to get ready to be sold in the market. The women not only earn enough by selling pigs, but the practice also adds sociocultural value to the community rituals. Bodo women buy piglets for INR 2,000–4,000 and sell them for around INR 10,000–30,000 within a short period of time.

Transformation in the Bodo–*Oma* Relations

The population of domesticated pigs in Assam was 21 lakhs (2.1 million) in 2019 and has recently grown to almost 30 lakhs (3 million), according to the census report of the Animal Husbandry and Veterinary Department.[8] The state is currently pushing for expanding piggery. Farmers are increasing their capacity to meet market demands and fulfil financial needs in general, avowing the social values in some tribal communities. While pig rearing and pig consumption are part of the tribal way of living among the Bodo, it has, however, led to the stigmatisation of their identity by the non-Bodos.

The influence of Hinduism in the region has led to the belief that Mahadev (a Hindu god) is a form of Bathou (a belief system followed by Bodo). There is an appropriation of the Bodo belief by the larger Hindu fold. Bathouism, the belief system of the Bodo, is based on paying homage to one's ancestors, and Mahadev represents the Hindu concept of a Trinity god, where Mahadev seems closer to the humans as he abodes on the earth, unlike Brahma and Vishnu, who live in mythical places, namely Brahmalok and Baikunthlok. However, some people consider that Mahadev is a tribal god because of his ash-covered body and tiger-skin clothes. Indeed, this parallel belief system continues to exist despite the separate religious characteristics of Hinduism and Bathouism. With the passage of time, Bathouism has been gradually assimilated into Hinduism and is now popularly known as Brahma Bathou. There is the presence of traditional Bathou followers who believe in two forms of Bathouism called Gudi Bathou and Bibar Bathou. Gudi Bathou is a type of Bathouism that believes in animal sacrifices while Bibar Bathou does not believe in animal sacrifices; instead, they make symbolic offerings of flowers to the Sijou plant. Hinduism follows the concept of *paap* (sin) and *punya* (virtue) and subsequently classifies society based on those who are *pure beings* and those who are *malign beings.* The Bodo's belief system, on the other hand, as a tribal religion, is based on nature, and all its followers are equal. The Sijou plant is a symbol of respect for ancestors' souls, who never die just like the Sijou plant, which can grow even after being uprooted or in any climate. These changes in the belief system have had an impact on the Bodo's relations with pigs.

There were two waves of religious campaigns against rearing pigs in Bodo villages, one during the 1925–1930s and the second in the 1970s, under the influence of Hinduism. The first wave of Brahma Dharma spread very fast among the Bodo people, and they campaigned from village to village against the killing of not just pigs but all types of household livestock. This campaign at one point became a social movement among the Bodo against keeping pigs and chickens at home. This was intended to standardise their lifestyle like other upper-class or upper-caste people. Once, a group of people randomly started visiting villages, killing and burying thousands of livestock, especially pigs and chickens, to pursue a 'life of dignity' resolution, guided by the principles of respect and cooperation, to strengthen relationships with the Brahma religion.

The Brahma religion among the Bodo is a Hindu practice that seeks to reform the traditional thought of the society in order to purportedly protect the Bodo community. It is a unique identity for the Bodo to rear pigs, so they stood against such livestock-killing activities. This form of Sanskritisation[9] by Brahma Dharma did not succeed in Bodoland. This form of resistance by Bodo was twofold. The first was to preserve the indigenous livelihoods in the community and the other one was to resist the caste hierarchy of Hinduism. The latter was intended to preserve the community's dignity by following native practices. However, resistance to dominance as well as preservation of the ethnic identity still exists in the larger Bodo community, though the traditional religion of the Bathou has seen certain changes recently.

Hinduism has created new sects and contributed some new rites and rituals to Bodo society. For example, Bathou is no longer a singular belief system but has instead evolved into different forms of Bathouism, such as Gudi Bathou, Bibar Bathou, Moni Bathou, Zangkhrao Bathou, and others, which are prevalent in the present community. Bathou deities are worshipped with sacrifices of chicken, pig, pigeon, duck and goat and offerings of rice beer in the most traditional form of Bathou worship, known as Gudi Bathou

Figure 7.1 Human–pig relations

or Bwli Bathou. Other forms of worship offer flowers to the Bathou (*sijou*). Among many flowers, the *aozaar bibar* (*Lagerstroemia speciosa*) has special significance to the Bodo community in its season-based worships. Therefore, the presence of animal meat – especially pork – becomes a key distinguishing feature of these multiple forms of Bathou.

Concluding Remarks

Animals have had a long association with different communities in human history. With the passage of time, this relationship has been changing as societies moved from agrarian to modern times. At present, scholars are carrying out studies on animal–human relations as a significant area of investigation.[10] In this context, this chapter has argued that the relationship between indigenous people and animals, particularly pigs, constructs cultural importance in the Bodo society. The present study demonstrates the importance of the presence of pigs in the Bodo society and in an integral part of sociocultural practices. Pigs are an important part of the indigenous economy, as they are a crucial source of livelihood for the Bodo people. Furthermore, pigs play a significant role in making them economically independent as they earn a livelihood by rearing pigs and it acts as a security during financial crisis. However, the relations between the Bodo and pigs are gradually changing under the influence of shifts in agricultural as well as socio-economic and cultural patterns. Studying the correlation between the pigs and the Bodo tribe provides insights into the cultural history of the indigenous people. The tribal or indigenous people are vulnerable and they struggle to preserve their relations with culture, tradition and even language for many reasons. The factors of modernity and the influences of other upper-class and upper-caste communities impact the lifestyle of the Bodo, which is reflected in their pig-rearing practices.

Notes

1. Bodo, also called Boro, is the largest ethnolinguistic group in Assam, India.
2. A. Brahma, 'A Study of Women's Human Rights of Bodoland Territorial Council, Assam', *International Journal of Innovative Research in Engineering and Multidisciplinary Physical Sciences* 6, no. 4 (2018): 563.
3. Sushanta Narzary, 'The Village of the Bodos: A Study on Socio-Economic Cultural Tradition and Change with Special Reference to the Bodos of Undivided Kokrajhar District' (unpublished PhD thesis) (Kokrajhar: Department of History, Bodoland University, 2020).
4. In addition to cowries, dead snails were used as currency earlier in Bodo society.
5. John S. Deyell, 'Cowries and Coins: The Dual Monetary System of the Bengal Sultanate', *The Indian Economic and Social History Review* 47, no. 1 (2010): 63–106, DOI:10.1177/001946460904700103.
6. W. J. Ripple, K. Abernethy, M. G. Betts, G. Chapron, R. Dirzo, M. Galetti et al., 'Bushmeat Hunting and Extinction Risk to the World's Mammals', *Royal Society Open Science* 3, no. 10 (2016): 160498.
7. Ambika Aiyadurai, 'The Mishmi Hunter of Arunachal', *Geography and You* 10, no. 60 (May–June 2010): 56–9, https://geographyandyou.com/ecosystems/the-mishmi-hunter-of-arunachal, accessed 15 October 2021.

8. Animal Husbandry and Veterinary Department, Government of Assam, 'Livestock Census Report 2019', https://animalhusbandry.assam.gov.in/information-services/livestock-census, accessed 15 September 2024.

9. A term coined by M. N. Srinivas, it is a process of adaptation from the cultural patterns of the higher castes to raise one's status in the caste hierarchical order.

10. Boris M. Levinson states that the study of human–animal relationships is respected but underdeveloped, with key research areas being culture, personality, communication and therapy, in the article 'The Future of Research into Relationships between People and Their Animal Companions', *International Journal for the Study of Animal Problems* 3, no. 4 (1982): 283–94.

8

Yaks and the Brokpa of Arunachal Pradesh

An Immemorial Nomadic Association

Khriengunuo Mepfhuo and Mihir Sarkar

The domestic yak is believed to have originated from its wild ancestor, the wild yak, as early as two million years ago on the Tibetan plateau.[1] The word *yak* comes from the Tibetan word *gyag*, which refers to the male yak. Yak-rearing regions in India include Ladakh, Sikkim, Arunachal Pradesh and Himachal Pradesh, with a few numbers reported in West Bengal. Yaks in India are mostly reared traditionally under the transhumance system[2] by the nomadic tribes who are mostly Buddhists in their religious orientation. Like in Ladakh, where it is reared by the Changpa, a semi-nomadic tribe, in Sikkim, it is reared by the Aho, Bho and Bhutia tribes, who are predominantly Buddhists. In Himachal Pradesh, the Buddhist tribes in Spiti are engaged in yak rearing, whereas in Kinnaur and Chamba districts, Hindus too are involved in rearing this bovine. Monpa, a Mongoloid Buddhist tribe, are involved in rearing Yak in Arunachal Pradesh.[3] They have close relations with animals, like other tribes, but have a special bond with the yaks. As per the 20th Livestock Census 2019, Ladakh has the highest yak population (26,221), followed by Arunachal Pradesh (24,075), Sikkim (5,219), Himachal Pradesh (1,940) and West Bengal (61). Internationally, apart from India, yaks are found in China, Tibet, Bhutan, Mongolia and Nepal.

In this chapter, we examine the relations of yaks with the people who rear them, that is, the Brokpa, to understand the role this bovine plays in the lives of the herders of this tribe – socially, economically and culturally. The word *brokpa* combines two Monpa words, *brok* meaning pastoral land and *pa* meaning people living on the pasture. Brokpa are a sub-group of the Monpa tribe of Arunachal Pradesh, a prominent tribe that engages in different livelihood generation activities, predominantly agriculture and livestock rearing. The Brokpa, a semi-nomadic group of this tribe, are engaged in pastoral animal rearing, including that of yaks, which occupy a special place in this landscape.

Unlike earlier times, when only the Brokpa would own and look after yaks, today they mostly act as caretakers for herds owned by others and sometimes include yaks owned by others in their herd. Usually, the yak Brokpas look after their own yaks but in certain instances they also engage in looking after the yaks belonging to their (yak Brokpa) relatives along with their own herd. This happens where their relatives have only a few yaks or if they are unable to lead their herd in the transhumance system.

Yaks favour alpine and sub-alpine regions with cold semi-humid climates, preferably between 3,000 and 4,500 metres above mean sea level (msl) and can also be found at around 6,000 metres. Anatomical and physiological adaptations of the yak to its environment include its sturdy and compact body covered with a thick outer coat of coarse hair and fine inner hair. Their large lungs and heart, in relation to the body size, and smaller body surface area per unit of body weight have enabled them to survive and thrive in extreme cold and high-altitude regions with low oxygen content and high solar radiation. Another interesting anatomical feature of the yak are the strong hooves with rough edges which enable them to climb steep terrain effortlessly. As a good pack animal, they are valuable in carrying loads through the steep hills. Though yaks are reared across many states and by different tribes, this chapter will be restricted to the rearing of yaks in Arunachal Pradesh and the significance of the role yaks play in the socio-economic and socio-cultural lives of the Brokpa. We focus on yaks in the Tawang and West Kameng districts of Arunachal Pradesh, which receive heavy snowfall, with winter temperatures ranging between a maximum of 14 °C and sub-zero minimum.

The yak is an excellent feed converter and can survive during the lean winter period when feed is scarce, despite losing body weight.[4] It is known to breed productively and can also be bred with the local hill cattle, resulting in a male animal known as *dzo* and a female called *dzomo*. This practice of hybridisation is followed for the purpose of increasing the milk quantity, which is generally low in pure yaks, yielding only about 1.1 kilolitres of milk in a day. However, it has to be mentioned that the yak female exhibits silent heat, and this can be a hindrance in assisted reproduction techniques like artificial insemination. Nevertheless, this poses no problem in a herd that follows natural mating. The yaks are known to have a gentle disposition with no tendency to panic unnecessarily, and a close bond is formed between the yak and the herder through the feeding of salt. Undoubtedly, over many years, the yaks have found a special place in the hearts and homes of its herders, especially the Brokpa of Arunachal Pradesh.

Yak and Brokpa Association

The association between any animal and a community finds its reflection in folklore, especially in tribal societies where knowledge and customs are passed on from generation to generation through the oral tradition, which could be in the form of stories, songs or their depictions through dances. It is through these forms of storytelling that today we get to know of the many legends associated with a particular tribe and community. Such tales continue to be kept alive throughout present time and generations.

A popular story about how yaks came into existence that is known to people of all ages in this community is often performed in the form of a pantomime called the Yak Dance or Yak Cham. This pantomime is a huge attraction at every cultural event. Its characters consist of a ceremonial effigy, which is essentially a dummy yak with a wooden head and body frame made of bamboo, which is carried by two men who remain concealed by a black cloth. The country guardian, known as the Sungma, the village deity, sits on the back of the yak. The two men carrying the effigy dance to the beats of the drum and cymbals. Thoepa Gali, a mythical figure who is credited by legends as having discovered the yak, is present along with his family members, represented by five masked men. Gali narrates the story of the discovery of the yak and how it came to be a source of wealth and happiness for the community upon its integration into the lifestyle of the people in the form of a pantomime.

According to this story, the protagonist, Thoepa Gali, belonged to a place called Yaen Tsa in the Kongpo region of Tibet. His parents were Nyokpo Shindang and Sholmo Samkyi, who had three sons – Hawo Dhargey, Gawo Samdrub and Thoepa Gali. The two elder brothers inherit their father Nyokpo Shindang's properties, but Thoepa Gali, the last child, gets nothing. After pondering the matter for three days, he goes to his father, who gives him a torn cap when he asks for his share of the property. When he approaches his mother, she hands him a wornout tunic. When he asks his brothers Hawo and Gawo for his share of the property, they give him a *githak* (traditional white-and-black rope made from yak wool by herdsmen to tie the animals) and a disfigured shoe, respectively. After pondering over his fate for three days, Thoepa Gali crosses three plateaus and ends up in a place called Palmo Pelthang. He then crosses three passes to reach the highest pass, named Sigma La. From there he sees a lake below the peaks covered with snow. Thoepa Gali circumambulates the lake thrice from the right and thrice from the left, when he notices a divine white bird flying over the lake. At the spot over where he saw the bird flying, he finds three eggs – a white egg, a black egg and a dotted one. Thoepa Gali wipes the white egg thrice, when its shell breaks. He finds a white yak inside it, which is claimed by Lha Geychin Wangpo, the Lord of all Gods. On wiping the black egg thrice and breaking it open, a she-yak appeared before him. When Thoepa Gali wipes the dotted egg thrice and breaks it, the black she-yak that belongs to deities appears.

Thoepa Gali then goes on to narrate how he repeatedly throws a *lasso* fashioned from the rope given by his brother to capture the she-yak and finally succeeds. Throughout the song, Theopa Gali explains ways to tame and milk the she-yak. He describes the beauty of the yak, its utilities and the annual migration of the yaks. He also sings praises of three mountain peaks regarded as the three female deities. Thoepa Gali also describes in detail the items he possessed and sings their praises.[5] This legend beautifully portrays the close association between the Monpa people, particularly the Brokpa, and yaks. It illustrates the central role played by yaks in the culture and economy of the Brokpa people.

The Brokpa, with their nomadic lifestyle, are ideal herders and keepers of the bovine species that has an affinity for the snow and depends on alpine pastures for its sustenance. The Brokpa's pastoral lifestyle entails the movement of the animal herds from lower to higher altitudes in the summer months (mid-May or June to September), while in the winter months (October–March), they migrate towards the lower altitude regions in the temperate zone. Thus, yaks and the Brokpa have evolved a form of nomadic association due to their proclivities and lifestyle. The yaks gain the protection of the Brokpa, and the latter, in turn, gain social status and all such amenities that help to sustain their way of life socially, economically and culturally.

Yaks in the Sociocultural Lives of the Brokpa

The Brokpa, being semi-nomadic pastoralists, do not own land. On their journey through the migratory routes with the yak herds, they take shelter in makeshift houses along the routes for the purpose of halting. During winter, they stay put in the settlements in their native villages. The yaks are a source of status, pride, food and income for the Brokpa. The number of yaks owned by a Brokpa indicates their wealth.[6] The Brokpa obtain milk and meat products from the yak apart from its hair, which is used to make different products. From the yak's milk, *churpi* (fermented cheese), *churkham* (dry cheese) and *mar* (butter) are obtained. Yak meat serves to meet the protein requirement of the Brokpa, and the hide of the animal too is put to good use, mostly to make bags for storing the butter obtained from the yaks. Cloaks worn by the Brokpa are made from the skin of yak calves. From yak hair, caps, bags, mats, tents, tunics and ropes are made. The tail hair of the yak has religious value. The *chaur*, or sacred whisks used in gurudwaras, are made from yak tail hair. Shamans in other parts of Arunachal Pradesh use the yak's tail as a ritual item for animistic practices. For example, the yak's tail is attached to the hairband of the *igu* (the Idu Mishmi shaman) while chanting hymns asking the Almighty to endow the power of the mountains, where yaks are reared.

Yak cheese and butter are the mainstay of the Monpa tribe's diet and are obtained by other members of the community from the Brokpa. In olden days, the Brokpa would barter these products from the yak for other necessities. Nowadays, they sell it for cash, thus generating an income for themselves even as they use part of the produce for their own subsistence. However, it has to be noted that a yak provides only about 1 litre of milk in a day, which is a comparatively low yield. The Brokpa of Arunachal Pradesh therefore have taken to the practice of yak hybridisation, which is the crossing of the male yak with female local hill cattle. As the Brokpa do not own land, while moving from pasture to pasture with their herd during the summer months, they pay taxes to the clans and villages that own the pastures. The taxes are paid in the form of butter and cheese, the amount of which varies from clan to clan, village to village, and is largely determined by the herd size as well. At times, the Brokpa also donate yaks to the clans and villages. The yak milk products, namely butter and cheese, that are accumulated as taxes from the Brokpa are divided among the villagers and also donated to monasteries to be used in ceremonies and associated feasts. Since no feast or religious ceremony is complete without yak milk products, this ensures that the tributes from the Brokpa are put to good use, which in turn helps these nomadic people to partake in and promote the cultural and religious ethos of their tribe. All these practices are a source of pride and income for the herdsmen. Since time immemorial, the Brokpa have been known to rear yaks, and throughout this period, despite the many hardships involved, they, along with the yak herds, have migrated annually in search of green pastures for the herds.

In the past, the whole Brokpa family, including a Brokpa man's wife and children, would accompany him during the seasonal migration. However, in present times, with the advancements of the world catching up with this pastoralist community, the wives and children increasingly tend to stay back in their villages for the purpose of the children's education. The family members are known to drop off the Brokpa at certain summer halting points and aid in carrying essential items that will sustain them during their stay in temporary hutments along the route throughout the migratory period. In instances where the Brokpa are accompanied by their families, the wives lend a helping hand in yak-rearing activities like feeding, milking animals and preparing yak products. There are also instances where a Brokpa brings a helping hand along with him, who could be a hired help or a brother or relative. At times, the Brokpa may come down to lower altitudes to sell and/or barter yak milk products, or a family member may go up to the higher terrain to collect the products.[7] The Brokpa usually move as a single unit during the migration but may be joined by other Brokpa families in the pasture, in which case arrangements are made for joint grazing of their herds. The time required for covering the migratory routes varies from one grazing ground to another but usually takes about 2–15 days. As per the interaction of the authors with the Brokpa, on average, a Brokpa and his yak herd cover a distance of 25 kilometres. Some of the grazing grounds have motorable roads along the way, and in these cases, the Brokpa only have to travel a short distance along with the loads and animals by foot. Some grazing grounds are very remote, and reaching them poses great challenges.

As the winter approaches, the migration back from the higher to lower altitudes starts. This begins in the month of October. However, the time of the winter and summer migrations is subject to the Tibetan calendar followed by the Brokpa. Upon reaching the winter settlements, the Brokpa get involved in other engagements. The yaks are generally let loose during this season, and it being a lean period, yak-rearing activities are limited, which allows the Brokpa the time to attend to their familial and social obligations. This

Figure 8.1   Yak and the Brokpa

remains the best time to catch up with the Brokpa to hear tales of their valour and hardship in negotiating the treacherous terrain as they move along with the yak herds, traversing miles along the hills in search of pasture for their animals.

Concluding Remarks

Yak, the animal, and its herder, the Brokpa, both exist on the margins of society. The total yak population in India stands at 58,000.[8] As per the personal records of the authors, there are around 100 Brokpa in West Kameng district and about 300–400 Brokpa in Tawang district, as cited unofficially by people who are involved in yak rearing. The number is decreasing each year due to the difficulties involved in this occupation. Yak husbandry hold no lure for the younger generation and, considering the hardships involved, the economic gains remain minimal, especially in comparison to present-day standards. Migrating with a yak herd, ranging from 10 to 150 animals, entails many challenges.

The best grazing grounds in Arunachal Pradesh require crossing the Indo-Bhutan border. For generations, many Brokpa have favoured these grazing grounds due to the lush pastures they offer, but access to these pastures is a huge challenge. As found out by the authors while conducting the survey for a research project during the peak of the COVID-19 pandemic, the Brokpa who tried to cross the Indo-Bhutan border during the summer months faced untold hardships as movement along the border was restricted. Due to the stress on the animals, they reported that the size and health of their yak herds were affected. The factors threatening the future prospects of yak rearing in Bhutan, which include forage shortages, predation by other wild animals and the lack of successors to engage in yak rearing,[9] are the same factors posing challenges for the Brokpa in this part of the world. For the older Brokpa, this is the only way of life they have known since a very young age. Boys of this community continue to get involved in yak herding, but the future remains uncertain because there are fewer of them to take over the occupation. The erosion of their way of life would mean the loss of sociocultural identity for this community and would also result in a major void in the biota of India, as this region is one of the few places with the climate and topography conducive for yaks and, by extension, a home to its herders. Hence, it was observed by the authors when interacting with the Brokpa that the most daunting task ahead would be to ensure the continued rearing of this precious, durable bovine by this community to keep in perpetuity the social and cultural values associated with it while maintaining the essence of the way of life of its herders. The problems associated with yak rearing have to be addressed in a thoughtful manner and sustainable solutions provided to safeguard the yak population and the interests of its keepers – the Brokpa.

Notes

1. Zhang Rongchang, Wu Jianping and Han Jianlin, 'Yak production in China', *Asian Livestock,* no. 19 (1994): 115–18.

2. M. A. Kataktalware, R. Pourouchottamane and K. P. Ramesha, 'Traditional System of Yak Rearing in India', in *Yak: Moving Treasure of the Himalayas,* ed. K. P. Ramesha (Dirang: National Research Centre on Yak, 2008), 61–8.

3. K. P. Ramesha, Manajit Bora, G. Kandeepan and P. Chakravarty, *Indigenous Traditional Knowledge of Yak Rearers* (Dirang: National Research Centre on Yak, 2009).

4. R. Pourouchottamane, G. Krishnan, M. Sarkar and K. P. Ramesha,, 'Adaptations of Yaks to Harsh Environment of High Altitude', in *Yak: Moving Treasure of the Himalayas*, ed. K. P. Ramesha (Dirang: National Research Centre on Yak, 2008), 53–9.

5. Tenjin Jorden, *Thoepa Gali: The Origin of Yak* (Tawang: Monyul Preserve Culture and Promote Dialect, 2019).

6. K. P. Ramesha and M. Bhattacharya, 'Domestication, Distribution and Genetic Characterization', in *Yak: Moving Treasure of the Himalayas*, ed. K. P. Ramesha (Dirang: National Research Centre on Yak, 2008), 1–33.

7. Leema Bora, Vijay Paul and F. U. A. Ahmed, *Yak Pastoralists of Arunachal Pradesh* (Dirang: National Research Centre on Yak, 2012).

8. Government of India, *20th Livestock Census-2019: All India Report* (New Delhi: Ministry of Fisheries, Animal Husbandry and Dairying, 2019).

9. N. Dorji, M. Derks, P. W. Groot Koerkamp and E. A. Bokkers, 'The Future of Yak Farming from the Perspective of Yak Herders and Livestock Professionals', *Sustainability* 12, no. 10 (2020): 4217.

9

The 'Divine Animal' of Arunachal Pradesh

Changing Human–Mithun Relations

Abhishruti Sarma

Introduction

How do we explore the relationalities of an animal that is believed to be a heavenly body, a symbol of purity, power, identity and life – an animal that is also at once social, sacrificial, economically valuable and consumed? This chapter is based on my research in the hill forests of Arunachal Pradesh in northeastern India where I explore human–animal relations – more specifically, the ways in which the mithun (*Bos frontalis*) is entangled in the everyday lives and practices of many tribes in the region. Mithuns are semi-domesticated animals found in India's northeast – sparsely distributed across Arunachal Pradesh, Nagaland, Manipur, Mizoram – Bhutan, the Chin State in Myanmar and the Chittagong Hill Tracts of Bangladesh. Also known as the 'ceremonial ox'[1] of northeast India, the mithun is the most culturally, socially and economically valuable animal among many indigenous people in the region extending to southeast Asia. Festivals are celebrated and rituals are performed keeping the mithun at the centre of familial and spiritual relationships. The life and the existence of the mithun, thus, have become congruent with not only the structures of a village, tribe or community but also its forests, agriculture and people's food habits. Given the animal's significance in many tribal societies of the region, the focus in the chapter remains not on the practices of any specific tribe but on the connectedness of the narratives of different tribes across Arunachal Pradesh.

Questions of why a particular animal is so remarkably significant for an individual or a community are often associated with the work these animals do for them. In contrast, in Arunachal Pradesh, people who own mithun unanimously told me, 'Mithun ka koi kaam nahi hain, yeh kuch nahi karta hain' (in Hindi, translated as 'The mithun has no work to do, it does nothing'). In the many conversations that I had with people from the state (particularly the Adi, Mishmi, Aka, Nyishi and Sherdukpen tribes), I was told multiple times: 'Mithun project achche se karna, juwai bhaal milega'[2] (Do your research on the mithun well, you will get a good husband) or that it was the 'perfect' animal to explore as I would always be 'blessed'! These lighthearted stories from different parts of the state paint the animal as revered and 'sacred' – an animal that aids in crucial aspects of a person's life such as religion and marriage. The mithun finds primacy over other cattle among many tribes (particularly the Adi, Mishmi, Nyishi and Aka tribes) in the state. As a middle-aged Digaru Mishmi man from Loiliang in Lohit district quipped during a group discussion, 'Mithun nahi hoga toh insaan nahi hoga' (If there is no mithun, then there will be no humans), the others around him nodded in unison. Historically, the animal has been used as a form of exchange. It is still used as bride price. In the tribal cosmologies of animal hierarchy, it assumes the highest value and is often the last animal to be sacrificed. It is through the sacrifice and exchange economy that the mithun is deemed the most valuable of all animals, with its presumed similarity with human life adding further value.

But how did this come to be? In the unpublished manuscripts of Ivan Martin Simon, who was a part of the Directorate of Research at the North East Frontier Agency,[3] the mithun differs from other animals like the buffalo as its significance moves beyond its economic value to a 'magico-religious' realm. The use of the term 'magico-religious' by Simon is fascinating in exploring the context in which the mithun is viewed today. Different tribes associate themselves with the animal differently in terms of the mithun's significance in their communal and personal lives. Of course, the basis of the relationship with the animal may be the same across tribes – like its use as property, bride price, a medium of exchange or in sacrificial rituals. But the meanings attached to the animal, which mostly emerge from folktales of its origins, differ to a great extent in all the tribes mentioned earlier.

A brief biography of the animal might be useful in this context. Not only different tribes but different people within a single tribe may associate with the animal differently. It is interesting to observe how people remember their folktales or even think about their gods differently. Among many cultures in Arunachal Pradesh, once a mithun is sacrificed, the animal's skull with its horns is hung on the walls of the owners' homes. Houses are traditionally adorned with the skulls of mithuns along with those of other wild and domesticated animals. The mithun heads are often displayed separately from the rest of the animals. Each mithun head hung on the wall has a rich story about why it was sacrificed. A mithun sacrifice to the gods means the people are blessed with abundant prosperity, good rice and other harvests and no epidemic. It is believed that not everybody can rear the mithun, and this is regardless of one's economic standing in society. While it is true that owning mithuns is an important marker of one's wealth, the Adi believe that no matter how wealthy or poor a person may be, if they do not have God's (Dadi Bote in Adi language) blessings, they can never own a mithun. In such a scenario, the mithun, it is believed, either dies or cannot bear calves of its own. So, there are separate rituals that people perform to be able to own a mithun.

The mithun is, as I was told by many, an easy animal to rear. The only investment it requires is about 12 kilograms of salt a year. In terms of the animal's food habits, local people and mithun rearers believe that it does not eat anything from the ground or anything which is 'impure'.[4] Simoons and Simoons record the same: 'Unlike common cattle, the mithan [sic] is a browser. Given a choice, it will seek out the tender shoots and young leaves of the forest rather than the grasses of more open country.' While confirming such habits of the animal, a forest officer from one of the districts in the state also pointed out that he had seen mithuns eating plastic on the side of the road in his town. More importantly, how do these changing habits affect human–animal relations?

Human–Mithun Relationalities

Before we explore the changes, it would be important to have an insight into what a human–mithun relationship entails. Among the Adi, the Mishmi and the Aka, the mithun is essentially associated with the human. A common observation shared with me during my research by people across different indigenous groups was that the mithun greatly resembles the human even in its behavioural characteristics. The affection for the animal, then, also comes from its perceived human-like nature. An Adi farmer, GL, from a village in the district of East Siang, said, 'Eitu maanuh-jontu' (literally translated from Assamese as 'This is a human-animal').

Local people I spoke to believe that the mithun is a human-animal or a human's animal because a human's value and price can be measured against it. Further, its life is believed to be interwoven with that of its owner. The mithun is sacrificed to thwart threats pertaining to the life and well-being of its owner. It is believed that the animal takes on the threat to, and the bad omen of, its owner upon itself when sacrificed. The animal thus becomes a substitute for its owner when passing on to the other world so that its owner can live longer in this one.

Phrases often used in human–animal studies like 'living with' and 'becoming with' represent complex assemblages not just of humans, plants and animals but of different life worlds growing together and out of one another – of a continuity demarcated only by an 'appearance of separation'.[5] The human–mithun assemblage acknowledges the complex and dynamic processes that make this interspecies interaction possible – biologically, culturally and politically. This interspecies relationship, then, is *becoming* through the changing habits of both the mithun and the human. Both humans and mithuns are not only *becoming* with one another but these changes are also intimately embedded in historical processes of economic, ecological, religious and legal 'developments' within the state. However, one cannot single out any one of these processes in order to determine the cause and effect of how humans and mithuns relate differently. For instance, if we were to only look into people's food habits – the ways in which mithun meat is consumed – even within Arunachal there are differences owing to different traditional consumption practices of the communities. There are also issues of management and ownership of land that greatly impact the sociocultural and ecological life worlds of these communities. Therefore, the often-changing courses of the aforementioned processes have greatly shaped or altered human–mithun relations over the years – be it in the form of new laws, new markets or new religions.

Ecological Perspectives

Humans' relationality through everyday practices with the animal primarily occurs by giving it salt once a day or two. However, in many places, this has changed, as salt-feeding has been reduced to once a week or as and when the owner pleases. Until a few years back, so I was told, the animal would come to its owner's house for salt, which would be placed in a wooden log near their bamboo porch. However, this has become a rarity now. The mithuns now live farther away from human societies, given their need for colder, denser forests. On so many occasions, the 'ceremonial ox' would not pay any heed to its owner's musical callings This change can be attributed to the increasing gaps in interaction between the man and the animal.

In the course of my fieldwork, I had the opportunity to participate in an interesting group discussion on the practices of rearing followed in East Siang district. The districts along the Siang river in the eastern part of Arunachal have a lot of mithuns, as a result of which it is easier for the local people to exchange with or sell them to other tribes. I was told that mithuns were sent to the Buddhist-dominated West Kameng areas and sometimes even to their Mishmi neighbours, where the mithun population was lower. The group of Adi farmers I was in conversation with revealed how mithuns were now increasingly being taken or sold to other states in India. For instance, the Shiv Sena in Maharashtra is said to have taken the animal with the objective of rearing it for milk. Similarly, many animals including the mithun have been transported to be exhibited at the recently inaugurated world's largest zoo in Gujarat's Jamnagar. It is concerning then to think about how an animal which is specifically found at an altitude of about 3,000 metres will fare in the dry, arid plains of western India.

The story of course does not end there. In August 2022, I learned that the Krishi Vigyan Kendra of the College of Horticulture and Forestry in Arunachal's Pasighat, in collaboration with the Central Agricultural University and the North East Council, had recently started a mithun conservation project. What they are trying to do, with inputs from the Indian Council of Agricultural Research–National Research Centre (ICAR-NRC), is to domesticate the mithun, a semi-wild animal. A college professor who is a veterinarian and a part of this project explained that by domesticating the animal they could also be milked. However, this idea does not sit very well with many villagers because traditionally milk has never been used as a source of food or nutrition by the hill people.[6] Even though the professor acknowledged the gap in understanding between the farmers and the conservation scientists at ICAR–NRC on mithuns, they were hopeful that after some trials and errors, they might ultimately be able to strike a balance. However, in the course of our conversation, what concerned me, as well as the professor to some extent, was the manner in which they were planning to domesticate the animal.

In Pasighat, for instance, which is a plain area in the foothills of the Abor range in the East Siang district, the idea was to rear the mithuns close to the villages in the plains. Domesticating an animal ideally requires it to be kept tied for long periods, especially when it is wild. The conditions of domesticating the mithun are in stark contrast to the conditions in which the semi-wild animal generally lives in – thick, forested hilly areas with streams of water running nearby. The mithun is a shy animal. The only time it comes to places full of people is when the owner feeds it salt (which forms an important part of the animal's diet). The veterinarian at the College of Horticulture and Forestry asserted that in order for the mithun to be able to evolve to live on a farm, like cows, a couple of generations of the animal may have to die. But despite that, it is now an ongoing process in the foothills of Arunachal.

Therefore, when we talk about the mithun transitioning from a browser (eating fresh leaves) to eating plastic on the roads, we must take into account changes like these that have occurred. But this conversation also leads us to directly think about the changing climate and the movement of people along with their animals from the hills to the plains.[7] A conservationist friend from the Adi tribe did not take a moment to think about the reason for an increase in diseases like foot-and-mouth disease (FMD) among mithuns over the past few years. His quick response was 'climate change'. But it was not him alone. A lot of my questions on the mithun have invariably led the local people to talk about it. From changes in temperatures to transcending geographical boundaries, we are yet to see how the mithun evolves and, then, how mithun–human relations are further restructured. Already, many people in the state have stopped rearing the animal because of the high rates of FMD and other diseases.

On a trip to an Adi village, I was hoping to gather a handful of people for a group discussion. To my delight, the turnout was more than what I had anticipated. All the men were mithun rearers who seemed eager to speak to me. A few minutes into the discussion, I realised that the villagers had taken me for a veterinarian who had come to cure their ailing mithuns. On figuring out that I was a researcher and not a doctor, all of them got upset. Given the increasing number of diseases among the mithuns, they had been waiting for a veterinarian or some government official for a long time. This raises some important questions about the state of the mithun in many places and why people are beginning to sell them. Of course, as we discussed earlier, rearing the mithun does not cost a lot of money, but it definitely costs labour – feeding salt, taking care of the calves, fencing the villages during crop season and going deep into the forests to find and look after them are only some of the responsibilities of the mithun rearer.

Changing Laws and Human–Mithun Relations

For Arunachal Pradesh, the development discourse(s) have been largely about attempts at nationalising these frontier spaces, which are also biodiversity hotspots, abundant with natural resources. Arunachal Pradesh's strategic location along the China border and the bitter memories of India's war with China in 1962 have only hastened the nationalising process, which is largely shaped by concerns of national security.[8] As a consequence, rapid road-building projects (a prerequisite to development) and marking areas as wildlife reserves for nature conservation have gained momentum in these areas. These processes have greatly altered the forested, mountainous landscapes of the region and the human–animal relations found within them.

For instance, in the West Kameng district of Arunachal Pradesh, the building of a 600 megawatt power dam by the state-owned North Eastern Electric Power Corporation Limited (NEEPCO) in the first decade of the twenty-first century has disrupted Aka cultural practices. Different kinds of jobs were offered to the villagers by NEEPCO. Money flowed abundantly in a cash-starved region as a result of the compensation given by the company for land acquisition to build the dam. I say 'abundant' because prior to that, as I was informed, no one in the region had seen so much money together ever in their life. Digging from my respondents' memories, the compensation figure stood at around INR 54,000 per household, doled out in four Aka villages – Bichum, Buragaon, Kimi and Khuppi. Besides the money that came with the building of the dam also came contractual jobs which ultimately contributed to people abandoning their agricultural fields and practices such as mithun rearing.

Thus, the NEEPCO project did not simply change their ritualistic practices but also cultures of eating, preparing food and singing songs. All the activities that had traditionally been tied to agriculture and cattle rearing gradually came to a halt. For instance, many upland tribal communities, including the Aka, would make fences at the beginning of their harvest seasons. The making of these fences used to be a community activity, usually done to prevent the mithuns from entering their fields and destroying their crops. However, agriculture, once an activity for self-sustenance, has now become a commercial endeavour; common lands have fragmented into individual plots through private fences built by farmers around their plantations, horticulture and other cash crops. The result of such transformations is a spike in conflicts with animals like the mithun in indigenous societies. For instance, if a mithun goes to the fields of someone other than its owner and destroys the crops, the animal is immediately shot at. This is true of almost every district in Arunachal Pradesh nowadays. This is not to say that such conflicts had not occurred earlier. In fact, the idea of community fencing was vital to keep animals out of their farms. But now with individual lands and crops being increasingly commercialised, these conflicts also seem to have increased. A lot of people have stopped rearing the mithun for the 'menace' it brings to their income.

It would be important, at this juncture, to examine how the state government is or could be working towards solving an issue like this. Additionally, for the mithun and the mithun rearers, there is also conflict with other animals such as Asiatic wild dogs or dholes (*Cuon alpinus*). Over the years, there has been a flurry of complaints from across the state that dholes have been preying on mithun calves or sometimes even adult mithuns. In monetary terms, the villagers thus incur a great loss as the mithun is their most economically valued animal. In an event like this, the villagers used to, or in some places continue to, hunt down the wild dog(s) altogether. Especially in the district of East Siang, there is now a reluctance to hunt these animals because of the growing pressure from local conservation groups – villagers fear being severely fined as hunting has been restricted to its 'traditional' ways, limited to a season/number of days/number of animals one can hunt at a given time. However, there seems to be no policy or concern among conservationist groups or forest officials about the value of the mithun and what the villagers might be losing when their mithuns are killed. So, the questions that then arise: What kinds of animals are important enough to be conserved or made policies for? And where does an animal like the mithun find its place in studies of human–animal relations in anthropology or wildlife sciences and among the tribal communities of Arunachal Pradesh?

In fact, the ambiguous status of the mithun as the state animal directly adds to this problem. While most of the local villagers I spoke to across Arunachal believe that the state animal is the mithun, forest officers, conservationists and government officials say it is the hoolock gibbon. There, however, seems to be no official documentation that corroborates either of the two claims as of now. When the decision to make the hoolock gibbon the state animal was initially made, it caused an uproar in the state. The Arunachal Pradesh Students' Union requested the state to review this decision and give the 'honour' back to the mithun.[9] Despite the directive of the Wildlife Protection Act of 1972 being in place, which stated that a state animal must be 'purely wild' or 'undomesticated', the mithun was given the 'honour' because of its cultural significance. Forest officials, conservationists and veterinarians alike have argued that it cannot be a state animal because we eat it! It is curious to note here that because the mithun is a 'domesticated' animal, it was removed from the premises of the state zoo in Itanagar.[10] It is even more ironic that the animal is being taken all the way to Gujarat to be displayed in a zoo because it is endemic to the forests of northeast India.

Culture, Religion and Economy

The mithun in many parts of the region is now also a commercialised animal. In the western part of Arunachal Pradesh, in the districts of West Kameng and much of East Kameng, the animal has mostly retained its economic value. It is kept as a security for emergencies – for example, medical or educational. The economic value of the animal is high (fetching anything between INR 70,000 and INR 100,000), given the high demand for its meat, among other things, in many tribes. This high demand similarly dictates its price in other regions of the state too.

Much of the increase in price could also be attributed to changes in religion. The practices of rearing, consuming or being with the mithun have changed over time – either gradually due to subtle influences of religions such as Hinduism or drastically due to high rates of conversion to Christianity. In Arunachal Pradesh, many people have converted to Christianity because they believe that their traditional religion has become increasingly expensive. In the Aka areas, for example, I was told that a lot of valuables had to be given to priests who performed the rituals in the villages. In the Mishmi areas in the Lohit district, I was told that people now wanted to shift to an 'easy religion'. Indeed, the need to ritually sacrifice a costly animal like the mithun meant that the indigenous religion was becoming unaffordable to the ordinary person. Villagers argue that if there is a religion (be it Christianity or Hinduism) that does not cost them their life's savings but helps them in the same way that their traditional religion does, then it is only natural that people would want to shift to new religions. It is therefore worth exploring how these changes in religion are reshaping human–mithun relations in the region.

In eastern Arunachal, especially in the Mishmi and Adi regions, there is an underlying influence of Hinduism. Many local people have associated their deities with the Hindu god Shiva. One of my respondents said, 'Humara dharm toh Hindu jaisa hi hai, bhagwan bhi aap logo ke Shiva jaisa' (Our religion is much like the Hindu religion and our gods are like your Shiva). 'Hum toh Krishna bhagwan ko maante hain' (I believe in Lord Krishna), said another. In this part of the state, right-wing Hindu groups have also been gaining ground gradually. A conversation with three members of the Akhil Bharatiya Vidyarthi Parishad (ABVP), who hail from northern India, in Pasighat (East Siang), an Adi area, revealed that they did not intend to change people's food habits and cultures of living.[11] 'Hum education pe zyada dhyan dete hain' (We focus more on education), said one of them. However, the Adi Baane Kebang (ABK)[12] has been making major changes to customs regarding mithun exchange, consumption and sacrifices. For instance, one farmer said that the amount of mithuns to be given as bride price has been limited now to one or two. Similarly, mithun sacrifices have also greatly come down in the region because of the Kebang's diktat. This, as argued by an ABK and ABVP member, also helps conserve a precious animal like the mithun.

The changes in religion have led to other changes in traditional indigenous practices too. Taking the example of meat consumption again, within Arunachal Pradesh alone, there are different ways of consuming the mithun meat. Traditionally, the meat would be consumed only after a sacrifice was made: that is, when a ritual centred around the mithun was performed or during harvest festivals and marriages. Tribal communities like the Adi and the Mishmi still follow these traditions of meat consumption, wherein it is considered a taboo to kill, sacrifice or eat the mithun on any other occasion. Yet the age-old practices of mithun rearing and consumption have changed. Through interviews and participant observation, during my fieldwork, I observed that in the Aka areas, where a majority of the population is Christian, the manner of consuming or simply being with the mithun has changed. In fact, these differences can be observed now even between the

Akas who follow their traditional religion and those who have converted to Christianity. For instance, during important festivals, parts of the sacrificed mithun are given only to the households that still follow the traditional religion. However, the mithun is still a socially valuable animal, sacrificed in festivities and exchanged during marriages. It is because they believe that it is an important part of their culture, even if their religion might have changed. The Aka account is interesting because it outlines the ways in which religion and culture coalesce and yet form distinct parts of people's lives. In fact, the Aka folktale of how the mithun came to be so valuable in society gives us a better understanding of human–animal relations formed on the interface of nature and culture.

The priest in Buragaon, an Aka village in West Kameng, narrates a story of the mithun, which is also linked to their gods. According to this folktale, the mithun used to be a girl who turned into the animal after a fight with her mother. The mother was infuriated with her daughter as the latter would not do household chores like fetching water or bringing in vegetables. The angry mother is believed to have hit her daughter with the kind of rope that came to be used to tie mithuns. Weeping, the daughter left to fetch water and turned into a mithun by the well. She then went to the forest to live with the other forest animals. Years later, when her father fell sick, the priests got a spiritual vision that the sacrifice of the girl-turned-mithun was the only way to cure his illness. This story shows how the mithuns became an important aspect of ritualistic sacrifices for the Aka.

However, this is only a snapshot of a narration that the priest warned would take four–five hours in its original form. Among many tribal groups, stories surrounding the birth of the mithun or its importance to spirits and humans alike are narrated for days at a stretch during harvest festivals. But when we carefully look into this particular folktale, we find that the girl had to turn into a mithun in order to serve the purpose of giving back to the spirits of nature. AJ, an Aka woman who has been working on developing a script for their language for years now, argues that it is not merely a story of the gods. Of course, indigenous deities figure in this tale, but beyond that, this folk story is more about how humans are connected to nature through spirits.[13] There is a need to give back to nature – it is done through the sacrifice of the girl-turned-mithun and with the help of the indigenous deities. So, when we look into the folktale through this perspective, we find that the mithun becomes a bridge between nature and culture, between humans and spirits, and between the domestic and the wild.

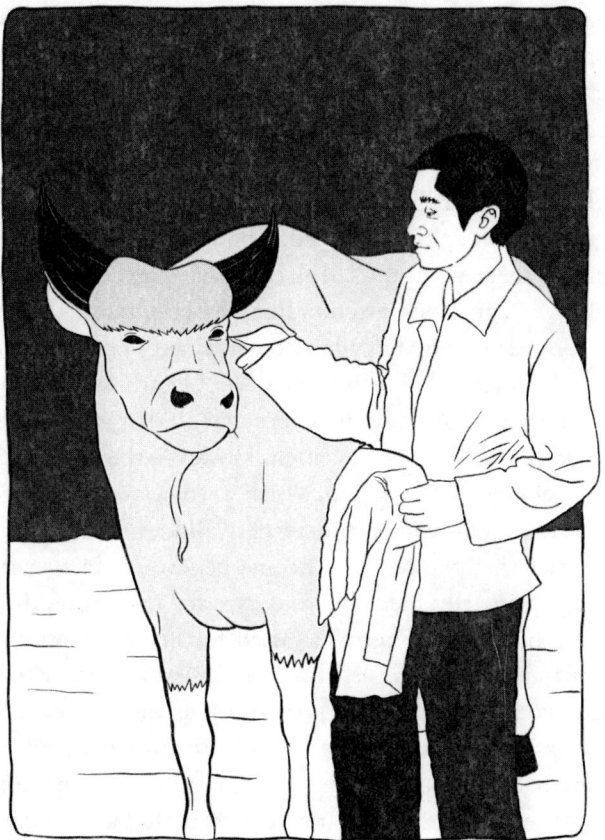

Figure 9.1   Human–mithun relations

Concluding Remarks

Circling back to where we began – has the mithun still retained its magico-religious character? As discussed earlier, this characteristic comes from the stories of its origins. For instance, in the Aka folktale, the girl had to turn into a mithun to serve as a gift to the forest spirits. The Adi believe that the mithun originated from an inanimate object – some believe it was a rock, while others say it was a gourd – which coincided with the formation of everything else in the world. From the bodily parts of the animal formed things that became important material for all Adi households like bamboo, leaves and baskets, among others. In the many folktales that I have come across in the region, the indigenous deities facilitated the birth of or transformation into the mithun in order to mediate relationships among humans, spirits and gods. There, indeed, is an economy of reciprocation between the humans and the spirits, but beyond that there is a relationship of respect and honour between the two realms.

These relationships of the human–mithun–spirits bring forth interesting ideas about the domestic and the wild. The mithun alone embodies varied interpretations of these two terms. The emphasis on the animal being 'semi-domesticated' is a conscious attempt to also emphasise the fact that the binary of the domestic and the wild is determined by where human agency is presumed to be located.[14] For instance, the Digaru Mishmi people in the Lohit district of Arunachal Pradesh believe that all that is wild belongs to men and all that is domestic belongs to women. However, the mithun despite being semi-domestic belongs to the women, which is why women do not eat the meat of the animal. The men–women binary here alludes to the indigenous male and female deities that the Mishmi people believe in. However, it is worth mentioning that primarily men rear and care for the animal in that region. Therefore, the fixity of these terms as used for humans and animals is not constitutive of indigenous peoples' lives and relationships with non-human beings in the region. For instance, for tribes in upland Arunachal, each forest and mountain has an individual owner or are owned communally. These forested mountains are spaces of food and agriculture, clothes and shelter for these tribes. Therefore, the boundaries between the domestic and the wild are subverted through their everyday actions and interactions with other life forms. In these landscapes, the fixed realms of wilderness and domesticity as states of being become extremely unstable.[15] Wildness and domesticity, then, are not properties of landscapes or places as much as they are qualities that come to be present or absent in particular relations between people and other beings.[16] Moreover, the domestic and the wild cannot form fixed categories in the context of indigenous cosmologies because of the presence of spirits. Alexander Aisher notes from his work in the Nyishi community in Arunachal Pradesh that the same animals that hunters value as prey the spirits value as livestock.[17] In the same vein, the humans' livestock is prey to the forest spirits. Therefore, it also becomes necessary to keep them appeased so that one's crops do not fail or domesticated animals do not die. The mithun, then, is semi-domestic or semi-wild because of its capacity to transcend both worlds.

The social and material landscapes of Arunachal Pradesh are rich with the mithun's presence. Even before I began discussing my research questions and concerns with the local people, the mithun had become a part of our conversations. Arunachal Pradesh is an interesting site to explore human–animal relationalities as age-old traditions centred around the mithun still find resonance among many indigenous groups in the state. Despite it being so important, the mithun has received scant attention in conservation practices as well as in the discourse of multispecies ethnography in the region. This chapter is an attempt to address the gap by exploring the changing affinities of the 'divine' animal vis-à-vis its state of entanglement in a web of relations with people, forests, the state and capital.

Notes

1. F. J. Simoons and E. S. Simoons, *A Ceremonial Ox of India* (Madison: The University of Wisconsin Press, 1968).
2. This language is a mix of Arunachali Hindi and Assamese.
3. The North East Frontier Agency (NEFA) was an administrative division of British India and later independent India, until 1972. This frontier province became a union territory and was named Arunachal Pradesh by Mrs Indira Gandhi, the then prime minister of India, on 20 January 1972. Arunachal Pradesh became a full-fledged Indian state in 1987.
4. Simoons and Simoons, *A Ceremonial Ox of India*.
5. Henry Lefebvre, *The Production of Space*, trans. Donald Nicholson-Smith (Oxford, UK and Cambridge, USA: Blackwell, 1991), 87.
6. A strategy of mithun rearing that I came across during the course of my fieldwork was in Shergaon in the West Kameng district of Arunachal Pradesh. Historically, the Sherdukpen were never known to have reared the animal or even eaten its meat. With the efforts of the veterinary department and the state government, they began rearing the mithun in 2011. The weather and topography of Shergaon are well suited for the mithun. The Sherdukpen use the animal for the sole purpose of producing meat, milk and cheese, and they believe that the animal has brought the community together through food.
7. For a detailed discussion on the villagers' perceptions of the interconnections between growing diseases among the mithuns and climate change, see Abhishruti Sarma and Joseph Zoliana, *Changing Affinities: Ecologies of Human-Mithun Relationships in Northeast India* (Guwahati: North Eastern Social Research Centre, 2023).

8. Sanjib Baruah, *Durable Disorder: Understanding the Politics of Northeast India* (New Delhi: Oxford University Press, 2005), 38.

9. Ambika Aiyadurai, *Tigers Are Our Brothers: Anthropology of Wildlife Conservation in Northeast India* (New Delhi: Oxford University Press, 2021), 123.

10. Aiyadurai, *Tigers Are Our Brothers*, 123.

11. However, in September of 2024, there was a media uproar in Arunachal Pradesh, when fringe Hindu groups moved to ban cow slaughter in the state capital of Itanagar.

12. The Adi Baane Kebang is the self-governing apex council of the tribe.

13. Aiyadurai, *Tigers Are Our Brothers*, 15.

14. Shaila Seshia Galvin, 'Interspecies Relations and Agrarian Worlds', *Annual Review of Anthropology* 47, no. 1 (October 2018): 233–49.

15. For more on this, see Radhika Govindrajan, *Animal Intimacies: Interspecies Relatedness in India's Central Himalayas* (Chicago and London: The University of Chicago Press).

16. Galvin, 'Interspecies Relations and Agrarian Worlds', 240.

17. Alexander Aisher, 'Voices of Uncertainty: Spirits, Humans and Forests in Upland Arunachal Pradesh, India', *South Asia: Journal of South Asian Studies* 30, no. 2 (December 2007): 479–98.

ANIMALS AS COMPANIONS

10

Pastoral Practices and Human–Animal Relations

A Case Study of Dhangars in Maharashtra

Ashwini Labde

Introduction

> It is our duty to migrate, we can't live in one place for long, and our life is on the move.
>
> – Dhangar herder from Kolhapur district, 2021

Estimates reveal that South Asia has the world's largest nomadic population.[1] India has roughly 10 per cent of the population classified under Nomadic and De-notified Tribes, comprising 150 De-notified Tribes and 500 Nomadic Tribes. While the De-notified Tribes have gradually become sedentary in various states of India, the Nomadic communities remain largely mobile in following their needs.[2] Of the nomadic tribes, the Dhangar are a semi-nomadic (nomads with fixed habitations to which they return after completion of the annual cycle of migration) pastoral community in Maharashtra. One of the defining features of semi-nomads is the presence of animals, mainly livestock, in their midst. The Dhangar begin migrating after the monsoon harvest and return to their respective villages just before the onset of rains. For eight to nine months, when they are out of their settlements, moving with their animals in search of pasture, their houses either remain locked or the men leave behind women, children and the elderly to look after their homes, but also to sow winter crops, if any.

The report released by the non-profit League for Pastoral Peoples and Endogenous Livestock Development (LPP) on 30 September 2020 stated: 'There is no official data on the number of pastoralists in India; although a figure of 35 million is often quoted, but without a source. An older, much-repeated figure is that pastoralists make up for six per cent of the population.'[3] One among them is the Dhangar, a community that consists of several sub-groups. Pastoralism is deeply ingrained in the cultural identity of these communities. Their traditional songs, dances and rituals often revolve around the themes of herding, livestock and their nomadic way of life. These cultural practices play a vital role in preserving the heritage and traditions of Maharashtra's pastoralist communities. According to the status of Nomadic Tribes (NT) in 1993, with an estimated population of 2 million (7 per cent of the state population), they are found in various parts of western India, mainly in the state of Maharashtra.[4] Reginald Edward Enthoven, an administrator in the Indian Civil Service during the British period, listed twenty-two different Dhangar groups (in 1920), who, in their oral traditions, are collectively called Bara Hatti, meaning the country of twelve Hatkar Dhangars. *Bara* means twelve, and *hatti* means Hatkar. In this chapter, I aim to examine the cultural context of the Dhangar community and their relations with animals, with reference to sheep, in terms of how their lives are tied to animals for sustenance and livelihood. My positionality of being a Dhangar myself helped me to understand better the lived experience of my community and their traditional occupations, the livestock they keep, annual migration patterns and livelihood issues. Using in-depth interviews and participatory observation with respondents, I will show how the everyday lives of the Dhangar are tied to animals in multiple ways. I lived and worked with them and, using participatory observation, collected information which gave me insights into human–animal relations in Dhangar society. As part of a project, I worked with the Dhangar community as a researcher based at Anthra, a non-governmental organisation working for pastoral communities in the state of Maharashtra. As a woman from the same caste as Khutekar Dhangar, a sub-group of Dhangars whose main occupation is weaving woollen blankets, it has greatly helped me enhance my understanding of animals and how they are part of the community's identity and livelihoods. Such a background also allows me to bring out native or subaltern perspectives of nomadic tribes, our history and culture.

The descriptive analysis I provide in this chapter acknowledges the reality as it is experienced by the Dhangar as a community and as individuals, their relation with their animals, while enabling an understanding of pastoralism as a source of livelihood. I conducted the interviews at their temporary residential location, called *wada*, which also gave me an opportunity to stay with them to understand their daily lives better. I have anonymised the names of my respondents.

Study Area and Migration Pattern

The fieldwork was undertaken in the western parts of Maharashtra, which is also my home state. My knowledge of my native language (Marathi) was an advantage while undertaking the research. This study was specifically based in Pune, Ahmednagar and Kolhapur districts, where pastoralists undertake varying migration routes. In Pune, most of the shepherding families migrate within the district, travelling distances of around 50 to 100 kilometres, with some of them following their traditional route to Raigad (Konkan division). In Ahmednagar district, shepherds from Dhawalpuri village migrate to the Konkan region (Wada, Dahanu, Bhiwandi, and so on), with the longest migrating groups travelling approximately 280 to 300 kilometres. In Kolhapur district, shepherds are sedentary in nature and call themselves Dange Dhangar. They are known as goat and cattle herders. They differentiate themselves from the others by the animals they keep. They say, 'We [Dhangars] keep goats and cows. We never migrate with our livestock so far, we lived near jungle areas and therefore choose to go to the jungle every day for grazing.'

Animals as Cultural Symbols

German ethnographers Günther-Dietz Sontheimer observes that the word 'Dhangar' (derived from *dhang*, Sanskrit for mountain/hill) refers to hill-dwellers. In Maharashtra, the Dhangar were officially recognised as a nomadic tribe in 1993. The Dhangar believe that they belong to twelve sub-castes known as Bara Hatti Dhangars, which are Dange, Gatri, Hande, Telwar, Hatkar (shepherds), Shegar, Sangar and Khutekar (wool and blanket weavers), Telangi, Tellari, Gawali (cattle herders) and Konkani. All sub-castes do not migrate, but some of the Hatkar Dhangar and Gawali Dhangar continue to migrate. Some of Khutekar Dhangar have livestock (sheep, goat and cow) but do not migrate far, limiting themselves to migration within the district or around the village and also engaging in agricultural activities.

A popular folk story about the Khutekar and Hatekar Dhangar is retold by Sontheimer as follows:

> Formerly the deity Biroba had entrusted the Khutekars with the tending of sheep. Many years passed but one day a Khutekar Dhangar wanted to attend a marriage. He did not find anybody who was able to take care of the sheep properly. So he put them into the holes of an ant hill and covered the ant hill with branches of a thorny, dry bush. The anthill was situated in a field and the farmer came to plough it. The anthill was hit by the plough and the sheep came out like ants (i.e. one after the other in a row). The farmer wondered what they could be and he set fire to the branches. Thus some of the sheep were burnt black, some turned red, some snuff-coloured patches and so on, in various shades of colour. Biroba decided that the Khutekar were not able to keep the sheep properly so he called the Hatkars, and entrusted them with the care of the sheep, whereas the Khutekar were to weave clothes (i.e. the *ghongadi*) out of the wool of the sheep. But the Khutekars objected and said that they had been in charge of the sheep from the beginning and that they would not leave their ancestral profession. To resolve the dispute between the two groups, Biroba resorted to an ordeal. Hatkars and Khutekars were to stand side by side and to whom the sheep would turn, to him the right of keeping the sheep would go: the sheep went to the Hatkar.[5]

Interestingly, I had heard a similar story from my father during my childhood. When I asked him who we were, he responded that we were Khutekar Dhangars. I asked him what he meant by Khutekar. He told me about the sub-groups of the Dhangar, one being the Hatkar and the other Khutekar. Both reared sheep, but we reared the black sheep, and the Hatkar reared white ones. At my uncle's *wada*, I noticed some white, black and brown sheep. Since we have some white, brown sheep along with black sheep, do we now become Hatkar Dhangar, I asked him. 'No,' he responded, 'these days, everything is mixed, and sub-castes cannot be changed by the color of the sheep.' He further added that those who migrate were known as Hatkar Dhangars, and the shepherds who settled or who hardly migrated were known as Khutekar Dhangars. Further, they are distinguished by their traditional clothes: a yellow turban is worn by the Hatkar and a pink turban by the Khutekar. There is another story about turbans; those who worship the Khandoba (a clan deity) of Jejuri, near Pune, wear yellow turbans, and those who worship the Khandoba of Pali, near Satara, wear pink turbans.

The identity of the Dhangar is in consonance with the shepherding occupation and their nomadic way of life. Having livestock is a symbol of wealth, entangled with various animals such as sheep, goats, horses, dogs and chicken. In addition to their primary source of income from the livestock they keep, they also generate income by selling meat, milk and providing animal manure to farmers. In exchange, they receive rice, *jondhal* or *jowar* (*Holcus sorghum*) and *bajari* (*Holcus spicatus*) under the traditional barter system.

Shepherds in Maharashtra typically employ traditional animal husbandry practices that are passed down through generations. These encompass feeding, milking, grooming and managing the health of the animals. The close relationship between shepherds and their animals ensures that these practices are carried out diligently and with care. The Dhangar keep many animals, and their relations with them are explained in the following sections.

Sheep (*mendhi*): Sheep are an important part of the culture and identity of the Dhangar community. In everyday communication, *dhangar* means sheep, and when one says 'sheep', it also means Dhangar. This is how intricate the relationship between the Dhangar and sheep is. *Dhan* also means wealth in the vernacular language, signifying that sheep and any other livestock are equivalent to wealth. They keep the Dakhani/Deccani breed of sheep (*Ovisaries*), an indigenous breed of Maharashtra. They are prized for their high-quality wool, used mostly for making *jen,* a type of carpet made by felting, and *ghongadi,* which are mats meant for everyday use but are also important during special occasions and rituals. They shear the sheep twice a year. They mostly prefer to keep female sheep because they (*mendhi*) can be used to increase the herd. Primarily, they sell the male sheep known as *balingya*. In a group of 100 to 150 sheep, they keep 7–8 good male sheep for breeding.

During my fieldwork, I asked a couple how they felt about doing shepherding? The man replied that when he got good value for his lamb in the market, he felt happy. When I asked the same question to his wife, she replied that when a sheep gave birth to two lambs, she felt happy. There is a gendered outlook on why people rear sheep, but what is more important is how intricate the animals and their relations to the Dhangar are, and how the community is dependent on these animals.

The Dhangar's reasons for rearing sheep go beyond the economic. These animals are very much a part of Dhangar rituals – for example, the ritual slaughter of sheep during festivals. Twice a year, one *bokad* (ram) and *kombda* (rooster) are sacrificed to appease their male and female deities, Mhasoba and Kuldevi.

Goats (*sheli*): Although the Dhangar are identified with sheep, goats also form an important part of their lives. It is believed that goats are known to lead the flock, so the shepherds say, 'Goats are leaders and sheep are followers.' Reared mainly for milk, they are traded as well. One respondent said that while searching for grass, they eat some medicinal plants as well, which makes for healthier and more nutritious milk. After extracting a certain amount of milk from the goats, the rest is left for the lambs. They might sell the milk when there is demand, but this is very rare. From a group of ten–fifteen goats, a healthy male goat is reared for the purpose of mating. A flock of hundred sheep would have ten–twelve goats accompanying it. Apart from the Dhangar, other backward, Scheduled Caste and Scheduled Tribe communities also keep goats, which are low-maintenance animals reared mostly for milk and meat.

Horse (*ghoda*): Horses are maintained largely by the nomadic or transhumance shepherds of the Dhangar community, who use them as pack animals. However, the Zende Dhangar, a sheep-keeping caste that is based near the hilly and deciduous forest regions near Kolhapur and Sangli, are known to have bred horses for the army.[6] Apart from holding utmost importance as a pack animal in nomadic pastoralist communities such as the Dhangar and Kuruba who depend on them for their annual migration, horses also hold cultural significance. Before their annual migration starts from their native village, Dhangars create a small shrine (*dev*) that consists of freshly cut grass, a horse (made of brass) and a dog (made of brass), the trifecta that they and their sheep rely on for their survival and which they offer prayers to.[7] They worship the horse also because it carries their deities (Khandoba and Biroba), while the dog is the faithful protector of them and their livestock.

Khandoba, a god worshipped by the Dhangar is depicted as being seated on a horse with his consort(s) sitting alongside him, and often this imagery includes a dog (*kutra*). Incidentally, in Jejuri (in the Purandar *taluka* of Pune district), Khandoba and Biroba, the patron gods of the Dhangar, are both depicted as riding horses. At Pattan Kudoli, a village in Hatkanangale *taluka* in Kolhapur district of Maharashtra, an annual village festival takes place where each Dhangar family is said to place an offering of a small bronze statue of a rider on a horse at the temple.

For the Dhangar, horses are also symbolic of honour.[8] The horses they keep are an indigenous breed called Gawathi, known to be sturdy and capable of carrying heavy loads. Two respondents said they preferred to keep the males gelded as it was a risk if the mares got pregnant. A mare's pregnancy lasts twelve months, and while pregnant, she cannot be loaded. One of the respondents said it was a sin to make a pregnant horse carry a load. However, another group from Kolhapur did not share this view and would not hesitate to load a pregnant mare – it was the animal's duty to carry the load. One group of Dhangars stated that their family buys only males as it is believed that female horses are not suited for longer journeys because they get frightened easily and tend to run off.

Horses are an integral part of wedding ceremonies, because the horse is seen as an auspicious animal, which is also used in rituals to Biroba, the arch deity of the community. So, while Dhangar groups use the horse in wedding ceremonies, some families prefer not to use horses in their marriage ceremony because the horse is seen as an auspicious animal; it carries their arch deity, Biroba. Their thoughts are that as God Biroba sits on the horse, how could they sit on the same? So some families do not use horses for their weddings.

Dog (kutra): The dog plays the role of protector for the Dhangar, keeping their herd safe from wild animals and protecting their families from strangers. Usually, a family has two–three dogs in one *wada*. A Dhangar with a flock of around 150 prefers to have more than one dog. Gawathi, a local canine breed, is stronger than others and is used for long-route migration, as it does not get tired easily. The dogs stay around the *wada* and tend to the sheep throughout the day. One shepherd even claimed that their dog was the *senapati* (commander) of their *wada*.

One of the respondents explained to me the importance of dogs in their lives in the following way:

> Our life is in the open field, and hence, the possibility of fights and that of our valuables being stolen always remains high. Apart from this, there is always the fear of wolves and leopards and other wild animals lurking around to catch our sheep. On such instances, our dogs always warn us of impending threats or dangers. For example, the last time when we were in the village of Otur-Dingur, our dogs started barking upon seeing a tiger nearby. The tiger then attacked the dogs and took them away instead of the sheep, and now we are left with only one dog. A dog is a must for the Dhangar because we rely on our dogs for our

own security. If tomorrow ten people gather for a fight, then three of us can't fight them back; our lives therefore are entirely dependent on our dogs.

Cows (*gaai*) and buffaloes (*mhais*): The Hatkar Dhangar migrate for eight months, so they never keep cows and buffaloes, as these animals do not walk long distances. They are therefore kept in their home villages. The Gavali Dhangar or Dange Dhangar are non-migratory pastoralists in Maharashtra whose settlements are distributed along the forested hill tracts of the Western Ghats. Traditionally, they kept buffaloes; however, due to changes in habitat quality and a reduction in the carrying capacity of the habitat, the herd composition of the Gavali Dhangar has shifted from buffaloes to cattle and goats. They typically take their livestock for grazing daily in the nearby forest patches. More recently, they have also started cultivating land for subsistence as well as for growing cash crops such as sugarcane.

Livestock and livestock products contribute in many ways to every Dhangar family. Livestock rearing is an important activity that supplements incomes, offers employment opportunities and complements agricultural activities, in addition to contributing to the health and nutrition of the community through milk and milk products. The sale of sheep, goats, chicken, eggs, milk and dung are important economic activities. Cows and buffaloes are used for milk, bullocks are used for agricultural purposes and produce like sheep's wool is sold in the market. The sheep, goats and male goats and lambs are sold directly in the market for meat.

Interactions of the Dhangar with animals go beyond just the domesticated animal groups. They also have close encounters with wild animals. In other parts of the country, there are several problems in this sphere, such as that of human–animal conflict, but these are minimal in the case of the Dhangar, who have both culturally sanctioned and pragmatic relations with animals, not only with the ones they rear but also with their predators. In one of the interviews, a man told me that he 'never hated the wolves' (*landga*) despite them killing his sheep. Annually, the Dhangar lose about 2–3 per cent of their livestock to wolves. The man thinks wolves pick up the weaker sheep which keep other sheep healthy. Similarly, shepherds in the Deccan region do not perceive the wolf as their biggest threat. Many shepherds I met, in fact, claim that the presence of the wolf is beneficial for sheep rearing. The lambs which are lifted by the wolves are considered an offering to the deities

(Khandoba), and many shepherds mentioned how the wolves ensured that they keep constant vigil and take better care of their stock.[9]

During interviews, respondents often mention the names of deities, which is an important linkage to understanding Dhangar–animal relations. In *Pastoral Deities in Western India,* the noted German ethnographer Günther-Dietz Sontheimer writes, 'Sacrifice creates life out of death.... Similarly, as the sacrifice to the wolves increases the herd, the sacrifice of sheep to Khandoba promises life',[10] also indicating the belief that wolves are manifestations of Khandoba. As discussed, animals are central to the Dhangars' lives, livelihoods and identity. Living with animals enables the Dhangar to communicate and understand the animals better. In the next section, I will show the role signs play in communicating with animals and vice versa.

Dhangar: The Zoosemioticians

Communities that live with animals can often understand their animals' requirements and communicate with them through codes and sounds. From subtle differences in the sounds made by the animals, they can easily tell if something is wrong with their animals or if they are hungry, thirsty or sick. At night, if other wild animals or thieves come close to the herd, dogs bark differently, thereby warning the Dhangar of the lurking danger. Even the cries of sheep would be different from the usual in such instances, which immediately informs the herdsmen that their herd is in danger.

On a recent visit to Rashiwade, the village with the largest sheep population in Kolhapur district of Maharashtra, I met three young boys grazing their flock of about 250–300 sheep in a freshly harvested field. Two of them came to talk to us beneath a tree, and the third boy kept watch over the sheep. There were crops in the adjacent field, and the herd had to be watched to ensure that they did not stray there by accident and damage the crops.

During the interview, we were talking to them about herding, migration, the health of sheep and fodder problems when one of the boys who were speaking to us immediately left us and ran towards the sheep making a distinct sound. The sheep had strayed into the adjacent field, but immediately stopped eating the crops on hearing the sound and stood still in one place. It was amazing to witness how with a single sound the boy had brought all the sheep back to the previous field in a minute. When asked where he learned to make this sound, he smiled and said, 'I have been with animals since childhood. Every shepherd has a specific call for his sheep; animals also have a specific language, and not everyone can recognize it.' He made a certain sound again, calling out to his flock, and all the sheep started walking behind him without a fuss. This was a unique experience for me as I witnessed first-hand how communities that spend a lifetime with animals can understand them and communicate with them in ways impossible for others.

A closer study revealed that the shepherds had developed a unique form of communication with their animals. Through vocal cues, gestures and body language, shepherds can guide their animals, call them back to the herd or alert them to potential dangers. This communication helps guide the

Figure 10.1   Pastoral relations

animals to suitable grazing areas, keeping them together and ensuring their safety. This form of communication is a testament to the deep understanding and connection between the two. In addition, there is a special bond and personal connection with individual animals within their herds. They can recognise each animal by their appearance and sometimes name them according to colour, as when they dub black sheep as Kali, white ones as Dhawali and brown ones Bandi. Sometimes, sheep are named after their physical peculiarities; for example, a white sheep with big ears is named Fadkani Dhawali, while a brown sheep with small ears is called Ghuni Bandi. This familiarity allows shepherds to quickly identify when an animal is unwell, distressed or missing and take appropriate action to address the situation.

Concluding Remarks

Being a Dhangar myself, I have tried to exploit my epistemological and cultural advantages to explore the depths of the intertwined relations of the Dhangar with their animals. I have specifically focused on Dhangar communities from the districts of Pune, Ahmednagar and Kolhapur. As migration is an important part of Dhangar life, I traced the migration routes of the Dhangar community and the pattern they follow in the above-mentioned districts of Maharashtra. Migration patterns are determined by the types of animals reared and based on certain cultural and economic aspects and the types of labour they perform in relation to their animals. While the identity of the Dhangar is deeply connected to the sheep they rear, it is not just limited to a single animal. Different Dhangar communities share their lives with various animals, such as goats, horses, dogs, cows and buffaloes.

I have observed that for shepherds in Maharashtra, their animals are not only the source of their livelihood and critical to their economic survival but also an indispensable part of their psychological makeup and self-identity. Hence, it is argued here that the relationship of pastoral communities with their animals cannot be understood by using the narrow lenses of the modern economy where occupation or economic activity is alienated from the labourer and only limited to economic gains, holding little or no emotional value. Unlike this, the economic activities of the pastoral community cannot be separated from their emotional, social and psychological life world.

Hence, it is proposed in this chapter that while understanding the livelihood of pastoral communities, one cannot make a clear distinction between the economic and emotional value they carry, as they often overlap and are deeply intertwined.

For the pastoral communities, the products derived from their livestock, such as milk, meat, wool and hide, are used for personal consumption and traded in local markets. This economic dependence fosters a strong sense of responsibility and care towards the animals. Shepherds take on the role of caregivers and protectors of their animals. They ensure that the animals have access to water and suitable grazing areas. During times of inclement weather or threats from predators, shepherds prioritise the safety of their animals.

The relationship between shepherds and their animals in Maharashtra goes beyond utilitarian considerations. It is a complex and intricate bond that encompasses cultural, economic and emotional dimensions. This relationship is an integral part of the identity of pastoralist communities and has been sustained through generations as a testament to the resilience of these communities and their unique way of life.

Notes

1. Ministry of Social Justice and Empowerment, *National Commission for Denotified, Nomadic and Semi-Nomadic Tribe* (New Delhi: Ministry of Social Justice and Empowerment, Government of India, 2008).
2. Ministry of Social Justice and Empowerment, *National Commission for Denotified, Nomadic and Semi-Nomadic Tribe*.
3. Ishan Kukreti, 'How Many Indians Are Pastoralists? No official Data, but Report Says 13 Mln', *Down to Earth,* 30 September 2020, https://www.downtoearth.org.in/agriculture/how-many-indians-are-pastoralists-no-official-data-but-report-says-13-mln-73598, accessed 25 August 2021.
4. Kailash C. Malhotra and Madhav Gadgil, 'The Ecological Basis of the Geographical Distribution of the Dhangars: A Pastoral Caste-Cluster of Maharashtra', *South Asian Anthropologist* 2, no. 2 (1981): 49–59; Ajagekar Balvant Appaji, 'Spatial Pattern of Habitat, Economy and Society of the Dange Tribe in the Western Ghat Region of Kolhapur District, Kolhapur', unpublished PhD thesis (Shivaji University, Kolhapur, 2001).

5. Günther-Dietz Sontheimer, 'The Dhangar: The Nomadic Pastoral Community in a Developing Agricultural Environment', in *Nomadism in South Asia*, ed. Aparna Rao and Michael J. Casimir, 364–397 (New Delhi: Oxford University Press, 2003), 365.

6. Malhotra and Gadgil, 'The Ecological Basis of the Geographical Distribution of the Dhangars'.

7. Kalyan Varma, 'Life on the Move', *Peepli,* 20 May 2015, https://www.peepli.org/stories/life-on-the-move/, accessed 25 August 2021.

8. M. L. Murty and G-D. Sontheimer, 'Prehistoric Background to Pastoralism in the Southern Deccan in the Light of Oral Traditions and Cults of Some Pastoral Communities', *Anthropos Freiburg* 75, no. 1 (1980): 163–84; Günther-Dietz Sontheimer, 'The Mallāri/Khaṇḍobā Myth as Reflected in Folk Art and Ritual', *Anthropos* 79 (1984): 155–70.

9. Nitya Sambamurti Ghotge and Sagari R. Ramdas, 'Black Sheep and Grey Wolves', *Seminar,* no. 613 (September 2010).

10. Cited in Kisan Anna Shingare, 'Barriers in Development of Dhangar Community and Present Education Condition', *International Journal of Applied Research* 3(1) 2017: 1003; Suryasarathi Bhattacharya, 'Kalyan Verma's Documentation of the Dhangars Reveals Existential Threat', 9 March 2020, https://www.firstpost.com/long-reads/kalyan-varmas-documentation-of-the-dhangars-reveals-existential-threat-facing-the-pastoral-tribe-7707161.htm, accessed 25 September 2024.

11

Bull-Vaulting Sport in Tamil Nadu

Why PETA's Animal Welfarism Was Misguided

Saravanan Velusamy

Growing urbanisation in India has resulted in people getting inevitably exposed to new and different cultural experiences. Eventually, it makes people, who until then regarded themselves as natives of a place, loosen their grip on their local cultural identity and embrace a global civic identity. It has become routine for Tamil youth from the hinterland to migrate to the urban centre of Chennai, seemingly aspiring to participate not only in its growth story but also in embracing the lifestyle changes that come with it. Kwame Anthony Appiah has illustrated how in urban environments people encounter commercial artefacts and establishments that bring other cultures into close proximity to their own.[1] Such a shift happens mainly through a rapid process of urbanisation that includes migration, lifestyle changes and advancement in communication technologies. A cosmopolitan, according to Appiah, is someone who has learnt to live with their roots in a wider world, with mutual respect for other traditions. He suggested a co-existence of modernist values with respect for tradition among people in a globalized world. Moving forward, the intermingling of diverse cultures is also about the differences that emerge among them. As a result, natives often emphasise the uniqueness of their own culture against universalist values. This process is identified as 'tribalism' in anthropological terms or 'localisation' in sociological terms. Further, the pursuit of universalist values in a modern world has come to imply moving from the anthropocentric, that is, where human lives are deemed more important, to an ecocentric worldview, where all lives are deemed equal. This is not to say indigenous cultures were anthropocentric; in fact, many aboriginal cultures emphasised ecocentrism. However, contemporary debates on animal welfare seem to be adopting Western sensibilities to assess human relations with animals in non-Western societies. In this chapter, I discuss the discourse surrounding Jallikattu, a bull-vaulting sport of Tamil Nadu, where animal rights and cultural relations associated with the bovines are at the centre of the controversy. Notions of modernity, cosmopolitanism and the politics of cultural identity are played around the animal's body.

What Jallikattu-like situations imply is that the cosmopolitanism of a society does not necessarily lead to the negation of an ethnic identity. People do not always disconnect or alienate themselves from their cultural roots as one would think while adopting modernity, and often continue to participate in the sociocultural proceedings of their communities. In fact, it may be said that they participate in social festivals and tend to preserve their cultural heritage more aggressively when they are perceived to be threatened, even leading to a greater cultural consolidation and solidarity in some cases, as illustrated in this instance. However, the conflict between modern ethos and traditional values continues to create tensions in contemporary societies. The controversy over Jallikattu was one such phenomenon, since bovines are an inseparable part of the identities of some rural communities in Tamil Nadu. They not only have had social and cultural significance but also ritual and symbolic significance in the lives of Tamils for ages. Having said that, I would like to state that I do not justify animal cruelty, nor do I argue that animal welfare measures are useless per se. The aim of this chapter is to examine the discourse surrounding Jallikattu, where conflict between the growing ideals of animal welfare and cultural relations with the bovine led to passionate debates on the topic.

Chennai, the state capital of Tamil Nadu, witnessed this cultural uprising in 2017. Opposing sides consisting of pro- and anti-Jallikattu groups, in addition to the presence of the media, political parties and the public at large, made this movement into a national-level news. The case reached the Supreme Court of India. Each group presented their arguments and concerns over the sport, and after listening to the merits of both sides, the Supreme Court gave a judgment in favour of those who wanted to retain the sport. In this chapter, I recount the debate that unfolded over the sport, keeping the animal question at the centre, illustrating how the bovine became a tool of political assertion for Tamils.

Frame Analysis: An Approach in Social Movement Studies

This section discusses the points raised for and against Jallikattu and the contestation between sociocultural uprising represented mainly by Tamil youth and cattle rearers on one side and the international animal welfare organisation People for the Ethical Treatment of Animals (PETA) on the other. I analyse the pro-Jallikattu protests through discourse and frame analysis. As we know, protests and agitations can break out anytime if public angst builds up over an issue. Some of them emerge suddenly, while others evolve gradually. However, they need not always be sustained in the form of a social movement. There is an inherent absence of regularity and consistency in such social uprisings, especially in a multicultural society like India, where reality is shaped by multiple positions and perspectives of its heterogeneous members. Social uprisings in India are gradually becoming a middle-class phenomenon because various forms of conflicts are felt and experienced by those who have the political strength to mobilise, the cultural dominance to frame narratives and the resources to organise themselves effectively.

The need for social change usually arises from a certain dysfunction operating in the social system. The purpose of social movements in a society is to identify such dysfunctions and replace them with desirable alternatives and redeem order and unity. Smelser,[2] for instance, propounded that collective action emerges necessarily from favourable conditions. From structural conduciveness (awareness among the public, ability to identify issues and gather, and so on) to structural strain (social unrest, disappointments, and so on) and growth of a generalised belief about an issue (locating the source and cause of the problem) – these conditions ought to be in place for movements to emerge and gain momentum. He also talks about the role of precipitating factors and the emergence of leadership and social control agents as important requirements for the sustenance of social movements during their functional phase.[3] However, social movements have also emanated from conditions of adversity, for example, in cases of repression and control by totalitarian regimes, too (for example, the anti-Emergency agitation in India in 1976). The pro-Jallikattu campaign in Chennai did not lead to any major outcomes in terms of lasting social change, except it allowed the people to display their strength which compelled the state to act upon it. However, at the symbolic level, the protest led to dramatic results, which this chapter highlights.

Frame analysis is a useful theoretical tool to understand collective action and a unique tool to apprehend the diversity of thoughts and perspectives within movements and between them. The chapter also comprehends the nature and scope of frames as introduced by Goffman and developed further and utilised by his followers later in various realms. According to Goffman, people use frames to organise social experiences. It is their way of understanding and conceptualising the world around them (both natural and social). Goffman[4] suggested that individual actions are guided by the frames people use to understand their reality. Frames are '[s]chemata of interpretations that an individual uses to locate, perceive, identify and label a seemingly infinite number of concrete occurrences defined in its terms.'[5] He proposes the differentiation between what he calls primary frameworks, keys and fabrications. The first one refers to the norms and ethos that already exist in society; keying refers to the process in which individuals are predisposed to act in a certain manner; and fabrication is how they manipulate their actions to suit their assessment of the situation.

Robert Benford and David Snow[6] illustrate the varying degrees of motivation and intensity in individual participation in collective action by drawing our attention to variable features such as problem identification, locus of attribution, flexibility, interpretive scope and influence, and so on. One such variable within aspects of movement functioning is the concept of resonance, that is, how effective the frames offered are in resonating with the masses involved and how successfully such frames can garner support.[7] Credibility, according to them, has to be ensured at all levels: creating frames, operationalising them and the articulators must earn the trust of the masses. The problem of convergence and overlapping of situations and events that resembles collective gathering (mobs, crowds or other public gathering) can be solved by separating them and reasoning on the basis of collective action frames. Frames allow us to focus on both the logic of the agency and the structure, say, the reasons and motives of the individual participants and the cultural context and norms within which they are embedded. When there is a conflict of interests between two competing social movement organisations or groups, frame analysis comes as a handy tool to explain the phenomenon (Goffman calls it frame disputes). In our case, both the sides – animal rights activists and pro-Jallikattu protesters – wanted bovines to be protected; the former saw natives as a threat to the bovines' dignity and safety, whereas the latter saw PETA as wrongfully interfering into the culturally sustained indigenous breeds.

Understanding the Contentious Politics around Bovines

Let us trace the eventful pro-Jallikattu protests in Tamil Nadu until January 2017 (see Table 11.1) which saw a tussle between a global non-governmental organisation (NGO) that works for animal rights, namely PETA, and a locally garnered, leaderless movement led by youngsters who felt that banning their traditional sport was an assault on their culture. While PETA won the legal battle leading to a ban on the bull-vaulting sport, people ran successful counter-campaigns to assert their position by various processes of what social movement scholars call 'frame alignment and amplification'. This includes invoking other related issues concerning farmers, 'Tamil' identity and hegemony of north India over the south of India (related to issues of federalism), and so on.

The conflicted relationship between the federation and the south Indian states, especially Tamil Nadu, was one of the significant factors behind the dramatic turn of events around the Jallikattu protests. There were conflicts at different levels. First, the people of Tamil Nadu, after the death of the then chief minister, J. Jayalalithaa, started perceiving the ruling dispensation as weak. And second, because of a widespread feeling of the state getting a step-motherly treatment from the union government on various occasions in history after independence, the middle class in Tamil Nadu took cognisance of the widespread dissatisfaction among people to stage a protest and send strong signals to the governments at both the state and the central level. Although the official response of the government at both the regional and the federal level was quick and deliberate (allowing for revocation of the ban), this did not have much impact as governments were not the primary targets of the protesters in this case. While the anger against the then state government may be seen as an expression of declining faith in the ruling regime, and against the central government as an indication of the discontent with federalism that has accrued over the years, the outrage was also against the Supreme Court's decision to retain the ban.

The enemies identified were corporate-backed PETA and the government agency Animal Welfare Board of India (AWBI). This is especially significant when two debates remain as burning embers, one around farmers versus corporates and the other the issue of multinational corporations that produce soft drinks which are accused of exploiting river water. Third, PETA is a corporate-backed international NGO which could not pass the test of credibility among protesters and hence failed to earn the trust of the Tamil people despite their heavily funded campaign against the allegedly cruel sport. When PETA won the case and successfully imposed the ban on the bull-vaulting sport, the urban middle class, especially youngsters based in Chennai, openly expressed their dissent against the verdict. The ban was taken as an offence to Tamil sentiment with its targeting of their traditional sport that has roots in the agrarian economy and heritage. The corporate funding of PETA was highlighted to drive home the view that multinational companies like Pepsi and Coca-Cola were interfering and threatening local cultural practices. Overall, there were three levels of contentions involving various stakeholders. The protests gained momentum and reached intense proportions due to the various ancillary issues that were articulated and aligned to it, which were also identified with its 'enemies'. The contentious politics around these issues demand that the phenomenon be understood from different perspectives and dimensions to comprehend why people did not buy into PETA's animal activism.

It is argued that the pro-Jallikattu protest was not only about a cultural sport, but it suffused within itself an opportunity for the Tamils to communicate their grievances with the federal structures of power. The protest was staged not only as a resistance to the imposition of the ban but as a massive response to the aggregated dissatisfaction over several such events in the past. These have roots in the 1970s anti-Hindi agitation in Tamil Nadu and later over issues such as the Cauvery water dispute, the Kudankulam anti-nuclear protests and a severe agrarian crisis, which have caused the Tamil people to distrust the central government. Bovines have come to symbolise the sad state of affairs of cattle rearers and by extension the agrarian communities. Indigenous bovines have come to represent not just the plight of cattle rearers and farmers in crisis but also other protest subjects (as stated earlier) that remain embedded in the highly volatile political sphere of Tamil Nadu. This explains how the frames were aligned by the larger protesting mass in order to create critical consciousness in the public sphere.

The other side argued there is a great risk involved to the young men who take part in controlling the bull during Jallikattu. In four years alone, between 2010 and 2014, seventeen deaths of participants were reported, not counting the many that have been injured during Jallikattu. This was another reason that led the court to impose a permanent ban on the sport. The animal rights groups provided evidence that showed both the cruel treatment of animals and the players during the sporting event when a youngster, the son of Mr A. Nagaraja, succumbed to the injuries, and the father filed a suit seeking to ban the sport in the Madurai Bench of the Madras High Court in 2006. Thus, they presented Jallikattu as an archaic and barbaric sport that does not have a place in modern society.

AWBI v. A. Nagaraja & Ors (2014): The Ban

A senior counsel appearing for the AWBI in 2011 argued that the pain and suffering that the bulls have to undergo during the conduct of the sport falls within the definition of 'cruelty' and hence should be considered illegal and banned. The senior counsel who represented the Government of Tamil Nadu argued that 'unnecessary pain and suffering' does not mean infliction of all forms of pain. Hence, Jallikattu cannot be banned but only regulated. The lawyer appearing for the organisers of the events argued that a few violations of regulations should not be used to ban the sport completely since such sports have been conducted across the world with precautions. The judge noted that the issue was to be examined keeping in mind the interest and welfare of the animals involved. He noted that the bulls be treated as 'sentient beings' with consciousness and hence an equal life form.[8] Because not only the lives of the bulls but human lives too have been lost, the arguments were more in favour of a complete ban. The organisers were accused of attributing only an 'instrumental value' to their bulls. Sections 3 and 11 of the Prevention of Cruelty to Animals Act, 1960, do not confer any rights to the organisers but only to the animals. Such a view gains weight when seen with Article 51A(g), which persuades citizens to have 'compassion for living creatures', which is one of their fundamental duties. It was argued that animals have intrinsic worth like humans and, hence, any anthropocentric bias should be removed while deciding on this case. Animal behaviour studies were invoked during the court proceedings. Flight response, the herbivorous nature and the natural instincts of the animal were listed, along with abusive handling of bulls. Using animals for public entertainment and amusement does not come under the category of necessary right; hence, it was argued, bull-vaulting cannot be claimed as one.[9]

It further reiterated that all living creatures have an inherent dignity, a right to live peacefully and a right to protect their own well-being, which encompasses protection from beating, kicking, over-working, over-loading, torture, pain and suffering. The matter of bulls being depicted as vehicles of Lord Shiva in the scriptures was brought up and, hence, it was argued that Tamil tradition and culture do not approve of the infliction of pain upon them. The court looked at the differences between the practice of embracing the bulls (*yeru thazhuvuthal*) and over-powering them (*jallikattu*), which is a recent practice. The sport was also seen by the court as avoidable and non-essential. This decision by the court can be seen as a shift towards eco-centric principles that mandates recognising the rights of animals. Thus, not only the animal welfare camp but also the courts used compassion and empathy to non-humans and favoured the 'humanising' of animals to bolster its case. The pro-sport camp had a different set of arguments to justify its case that the sport does not mistreat the bulls.

Pro-Jallikattu Protests: Framing and Staging

In mid-January, Tamil Nadu witnesses the harvest festival called Pongal, where the sun god is worshiped with a sweet porridge served as an offering. The second day of the week is dedicated to the cattle, especially cows and bulls. These animals play a vital role in agrarian societies since the cattle economy complements the agricultural sector in rural Tamil Nadu. Jallikattu comes from the words *jalli* (silver or gold coins) and *kattu* (bags with cash tied to the horns of the bull). The sport is performed on the third day of the harvest festival, *mattu pongal* (a day dedicated to cows and bulls during the Pongal season), in specific locations in rural Tamil Nadu. Specially bred and reared bulls are released into a crowd of players, all men, wherein the one who successfully holds on to the bull for a certain period of time takes the prize money. Jallikattu is also conducted in villages during temple festivals and is hence considered to be an intrinsic part of village life in Tamil Nadu, especially in the southern regions. Tho. Paramasivam, a scholar in Tamil studies, has maintained that the various cattle breeds hold a historical and cultural significance for the Tamils and that the sport was intended to enable the rearing of healthy indigenous breeds such as the Kangeyam and Puliyakulam breeds that are near extinct today. The argument from the pro-Jallikattu camp is that bovines are reared like a family member and given enough care and attention; hence organisations such as PETA that never bothered otherwise to help people maintain these breeds should not have a say in the matter. According to him, these bovines that are part and parcel of rural agrarian societies have been considered as wealth (*selvam* meaning wealth) and accordingly safeguarded. Such a framing was a substantial defence against the accusation that bulls are being treated cruelly. When bulls and other bovines are taken care of by the rearers and the village communities they are a part of, as a 'human member', then the frame sought a relook of how bovine–human relations are being looked at by PETA and AWBI.

The pro-Jallikattu protest was organised by self-motivated youngsters, most of them from around Chennai. Alongside the organisers of the sport and cattle breed owners, the protests also saw participation from IT professionals, students (law graduates), Kollywood stars, TV personalities, radio jockeys, artists, environmentalists, nearby residents, government staff members, farmers and social activists. They assembled in the most peaceful way possible without obstructing the everyday life of the city. Water bottles and food packets were distributed to the people who protested on the beach. The garbage was collected and disposed of properly. This way, the urban-based protesters demonstrated civic sense and assembled without arms in order to urge the government to pass an ordinance to allow conducting the sport. A few untoward incidents would have been enough for the state machinery to act and disperse the crowd. Therefore, the burgeoning crowd of protesters quickly organised themselves and shrewdly conducted themselves in a disciplined manner to avoid getting curbed by the state forces. Protests in democracies require carefully crafted action and foresight for greater success. Though the January protest reminds one of the anti-Hindi agitations of the 1960s, it was, however, a non-violent one. The mobilisation of people into collective action stems from perceived dissatisfaction with an existing situation that has caused displeasure due to prevailing conditions in a society that has long deprived the affected sections of their rights and/or access to resources. Striving for recognition, members participating and co-ordinating in a protest have to avoid cynicism and any other conflicting dilemmas. Emotions like hope and pride need to be constantly reproduced to recruit new members and strengthen the resistance. They need to overcome fear and doubts, too.[10]

Benford and Snow[11] clear the air by denoting that framing as a process of meaning construction involves agency and entails that the work of a social movement can be contentious in the sense that its interpretive frames can differ or possibly even challenge the existing one. Moreover, frame analysis allows protesting individuals to process their readings of the event to fabricate and refabricate their actions to guide the protests. Henceforth, such an analysis is the only processual analytical scheme available in social science which allows for nuanced qualifications, elaborations and descriptions of transformations that could happen within an episode.[12] As citizens of modern democracies, the stance one takes depends on how contentions are staged and framed as well. Usually, diplomatic positions held that the sport be allowed to continue with restrictions.

The protesting Tamils articulated their grievance in a framework of injustice. Often, when members of a civic society identify and recognise an issue, they also sensitise their fellow members, leading to a shared belief and understanding of the situation. This leads to an organisation of the members to collectively agitate until an alternative arrives, in this case an ordinance to lift the ban. Eventually, the ordinance was passed, and the Prevention of Cruelty to Animals Act (Tamil Nadu Amendment) Act, 2017, came into being. The ordinance temporarily allowed the sport to be organised in the state provided adequate precautions and safety measures were followed as prescribed in the Act.

Six years later, by May 2023, the Government of Tamil Nadu appealed to the court that Jallikattu is 'not merely an act of entertainment or amusement but an event with great historical, cultural and religious value'. The Supreme Court thus noted, 'When the legislature has declared that Jallikattu is part of the cultural heritage of Tamil Nadu state, the judiciary cannot take a different view.'[13] A judge even stated that if we have not banned mountain climbing because people died climbing, then why should an adventure sport such as Jallikattu be banned? A compromise was reached between cultural tradition and animal rights protection in favour of the former, given the solidarity and collective staging of protests through the use of metaphors and symbolism of the declining indigenous cattle breeds and their deep-rooted relation with Tamils. Since the court is convinced that the Amendment Act does not allow for cruelty that was prevalent before the law, it upheld Jallikattu as a cultural right under Article 29(1). This provided legal sanction to Jallikattu and even various other sports involving animals and birds, such as cock-fighting, *kambala*, and so on. While these developments were directly a result of protests that broke out in 2015, they kept the debate around cultural identity alive.

A. Creative means of urging the State to act:

Protesters: Fasting, organising all, folk art at Marina beach, mass public participation, mobile when forming a human chain, silent protest, candlelight vigil, and art of bulls, other traditional sports like Silambattam were staged at protest sites.

State: Police cut power at the beach site, tear gas shelling, baton charge, Section 144 at Madurai.

Benford and Snow[14] define collective action frames as also serving an interpretive function but with respect to their intention to mobilise potential supporters and destabilise antagonists.[15] Social movement scholars who use frame analysis, such as Snow[16] and Benford,[17] point out that the success of a social movement depends on the way 'collective action frames' are aligned and realigned to suit the expectations and aspirations of the masses in society. It deals with how members within the social movement organisations engage with the issue and make sense of it in order to decide their further mode of action. The 'truth' location of the frame is in the mind of the social movement participant and, ultimately, frame analysis is about how cognitive processing of events, objects and situations gets done in order to arrive at an interpretation.[18] According to Nick Crossley, frames are principles of selection, emphasis and presentation composed of little tacit theories about what exists, what happens and what matters.[19] Frame analysis, therefore, consists of identifying recurring patterns and particular themes in the way members conceive their ideas, mapping the appropriate choice of words and phrases being used, the places where they lay emphasis, and looking for stylistic clues in their narratives. The following discussion points out how protesters were clear in their articulation of demand.

B. Demands of the protesters:
1. Conduct Jallikattu without delay
2. Amend Sections 22 and 27 of the Prevention of Cruelty to Animals Act
3. Scrap FIRs filed against protestors in Alanganallur
4. Ban the animal welfare organisation PETA in Tamil Nadu

Identifying problems and perspectives (called diagnostic framing), finding ways and means to solve and organise (called prognostic framing) and charting a plan of action (motivational framing) are three core tasks that frame analysts in social movements have recognised.[20] Differences of opinion can arise from any of the above phases since many organisations, supporters and bystanders are involved who represent diverse standpoints. Divergence of diagnosis or prognosis can lead to departure in motivational framing and further to a parting of ways during the course of the movement or after. Analysing collective action and individual participation through such disjunctures can be best captured by the contradicting frames they use. Core framing processes, claim Benford and Snow, are continuously being constituted, contested, reproduced, transformed and/or replaced during the course of the social movement activity.[21]

To understand the collective action and behaviour of the protesters in the pro-Jallikattu campaign, we need to see their 'act' as not in terms of means and ends and conditions favouring the act but 'action as social performance'. There is an absence of trust among the masses, given the short-sighted approaches to animal welfare activism, but also at multiple levels (corporates and NGOs as crooked, animal rights activists as Brahminical, state government as weak and central government as scheming, and so on). Distrust emerged as a strong factor that provoked the uprising. It was not that the people did not realise the importance of animal rights and welfare. Jeffrey Alexander and Jason Mast, in their introduction to cultural pragmatics, state that cultural practices are not just speech acts but the performance of which can constitute social reality through its utterances.[22] They inform us how looking at acts as social drama can bring analytical transformations and help us see cultural traditions as expressing motives.[23] They direct our attention to how Geertz described Balinese cockfights as a choreographed way of reaffirming authority structures. He takes a step back from a strictly anthropological view and views it in terms of its theatrical demonstration.[24]

The performance of the 'protesting public' as active citizens took place both in public spaces and on social media platforms such as Twitter (currently X) and Facebook. The sphere here was virtual and digital. Issues were discussed and debated live. Comments were posted and 'liked' across social networking sites. Opinions of experts were tweeted and retweeted. The media and the middle class went hand in hand with each other, taking upon themselves the responsibility of articulating each other in an era of information democracy. However, the problem with studying mass media is that they make it appear as if they occur as such in real life.[25] The protesters' opinions and views then become influential and could come to represent what reality is instead of a comprehensive understanding of the same.[26] In our case, the reality is that only the agrarian castes as landowners and cattle rearers own these bovines and have benefitted from it. These are intermediary castes categorised as 'Other Backward Classes' (OBC) in India. Whereas the Scheduled Castes and Scheduled Tribes were not the ones who could own and rear cattle, even now this holds true. So we are talking about the influential middle castes of Tamil Nadu when we discuss bovine politics. From the point of view of the marginalised sections of Tamil society, this is not a pertinent issue except as a matter of larger Tamil unity.

Limitations of the Study

Goffman's frame analysis has received scathing criticisms from within social movement theorists and generally from other disciplines. According to Davis, frames can be ambiguous, error bound and sometimes based on disputed ideas of reality, and hence cannot be a completely reliable tool for analysis.[27] Davis further states that events in people's lives need not necessarily be as fateful and relevant as Goffman makes them appear. Everyday reality is not a piece of unified fact but a loosely integrated frame; however, Davis believes that individual action should be seen as a direct indication of the individual's inner state and not necessarily an outcome of his being in a social setup. Finally, he insists that everyday reality can only be one of the many realms of truth but certainly not the fundamental whole.[28] According to Manning, Goffman's arguments in frame analysis often rest on the distinctions between the individuals' perception of reality (however faulty and arbitrary it may be) and its actual occurrences.[29]

Framing is used both as a natural process that various social entities engage in making sense of the issues being taken up and as a strategy to align different but related motives into a project in unison. This amplifies the frame, attracting new participants, thereby building a larger solidarity. A social movement or its potential event (such as a protest) attains strength and sustains itself because of such frame alignment and amplification. The process of alignment amplification in frame analysis explains why some movements or their objectives and strategies spread from one place to another (inter-spatial/inter-cultural spread of movements). Interaction

Figure 11.1   Bull-vaulting

in the public sphere is no longer only face to face; the increasingly digital worlds we live in mediate human social life. Earlier, television and other mass media shaped public opinion, and now social media acts as a powerful channel to spread news and views across the length and breadth of society and inspire action. Framing effects thus become an important tool because of such media influence in shaping collective action frames. Many papers that talk about Jallikattu acknowledge the role played by social media. With the unprecedented growth of media, it is increasingly difficult to locate the discourse and its frames, as interactions in the public sphere emerge from muddled representations of truth. This makes framing analysis complicated and challenging.

Table 11.1   Pro-Jallikattu protest: a timeframe

2011 – PETA challenges the validity of the Tamil Nadu Regulation of Jallikattu Act, 2009.

July 2011 – The Ministry of Environment and Forest exempts bulls from the performing animals list and allows the conduct of the sport with restrictions and regulations, keeping the 'historical, cultural and religious significance of the event'.

7 September 2013 – The Animal Welfare Board of India (AWBI) submits a report on the abuses involved in the sport. According to the report,

> Investigators observed that bulls were forced to participate and were deliberately taunted, tormented, mutilated, stabbed, beaten, chased and denied even their most basic needs, including food, water and sanitation.*

May 2014 – Supreme Court bans Jallikattu in 2014 under the Prevention of Cruelty to Animals Act 1960.

January 2016 – The central government notifies revoking the ban and allows the sport to be conducted. The Supreme Court stays the notification favouring PETA and others.

November 2016 – The Supreme Court rejects Tamil Nadu government's plea too. Protests start in the first week of January 2017.

January 7–8 – Organising the rally.

January 12 – The Supreme Court refuses to lift the ban before Pongal.

January 15 – Protest moves to Marina Beach.

January 23, 2017 – Tamil Nadu assembly passes an ordinance bill to lift the ban on Jallikattu.

May 2023 – The Supreme Court upholds the law allowing Jallikattu after deliberations.

Source: Author

Note:*K. S. Radhakrishnan and P. C. Kose, *Animal Welfare Board of India vs A. Nagaraja & Ors on 7 May, 2014*, Indian Kanoon, https://indiankanoon.org/doc/39696860/, accessed 15 October 2024.

Concluding Remarks

The chapter shows how the notion and importance of animal rights and well-being were relevant when it came to the Jallikattu issue, but since it was articulated without acknowledging the customs and traditions of local Tamils, it did not gain traction with the populace. Animal welfare organisations like PETA are powerful and often show a condescending approach towards natives. The court, in this case, eventually supported the pro-Jallikattu group by laying bare the upper-class and upper-caste bias among some of the PETA activists over the locals and their relation to bovines. Since some of them spoke a dialect that marks their identity as 'Brahmins' – the upper castes in India – it raised a suspicion among the non-Brahmin masses (the OBCs) that the ban was an assault on their culture. This Brahminical attitude of seeing the locals as 'barbaric' is what partly gave rise to the distrust that led to the protests.

This chapter, therefore, differs from the literature that has conferred the status of 'social movement' on the pro-Jallikattu protests. I would treat it only as a protest or an uprising to express grievances. The protests did not evolve into a social movement. It did not urge the government to draft a long-term plan for animal welfare, nor lead to any state-driven, concerted action towards supporting cattle rearers that would aid the well-being of these indigenous breeds in the long run. Hence, PETA and other animal welfare organisations should aim to work with the local people to get a wider social consensus towards the protection of animal rights rather than paying celebrities and corporate lawyers to get their goals fulfilled through the judiciary. In the end, Jallikattu continues to remain central to Tamil culture, and this chapter highlights a not-much-studied aspect of human–animal relations embedded in a traditional rural sport. Jallikattu should also be seen as embedded in the entangled world of human–non-humans in Tamil Nadu, where the indigenous bovines have acquired a totemic status in the agrarian and rural communities.

Notes

1. K. A. Appiah, *Cosmopolitanism: Ethics in a World of Strangers* (New York: W.W. Norton & Co., 2006), 101–13.

2. Neil J. Smelser, *Theory of Collective Behavior* (New York: Free Press, 1962).

3. Smelser, *Theory of Collective Behavior*.

4. Erving Goffman, *Frame Analysis: An Essay on the Organization of Experience* (Cambridge: Harvard University Press, 1974).

5. Goffman, *Frame Analysis*, 21.

6. Robert D. Benford and David A. Snow, 'Framing Processes and Social Movements: An Overview and Assessment', *Annual Review of Sociology*, 26 (2000): 611–39.

7. Benford and Snow, 'Framing Processes and Social Movements'.

8. Supreme Court of India, 'Animal Welfare Board of India vs A. Nagaraja & Ors.', *Indian Kanoon,* 7 May 2014, https://indiankanoon.org/doc/39696860/, accessed 8 December 2023.

9. Supreme Court of India, 'Animal Welfare Board of India vs A. Nagaraja & Ors.'.

10. Helena Flam and Debra King (eds.), *Emotions and Social Movements* (New York: Routledge, 2005).

11. Benford and Snow, 'Framing Processes and Social Movements'.

12. Peter, K. Manning, 'Book Review: Frame Analysis by Erving Goffman', *American Journal of Sociology* 82, no. 6 (1977): 1361–4.

13. Meryl Sebastian, 'Jallikattu: Supreme Court Upholds Validity of Tamil Nadu Law Allowing Bull-Taming Sport', BBC News, 18 May 2023, https://www.bbc.com/news/world-asia-india-65630617, accessed 16 December 2023.

14. Benford and Snow, 'Framing Processes and Social Movements'.

15. David A. Snow, E. Burke Rochford Jr., Steven K. Worden and Robert D. Benford, 'Frame Alignment Processes, Micromobilization and Movement Participation', *American Sociological Review* 51, no. 4 (1986):464–81, DOI: https://doi.org/10.2307/2095581.

16. Snow et al., 'Frame Alignment Processes, Micromobilization and Movement Participation'.

17. Benford and Snow, 'Framing Processes and Social Movements'.

18. Hank Johnston, *Social Movements and Culture* (London and New York: Routledge, 2013), 218–45.

19. Nick Crossley, *Making Sense of Social Movements* (McGraw-Hill Education [UK], 2002), 127–47.

20. John Wilson, *Introduction to Social Movements* (New York: Basic Books, 1973).

21. Benford and Snow, 'Framing Processes and Social Movements'.

22. Jeffrey C. Alexander and Jason L. Mast, 'Introduction: Symbolic Action in Theory and Practice – The Cultural Pragmatics of Symbolic Action', in *Social Performance: Symbolic Action, Cultural Pragmatics, and Ritual* (Cambridge: Cambridge University Press, 2009), 1–28.

23. Alexander and Mast, 'Introduction', 10.

24. Alexander and Mast, 'Introduction', 12.

25. Alexander and Mast, 'Introduction'.

26. Robert D. Benford, 'Frame Disputes within the Nuclear Disarmament Movement', *Social Forces* 71, no. 3 (1993): 677–701.

27. Murray S. Davis, 'Review Work: Frame Analysis: An Essay on the Organization of Experience by Erving Goffman', *Contemporary Sociology: A Journal of Reviews* 4, no. 6 (1975): 599–603.

28. Davis, 'Review Work: Frame Analysis: An Essay on the Organization of Experience by Erving Goffman'.

29. Manning, 'Book Review: Frame Analysis by Erving Goffman'.

12

Dalit Ecologies and Animal Rights

Caste, Body, Metaphor

Susan Haris

Dear Karuppi, my Karuppi
Your paw scrapes are my trails
In the wilderness without you
How will I find my way?

This powerful lamentation follows the death of Karuppi, the beloved pet dog of the eponymous protagonist in the 2018 movie *Pariyerum Perumal BA BL*. The dog is a crossbreed of Chippiparai, a local breed in Tamil Nadu famous as a hunting dog. In a chilling scene, Karuppi (the black one) is tied to the railway tracks by men from a higher caste, and the protagonist runs to rescue her from being run over by the train but does not reach her in time. Her death inaugurates a series of violent encounters that progressively dehumanises the Dalit protagonist until the lives of dog and human become comparable. In this sense, the dismemberment of Karuppi's body establishes, beyond doubt, the inhuman treatment of the Dalit community at the hands of the upper castes.

For millennia, Dalits have been marginalised and oppressed in Indian society through an association of negative attributes which also include animality. The deployment of the 'animal' as a trope makes sense in a caste-structured narrative but it is a troubling metaphor because of the intimacy in life and death the animal shares with the human protagonist. This chapter centralises this two-pronged trope of animality that may signify the intimate relationship, the intimate knowledge that Dalits have of actual animals, and how this very association or affiliation is used to symbolically and materially dehumanise them. Thus, the trope has a twin function: it grounds Dalit experience ecologically and it debases Dalit experience. In the context of intersectionality, which would seek a coalition between animal rights and Dalit ecologies, I suggest that the knot in this problem is the question that emerges from the forked trope that I have described above. Or, to put it simply, how can a claim for animal rights be made in India when the trope of animality is entwined with the trauma of caste?

To respond to this question, I suggest examining the vexed interplay between caste, its (animal and human) bodies and metaphor. I build upon Mukul Sharma's[1] conceptualisation of Dalit ecologies as opening up a 'new ecological universe' outside of dominant frameworks and contributing to our understanding of environmental justice with their political assertions on land, water and commons.[2] Sharma asserts that the Dalit ecologies are shaped by caste markers of purity and pollution, body, touch, space and place, leading to alternate conceptions of environmental justice that are modulated by the 'language of experience, feeling, humiliation and dignity'.[3]

I argue that the animal body is in a metaphorical relation with caste, and that Dalit ecologies can point us to a phenomenology of animal life that may not correspond neatly with the animal rights movement but can nevertheless open up spaces for multispecies justice. In the first section of the chapter, I provide a brief account of how the field of Dalit Studies situates the question of the animal in relation to wider ecologies such as that of space, environment and tradition. The next section outlines some attempts from different disciplinary standpoints to unshackle the animal metaphor so as to foreground the animal qua animal. I then follow the recent rise in fortune of the Chippiparai breed in Tamil Nadu and examine the overlap of caste identity with anti-colonial sentiments and a concomitant concern for indigeneity. In the final section, I outline the difficulties and possibilities that my reading raises for an alliance between Dalit ecologies and animal rights. I suggest that delinking the animal body from metaphor may not be enough, as the limits of non-anthropocentrism may be found in the human body and its experience.

Introduction: Animals in Dalit Ecologies

When Karuppi appears before the protagonist after her death, she is blue in colour, attesting to the psyche-splitting phantasmagoria of humiliation and violence that befalls the hero. Why does Karuppi return, and what is the mode of profound doubling that characterises her relationship with Pariyan? As the lines I quoted in the beginning show, Karuppi is not unlike a 'familiar' from European folklore where spiritual entities can manifest in animal forms to serve as guardians or guides. They also show Pariyan's grief, and in mourning her death celebrates the powerful connection between the two. Yet the song also opens up another meaning in these lines:

> Where do I see you now?
> Who is it lying broken in the forest?
> Is it you or me
> Is it me or you
> You ... me ...
> Me ... you ...
> Karuppi! `

The doubling between Karuppi and Pariyan is significant because the relationship suggests an interchangeability that is different from standard depictions of self–other relationships where the othered animal serves merely as a metaphor or a trope for the evils in a caste-ridden society. It is also not the same as a Dostoevskyan double where the double is a malignant entity or a Stevensonian double which is manifested as a physical split. Karuppi as the double is the self that is encountered not as an intractable other but as something closer, a not-yet-another. In the hermeneutic of selfhood that emerges in the movie, Karuppi cannot be othered because she is identical with Pariyan, and this intimacy of the self with the other gestures towards an interchangeability. This non-anthropocentric interchangeability, premised on love and certainly, in the mode of an interspecies companionship is what impels her appearance after death.

The animal presence and the proximity of animality to caste are configured as a potent trope and subversive strategy. In relations of intimacy and its offshoots such as grief, anger and mourning, such as in the film that we are examining, the animal figure appears to evince new, overwhelming levels of analogy. However, the animal figure remains spectral and shadowy in critical readings despite their often resplendent corporeal presence. What happens if we take the corporeality of the animal seriously, as something non-negotiable that cannot be bypassed or be set aside for later discussion? Allegorical representations of animals are often taken to speak for real caste politics of humans outside the text – if that is so, these representations can also speak to real animals in our world.[4]

Caste has come to be associated since at least 1920 in India with identity politics and issues of representation, which are framed in terms of social exclusion. In turn, caste is seen as an issue of culture and politics rather than as an environmental or animal question.[5] In an article she wrote in 1997 called 'Why Dalits Dislike Environmentalists', Gail Omvedt argued that the environmental descriptions by environmentalists of pre-British times described a world of harmony with nature which grossly overlooks how those very worlds were structured on the basis of inaccessibility and deprivation for the Dalits. Though Indian environmental politics is characterised as exemplifying environmentalism of the poor and indigenous environmentalism, it frames itself as concerned with poor, marginal and vulnerable populations while displacing caste as an important lens through which we can understand India's ecological crisis.[6] Ironically, India's environmental politics has been criticised for being Brahminical and Hindu, ignoring and excluding Dalit perspectives.[7]

Animals are considered a part of the environment, whereby the animal question is elided in favour of a discourse on forests, select charismatic species and conservation. The near absence of work on animals in Dalit Studies resembles a gap in postcolonial studies, which stems from a fear of metaphor, or of making the non-human animal and the colonized human comparable.[8] This comparison or equivalence is unwelcome because a fixed species boundary is critical to maintaining the autonomy of the once-dehumanised colonised over the non-human.[9] In addition, the discourse of vegetarianism is often aligned with the Hindu Right, and the claims for animal resources and forest rights frustrate a possible alliance between animal rights and Dalit rights.

The paramountcy of food as a metaphor in caste discrimination implies that the animal body is already transformed into food. Efforts to dissociate the body from its symbolic role as food are viewed as a means to reinforce the ethical and cultural practices of upper-caste Hindus.[10] For example, Pandian[11] argues, in this context, that vegetarianism in India arises out of a 'heightened concern for the conservative ethics of Purity'.[12] The Dalit embrace of beef-eating recognises that Hindu vegetarianism is a way of encoding caste by 'other means'. Similarly, untouchability executed and reinforced by withholding access to land, water and other natural resources means that Dalits are not very sympathetic to modern environmental causes that seek to protect forests[13] and their animal inhabitants.[14]

Theorisations of Dalit ecologies propose frameworks that can simultaneously examine caste-based exploitation and appropriation of Dalit ecological knowledge and how the global climate change crisis affects the lower castes disproportionately.[15] However, such formulations do not adequately account for animal bodies and do not endorse animal rights to be a crucial component of Dalit intersectional activism. Dalits perceive the nascent animal rights movement to be socially elitist in nature and that the narrow definitions of animal rights do not engage with Dalit environmental thought and unique ways of understanding our environment, as evidenced in the rich eco-literary traditions of Dalit literature.[16]

Rerouting the Metaphor

In consideration of these difficulties and dilemmas, there have been numerous attempts to rescue animals from the clutches of the metaphor. Such readings of animal metaphors typically see the animal body as a site of *multiple* meanings for the human characters. Animals hold within their bodies abstract meanings standing for oppressed human characters whereby their suffering becomes real and material. To resist such an essentialising erasure, critics ground the animal bodies as real and demonstrate that the trope does not uphold one singular meaning.

In his essay on the animal in Dalit autobiographies, Aniruddha Mukhopadhyay suggests that animal representations serve as a rhetorical trope that demonstrates the dehumanisation of Dalits.[17] The non-human animal is deployed as the 'constitutive limit of the Dalit subject', and the question becomes how the Dalit can be more than animal and become properly human.[18] The focus is not on why the animal is pitted as the 'other' in Dalit autobiographies because the analogy draws attention to caste exploitation and depicts the growth and transformation of the author as protagonist. The analogy in the autobiography also invokes its use by colonial and native oppressors alike: on the one hand, the dog is treated as vermin by the British rulers and, on the other, animal analogies have been weaponised to humiliate the lower castes by the hegemonic Hindu society. For these reasons, Mukhopadhyay points out that in the Dalit reconstitution of self, freeing and standing up against oppression results in a new identity which can inadvertently erase the animal. In his 'interruptive reading' of Dalit autobiographies, he resists this reading to show how the animal trope in fact shows a 'deep familiarity or relatedness of Dalit life with non-human animals'.[19]

This is true in the case of Karuppi, whose death is mourned by the entire community and not just Pariyan in the film. The villagers participate in the lament alongside Pariyan, as we see flashbacks of happier times where Karuppi and Pariyan frolic with other hunting dogs and human friends. They belong to different species but the time spent together forms bonds that are culturally unique, significant and grievable. The moving image of Karuppi's body wrapped in a shroud and tenderly carried along evokes images of a child's body due to its size. Animal death is neither an ordinary occurrence nor culturally endurable like, say, animal sacrifice is in some cultures. Karuppi's death means something in its irreducible gravitas.

Having said that, Karuppi's death opens up the thorny question of why she had to die in the first place. Did she die and become blue in service of the trope – to become a hard-hitting symbol of Dalit activism? But if she did not die and appeared by Pariyan's side throughout the film, parallels would still be invoked, and she would still be a critical trope. In his 1980 essay, 'Why Look at Animals?' John Berger's startling claim is that the relationship between humans and animals is foremost a metaphorical relation and that the animal is the first metaphor. In that sense, since the movie opens with her death, Karuppi could be called its originary metaphor.

However, her death happens on railway tracks, a spatially critical location where the antagonist tries to kill the Dalit hero later in the film. Gopal Guru, in discussing the pervasive forms of Dalit marginalisation, comments that Dalits are pushed physically to the margins and that Dalit homes are frequently located near sites of drainage and garbage, railway tracks, and so on.[20] At the same time, the railway track is a sacrificial site used to murder Dalits. Several commentators have pointed out that the attempted murder of Pariyan at the railway tracks references the real-life murder or suicide of Dalit youth Ilavarasan, whose marriage with a girl from a higher caste had provoked caste clashes in Tamil Nadu in 2013.[21] Karuppi's death at this spatially loaded site is thus symbolically generative.

It is salient to note Akira Lippit's striking thesis that cinema incorporated and developed the animal metaphor as a gesture of mourning for vanishing wildlife in modern societies.[22] Referring to Derrida's work on metaphors, Lippit claims that metaphors are 'a priori figures of mourning' because they encapsulate their own finitude and predict their own disappearance.[23] Terming it the animetaphor, Lippit finds a transversality between the animal and metaphor where the 'animal is already a metaphor, the metaphor an animal'.[24] The animetaphor, which is metaphor made flesh and therefore a living metaphor and, by extension, not a metaphor, incorporates in film 'the speechless semiotic of the animal look'.[25] The film plays this 'speechless semiotic of the animal look' again and again through full shots, medium shots and close-up shots of Karuppi. These shots situate Karuppi on the screen at the centre, showcasing her physicality, and the viewer experiences remorse, anxiety and empathy for her. These are the same set of emotions that the protagonist Pariyan evokes in his thorough humiliation and quest for dignity. A striking parallel unfolds between the dismemberment of Karuppi's animal body on the railway tracks and the physical and psychic violence inflicted upon the human body by upper-caste men and corresponding institutions.

At first glance, it may appear that the flow of power in a metaphor is unidirectional. For example, if I say, 'I am a stone', it means that I, a human, have taken on some qualities of a stone, but it does not imply that the insentient stone takes on my human qualities. There is an implicit 'animacy hierarchy' at play which arranges animals, plants and humans in logics of differential value.[26] Amit Baishya takes a different tack when he considers representations of canine corporeality to look beyond the symbolic mode of figuring animals, which is equally common to postcolonial literature.[27] He contends that anthropocentrism is subverted by 'zoomorphic figurations' that ensure that the progress of characters is not from animal to human but to a hybrid humanimal, thereby opening up alternative modes of political agency.[28] He tasks the 'polyvalent-reversible usage of animal metaphors' that allow the dehumanised colonised to articulate ways of becoming human.[29]

There are two ways in which dogs are used as a trope in the film. The first one is the popular troping of the dog to express how Dalits are treated like dogs – like an animal, with the interchangeability magnifying the abject wretchedness of their existence. The second troping, in contrast, is the friendship between Karuppi and Pariyan, which is a rejection of caste assignations. David Gordon White's chart, illustrating how the canine comes to acquire negative caste connotations of stigma and impurity, is useful in this regard:

Brahman	Svapaca[30]
Pure	Impure
Cow	Dog
Bovine milk	Canine milk
'Cooked' milk	Canine saliva/flesh[31]

Yet another way to read animals as more than a metaphor in caste politics is to look at the animal body and examine the material effects of caste oppression on animal bodies. Yamini Narayanan argues that 'animals are instrumentalized as core political metaphors to sustain the typologies of polarizing caste, and maintain adversarial caste positionalities and hierarchies'.[32] Here, metaphors carry meaning for both humans and animals. She argues that cows are subject to caste politics because of the way some Right-wing groups deploy the sacrality of the bovine body to mobilise a politics that is premised on a pure Hindu nation that excludes undesirable castes and communities. Cow slaughter is then vilified as an attack on Hindu identity, thereby demonising those communities whose livelihood, often caste-based, is dependent on cows. Cow protectionism sits uneasily with the animal advocacy movement in India because of its endorsement of casteism, sectarianism, patriarchy and speciesism.

Caste as Indigeneity as Pedigree: Species History and Metaphor History

We know that by attributing to them animal characteristics, the subjecthood of certain humans emerges precisely in relation to ideologies and practices of race, gender and sexuality and situates them specifically as raced and gendered subjects. That is, a charge of animality is always a racialised and gendered charge specific to time–place coordinates. Then, one of the questions that can animalise Dalit ecologies is to ask what would a postcolonial caste politics that oppresses animals look like by situating a species history and metaphor history in relation with each other.

Dogs have been subject to the vagaries of caste politics and hierarchies that have rearranged relations between humans and different species. Wendy

Doniger traces these changes in fortune and suggests that binary notions of impurity or sacredness cannot capture Hindu attitudes towards animals. She argues that dogs had a positive reputation in the *Rig Veda*, as indicated by the presence of Sarama, god Indra's dog. In the *Skanda Purana* from 800 CE, dogs are depicted as aiding sinners in achieving salvation. But by 900 CE that had changed due to the increasing importance of caste, through which dogs began to be seen as impure eaters and polluters of sacrificial rituals.[33] In the section titled 'Dogs as Dalits in Indian literature', she argues that dog narratives are about Dalits since some Dalit groups called 'Dog-cookers' (Shva-Pakasii) were thought to eat dogs, and like dogs, they were perceived as being indiscriminate in what they ate.[34] Sanskrit epic authors used dogs as symbols for a group of people derogatorily referred to as 'dog-cookers'.[35] Doniger also highlights that dogs are associated with Adivasis, and terms like 'pigs and dogs' are used to demean manual scavengers, tanners and certain workers. The double impurity by connection with the lowest animal and what the lowest animal is associated with is a particularly inflexible and compressed association which condemns the lower castes and the dog to be subject to injustice.

As noted, Karuppi is a crossbreed of a Chippiparai dog. She wears a leopard collar worn by hunting dogs. Hunting dogs in forests wear a wide collar of light metal like tin or thick leather to protect their necks from leopards who have a penchant for attacking them by striking at their throats. Hunting, along with other animal sports such as rooster fights and *jallikattu* (bull-vaulting) and *rekla* (cart race), played a central role in Tamil Nadu's local culture. Dogs like Chippiparai were raised by communities that would earn money by selling bush meat. After her death, when Karuppi reappears, her body undergoes a transformation. No longer black, it takes on a blue hue, symbolising both death and Dalit resistance.

In 2020, in his popular monthly radio program *Mann Ki Baat*, the prime minister of India, Narendra Modi, exhorted his listeners to bring home dogs of local breeds.[36] This was during the time of Unlock 4.0, when the Indian economy was slowly being reopened after the 'lockdowns' during the coronavirus pandemic. Since all movement was restricted, the prime minister's monthly radio programme became a major source of news and government policy. Thus, topics discussed by Modi were assumed to be of national importance and bestowed additional credibility on them. In this particular episode, Modi praised two Indian dogs in the army – namely Sophie and Vida – reiterating the vital role dogs play in security operations.

He added that local breeds of dogs should be adopted by citizens, implicitly urging the listener to reject western pedigree dogs. As people worked from home during the pandemic and often experienced feelings of isolation, a sudden spike in the adoption of dogs was reported. Modi's mention was meant to be a shot in the arm for domestic breeds as part of his Make in India initiative.[37] The government of India also banned the import of dogs for breeding and other commercial purposes in 2016 to discourage the adoption of foreign breeds which are generally perceived to be superior. In 2022, the Mudhol breed of Indian dog was inducted into the Special Protection Group (SPG) for their strong hunting and guarding skills.[38]

As with dogs, caste is also extended to the bovines, such that society's hierarchy-based structure can be located among different breeds of cows as well. For example, the *gaushalas*, or cow-shelters, prefer to house only native Indian breeds whose 'purity' is explicated through a casteist logic of apparently higher spiritual value as opposed to the low-caste, mixed and, therefore, impure nature of the Jersey and Holstein Friesian cross-breeds.[39] The native cow's milk was attributed a spiritual value that was further elevated by highlighting the tainted nature of other bovine milk. This revulsion is often based on behaviour-based valuation, taking the form of a prejudice that is wholly birth-based, such as in the form of caste. Thus, routine, species-specific behaviours such as coprophagy or ingestion of its own excreted faeces saddle buffaloes with an impurity similar to the association made with untouchability.

Following the prime minister's mention in September 2020, the Indian Council of Agricultural Research (ICAR)-National Bureau of Animal Genetic Resources (NBAGR), Karnal, the nodal institute for registration of new livestock, registered dog breeds for the first time in December 2020. These include Rajapalayam and Chippiparai of Tamil Nadu and Mudhol Hound of Karnataka as indigenous breeds of India. They characterise the Chippiparai dog breed as a medium-sized indigenous sighthound found in the Thoothukudi, Tirunelveli, Virudhunagar and Madurai districts of Tamil Nadu. Scientists at NBAGR have claimed that gazette notification for livestock and poultry breeds was started in 2019 'after realizing the need to protect the valuable agricultural genetic resource biodiversity specific to indigenous farm animal germplasm in the country and claiming its sovereignty over the germplasm'.[40] This sovereignty – national and regional – is premised on being able to establish breeds of its own. The registration of new breeds generates legitimacy, thereby allaying fears and anxieties about lineage and parentage. Such autochthony repudiates aspersions cast by upper castes on dogs as impure and polluting animals but, crucially, it also rejects the colonial ideology which deems all Indian dogs to be local, mongrel and characterless.

Aaron Skabelund traces this genealogy along with other dog histories when he traces the connection between imperialism and animals and how the idea of a colonial dog was constructed.[41] The dynamic Skabelund is referring to is the different orders of relationships between the coloniser and the colonised, between the dogs who came with the human coloniser and the canines who already lived in pre-colonised regions and the resultant types of human interactions with dogs. Though Skabelund's examples are from Japan, the dog in colonial India emerged from dog-keeping practices in Britain in the nineteenth century which spread to other parts of the world. He points out that this idea of a native dog is itself problematic because of the colonial arrogance it embodies, much like other terms such as 'pariah' dogs to designate these dogs, which were also used to denigrate humans. The explicit inferiority and the sameness of the native human and the native canine were central features of colonial discourses.

Indeed, colonial legislation such as the first Act for the Prevention of Cruelty to Animals for Bengal, which was passed in 1869,[42] sought to protect the Indian dog from cruelty at the hands of native Indians, and it coincided with the passage of the Criminal Tribes Act, which criminalised numerous low-caste groups for their 'criminal' nature two years later. Policing of these tribes was based on wanting to govern the perceived animal qualities of these humans and the hereditary lack of moral restraint among these people, which needed imperial control.[43] Vanja Hamzić[44] lucidly summarises this cruel irony, 'in which the bare existence of certain groups of humans effectively became less valued, and legally protected, than that of mongrel dogs'.[45] The metonymic power of caste means that the dehumanising, subhumanising and animalising of humans are concomitant with the dehumanising, subhumanising and animalising of animals.[46]

Moreover, during the colonial period, various European breeds were imported due to the popularity of hunting as a pastime for the British administrators in India. Hunting required retrievers and pointers, and the Indian breeds were not useful as they had been bred to chase and corner quarry. Scientific studies on indigenous breeds, however, challenge such perceptions. For example, in a paper titled 'A New Methodology for Characterisation of Dog Genetic Resources of India', K. N. Raja and others argue that the indigenous dog breeds such as Combai, Chippiparai,

Rajapalayam and Kanni are important components of the nation's animal biodiversity.[47] Distinguishing indigenous dog breeds from exotic breeds kept for companionship, the authors emphasise their utility in livestock and agricultural farms. They call for phenotypic characterisation[48] of the indigenous dog breeds so as to contribute to our knowledge of Indian dog genetic resources – to fill up gaps in existing knowledge to contribute to a database of indigenous genetic resources.

Vikhar Ahmed Sayeed[49] has put forward two reasons for the initiative by the Canine Research and Information Centre (CRIC) to preserve the Mudhol breed. This 'canine eugenics' is aimed at reviving the Mudhol Hound and encouraging 'alternative animal husbandry practices with a built-in social welfare agenda'. What he means is that since Mudhol dogs are found in villages belonging to Scheduled Caste or Scheduled Tribe communities, breeding these dogs can provide them a source of income. We see again an overlap between caste and indigenous breeds, which is verified and documented through accepted and standardised measures of canine classification. The distinct characteristics of indigenous animal breeds have a phenotype that requires international recognition in order to assert Indian canine sovereignty. Sovereignty[50] is asserted through regional indigeneity, culture and tradition. At the same time, indigeneity is interconnected with certain traditions of lower-caste communities which are seen as vanishing. This nexus is then connected to social welfare schemes to advance particular modes of animal husbandry practices, which can replace those caste practices that are no longer practicable in modern India.

Most prominent among them is hunting, which is one of the main reasons dogs were bred by lower-caste, pastoral and nomadic communities. Theodore Baskaran[51] indicates that hunting dogs were an important part of the life of farmers since people continued to offer terracotta cattle figurines to local deities like Ayyanar for the good health of their domestic animals and terracotta dog figurines for seeking protection for their dogs. He notes that hunting could be extremely dangerous for the *pullaikanni* or *vettai nai* (hunting dogs). Two types of hunting were practised: *thangal vettai* (camp hunt), led by a single person with a few dogs, and *koottu vettai* (combined hunt), led by a number of men with many dogs. The push for alternative husbandry practices also follows the ban on hunting by the Wildlife Protection Act 1972.

Theodore Baskaran reminds us that the concept of breed is a recent one, and, previously, various other ways were used to distinguish between breeds. Interestingly, in Tamil, the word *jathi* for 'caste' is also used for 'breed'. As we have seen from the drive to protect India's germplasm, animal husbandry practices rely on the scientific characterisations of breeds identified through genes and behaviour. The description of the Chippiparai breed is telling: 'The utility of this dog is mainly for guarding and hunting, but they are also kept as a hobby and pride by the owners. These dogs are high in obedience and easy to train.'[52] What happens to those dogs that do not fit in the category of the breed? W. V. Soman[53] considers several sources in his chapter on the pariah and the mongrel to conclude that they are two different types of dogs.[54] In a brief discussion of the etymological difference, Soman claims that the word 'pariah' is applied to an aboriginal people who are not outcastes or untouchables, whereas the word 'mongrel' is from the word 'mang', meaning mixture. Hence, this distinction allows Soman to preserve indigeneity as belonging to a particular group of people who are not untouchables, and Soman warns that if the pariah dogs are not protected from indiscriminate mixing with local dogs, then they will become mongrels.[55] The indigenous breed, standing for caste-based traditions and community practices, must be superior or equal to the western pedigree dog but different from the mongrel dog.

In this connection, the drive towards the preservation of indigenous dog breeds tries to make an anti-colonial move which attempts to dismantle the 'canine cartography' that was established in the late nineteenth century by imperial Britain.[56] By identifying Indian breeds and by rejecting the imperial hierarchy that places western pedigree breeds on top, they successfully make a case for the preservation of indigenous breeds. Worthy as this endeavour may be, it could be useful to examine the criteria for these newly elevated breeds of dogs and explore what kinds of exclusions such scientifically rigorous selections entail. For example, how can we explain the fact that indigenous breeds are hounds with masculinised attributes, excelling in hunting and guarding, and can be employed by the modern state for security tasks? Their physical characteristics are complemented by exemplary behaviour characterised by obedience (and apparently, restraint), challenging the prevailing notion of foreign breeds as inherently trained and disciplined. In the project of self-rule and nation-building that these indigenous breeds are supposed to help advance, we see similar patterns as those that guided the logic of the colonial dog.[57]

In one sense, the focus on indigeneity is at the core of a Hindu politics that must unify the nation and marshal its natural resources, such as animal breeds, to work towards its vision of prosperity and glory for its true inhabitants. However, as we have seen, caste, anti-colonial politics and

Figure 12.1 Interspecies companionship

animal husbandry come to operate on the animal body to advance diverse metaphors.

Concluding Remarks: Animals Are Not a Metaphor

Historical processes, systems and structures render animals into powerful metaphors with unpredictable effects on their bodies. Can we think of animals non-metaphorically without abandoning interconnections? Can we think of animals non-metaphorically alongside caste? What kind of intersections surface between animal rights and Dalit rights on such occasions?

Keeping in mind the alternative modes of political agency that Baishya alerts us to, and the interagency[58] that Vinciane Despret describes, we can think of interchangeability as that which speaks to us about Karuppi in lieu of a stony silence. Karuppi is endowed with attributes such as beauty, agility and dignity, but they are also qualities that are repeatedly crushed out of Pariyan's reach due to the relentless humiliation and violence that come down upon him. To read this aspect metaphorically alone would be to endow the animal with abstract qualities, but as we saw earlier, these qualities are attributed to the breed, Chippiparai. As such, the bond between them intimates a complementarity and partnership that cannot be dissevered even in Karuppi's death. The wholeness of Karuppi's phantom body appears before Pariyan as his body and soul are being fissured by malevolent forces, and his revival is reliant on their friendship.

In this regard, the interchangeability draws on Pariyan's memory of Karuppi that emplaces her in the Dalit community where her death not only speaks for their suffering but where their suffering speaks for hers. Sundar Sarukkai, in advancing his argument on untouchability as constituent to Brahminhood, cites Merleau-Ponty's notion of reversibility, where to touch something is also and necessarily to be touched by it.[59] Merleau-Ponty's 'identity-within-difference' is like the relation between the mirror and the object, where the mirror exacts visibility by rendering a very particular reflection.[60] Sarukkai's important insight built around reversibility by establishing the interconnection between the toucher and the touched is that 'the real site of untouchability is the person who refuses to touch the untouchable'.[61] While both the Brahmin and the Dalit do not touch, the phenomenological experiences manifest very differently, with the Dalit afflicted with feelings of shame and humiliation and the Brahmin with power, rejection, and so on.

Merleau-Ponty's ontology of the flesh situates the body as the subject of experience to spotlight the radical 'experience of reciprocal encounter'.[62] The reversibility between the self and the other, or the mirror and the object, can yield standpoints and phenomenologies without folding it towards the human. This phenomenological experience of the world is participatory, emphasising experience as an active communication between the perceiver and the perceived. Coupling Sarukkai's use of reversibility to animals with a phenomenological reading of animal life,[63] we can highlight the intersubjective relations between humans from different castes and animals from different species to reimagine the Dalit experience of the everyday social *with* the animal. The phenomenology of caste thus revealed through the perception of human and animal bodies embedded in the oppressive system is that of a shared life.

For this reason, it is not enough to situate animals as metaphors or potent symbols in relation to caste or assimilate them as part of the environment with which humans have a unidirectional relation. Dalit ecologies cannot be the elucidation of a single metaphor through the prism of caste markers. It is, as we have seen, a sphere of multiple species modulated by the oppressive rhythms of caste. Similarly, animal rights activists may not find the politics of indigenous dog breeds appealing; nevertheless, they tap into this discourse to advocate for street dogs – the mongrels that neither the government of India nor the British government cared for. By framing street dogs as 'indie' and by gracing them with similar attributes that the government painstakingly equips the indigenous breeds with, animal activists attempt to subvert the casteist and the colonial logics that regulate our relations with animals. This sleight of hand mobilises the Indian street dog as an animal that deserves dignity, affection and respect because of its indigenous roots. Its empowerment is almost anthropomorphic in its subversion of the caste system: the Indian pariah dog sheds its caste to become the pan-Indian interlocutor of indigeneity and locality, the Indie. Multispecies justice in Dalit ecologies cannot be tidy correspondences between act, actor and justice. Instead, it is a mediation of historical processes such as caste and colonialism with varying effects on different species in the longue durée. Thus, to ask whether Dalit ecologies can ever engage with animal rights is perhaps the wrong question – it already does through the manifold relations between caste, bodies and metaphor.

In contrast, the facticity that seems to follow animal troping in a story that deals with caste should not be equipped with a transparency that affixes human and animal characters in fixed positions. There is no 'archaeology of untouchability' to be brought to light if the narrative, in casting the untouchable in relation to the animal, can pinpoint entirely the precise forms of caste oppression.[64] This folding and flattening are not conducive to a phenomenology of untouchability; rather, they prematurely deliver the most obvious message as meaning and ignore the animal. Furthermore, they misstate the caste system as a dyadic, irreversible system of singular oppressor and singular oppressed and ignore animals as equal, perceptive participants in our social worlds.

Notes

1. Mukul Sharma, '"God of Humans": Dina-Bhadri, Dalit Folktales and Environmental Movements', *South Asian History and Culture* 12, no. 1

(2021): 1–18; Mukul Sharma, *Caste and Nature: Dalits and Indian Environmental Policies* (Oxford: Oxford University Press, 2017); Indulata Prasad, 'Towards Dalit Ecologies', *Environment and Society* 13, no. 1 (2022): 98–120.

2. Mukul Sharma, 'Caste, Environment Justice, and Intersectionality of Dalit–Black Ecologies', *Environment and Society* 13, no. 1 (2022): 78–97, 79.

3. Sharma, 'Caste, Environment Justice, and Intersectionality of Dalit–Black Ecologies', 79.

4. Mukul Sharma, '"My World Is a Different World": Caste and Dalit Eco-literary Traditions', *South Asia: Journal of South Asian Studies* 42, no. 6 (2019): 1013–30; Aniruddha Mukhopadhyay, 'From Worse Than Dogs to Heroic Tigers: Situating the Animal in Dalit Autobiographies', *South Asia: Journal of South Asian Studies* 44, no. 4 (2021): 756–71.

5. Surinder S. Jodhka, 'Agrarian Studies and the Caste Conundrum', *Agrarian South: Journal of Political Economy* 11, no. 1 (2022): 14–36, DOI:10.1177/22779760211068254.

6. Sharma, *Caste and Nature*; Sharma, '"God of Humans"'.

7. Subir Sinha, Shubhra Gururani and Brian Greenberg, 'The "New Traditionalist" Discourse of Indian Environmentalism', *The Journal of Peasant Studies* 24, no. 3 (1997): 65–99; Sharma, *Caste and Nature*.

8. Susan Haris, 'Compassion, Hunger and Animal Suffering: Scenes from Kerala, South India', *Journal of Applied Animal Welfare Science* 25, no. 2 (2022): 139–52.

9. Graham Huggan and Helen Tiffin, *Postcolonial Ecocriticism: Literature, Animals, Environment* (New York and London: Routledge, 2015).

10. Gopal Guru, 'Food as a Metaphor for Cultural Hierarchies', in *Knowledges Born in the Struggle: Constructing the Epistemologies of the Global South,* ed. Boaventura de Sousa Santos and Maria Meneses, 146–61 (New York and London: Routledge, 2019).

11. M. S. S. Pandian, 'One Step Outside Modernity: Caste, Identity Politics and Public Sphere', *Economic and Political Weekly* 37, no. 18 (2002): 1735–41.

12. Pandian, 'One Step Outside Modernity', 1735.

13. Dalit Exclusion in the Forest Rights Act (FRA 2006) is an important case in question. Arpitha Kodiveri, 'Changing Terrain of Environmental Citizenship in India's Forests', *Socio-Legal Review* 12, no. 2 (2016): 9; Anand Vaidya, 'New Villages for Old: Collective Action and Conditional Futures

after India's Forest Rights Act', *PoLAR: Political and Legal Anthropology Review* 45, no. 1 (2022): 42–55.

14. Jodhka, 'Agrarian Studies and the Caste Conundrum'; Uma Chakravarti, *Gendering Caste: Through a Feminist Lens* (New Delhi: Sage, 2018); Prasad, 'Towards Dalit Ecologies'.

15. M. Bhimraj, 'A Dalit Critique of Environmental Justice in India', in *Contemporary Environmental Concerns: Multi-Disciplinary Aspects of Environmental Law*, ed. Renuka Soni, Souradeep Mukhopadhyay, Bhaavi Agrawal, Shreetama Ghosh and Anandita Bhargava (Patiala: Rajiv Gandhi National University of Law, 2020), 89–120; Malini Ranganathan, 'Caste, Racialization, and the Making of Environmental Unfreedoms in Urban India', *Ethnic and Racial Studies* 45, no. 2 (2022): 257–77.

16. Pramod K. Nayar, 'Indigenous Cultures and the Ecology of Protest: Moral Economy and "Knowing Subalternity" in Dalit and Tribal Writing from India', *Journal of Postcolonial Writing* 50, no. 3 (2014): 291–303; Prasad, 'Towards Dalit Ecologies'; Sharma, '"God of Humans"'; Sharma, '"My World Is a Different World"'.

17. Mukhopadhyay, 'From Worse Than Dogs to Heroic Tigers'.

18. Mukhopadhyay, 'From Worse Than Dogs to Heroic Tigers', 757.

19. Mukhopadhyay, 'From Worse Than Dogs to Heroic Tigers', 763.

20. Gopal Guru, 'Dalits from Margin to Margin', *India International Centre Quarterly* 27, no. 2 (2000): 111–16.

21. Karthikeyan Damodaran, 'Pariyerum Perumal: A Film That Talks Civility in an Uncivil, Casteist Society', *The Wire,* 12 October 2018, https://thewire.in/film/a-film-that-talks-civility-in-an-uncivil-casteist-society, accessed 18 May 2023; Sowmya Rajendran, 'Pariyerum Perumal': A Brave Film That Addresses the Omnipresence of Caste', *The News Minute*, 2 October 2018, www.thenewsminute.com/article/pariyerum-perumal-brave-film-addresses-omnipresence-caste-89322, accessed 28 May 2021; Ravichandran Bathran, 'Pariyerum Perumal: Examining the Anti-Caste Perspective of Mari Selvaraj's Critically Acclaimed Film', *Firstpost*, 14 October 2018, www.firstpost.com/entertainment/pariyerum-perumal-examining-the-anti-caste-perspective-of-mari-selvarajs-critically-acclaimed-film-5369831.html, accessed 11 April 2023; Deivendra Kumar A., 'Pariyerum Perumal: On the Caste Reality of South Tamil Nadu', *Round Table India*, 6 October 2021, www.roundtableindia.co.in/pariyerum-perumal-a-film-that-manifested-the-casteist-reality-of-south-tamil-nadu-deivendra-kumar-a/, accessed 11 April 2023.

22. Akira Mizuta Lippit, *Electric Animal: Toward a Rhetoric of Wildlife* (Minneapolis: University of Minnesota Press, 2000).

23. Lippit, *Electric Animal*, 169.

24. Lippit, *Electric Animal*, 165.

25. Lippit, *Electric Animal*, 197.

26. Mel Y. Chen, *Animacies: Biopolitics, Racial Mattering, and Queer Affect* (Durham: Duke University Press, 2012), 13.

27. Suvadip Sinha and Amit R. Baishya (eds.), *Postcolonial Animalities* (New York: Routledge, 2020).

28. Sinha and Baishya, *Postcolonial Animalities*, 64.

29. Sinha and Baishya, *Postcolonial Animalities*, 65.

30. A cynomorphising term meaning 'Dog-Cookers', 'Dog-Milkers' or 'Dog-People' to refer to outcastes. Susan McHugh, *Dog* (London: Reaktion Books, 2004).

31. David Gordon White, *Myths of the Dog-man* (Chicago: University of Chicago Press, 1991), 59.

32. Yamini Narayanan, 'Animating Caste: Visceral Geographies of Pigs, Caste, and Violent Nationalisms in Chennai City', *Urban Geography* 44, no. 10 (2021): 2185–205, 2186, DOI: 10.1080/02723638.2021.1890954.

33. Wendy Doniger, *On Hinduism* (New York: Oxford University Press, 2014).

34. Doniger, *On Hinduism*, 488.

35. Doniger, *On Hinduism*, 493.

36. Mayank Singh, 'PM Modi Encourages People to Adopt Indian Breed Dogs While Praising "Canine Soldiers" in Address', *The New Indian Express*, 30 August 2020, www.newindianexpress.com/nation/2020/aug/30/pm-modi-encourages-people-to-adopt-indian-breed-dogs-while-praising-canine-soldiers-in-address-2190329.html, accessed 8 April 2023.

37. A paper could be written about how state heads impact popular perception of animals by lending their support. In Kerala, for instance, the chief minister's support encouraged people to be compassionate towards street dogs. See Haris, 'Compassion, Hunger and Animal Suffering'.

38. Basavaraj Kattimani, 'Mudhol Hounds 1st Desi Breed in PM's SPG Squad', *The Times of India*, 18 August 2022, timesofindia.indiatimes.com/city/hubballi/mudhol-hounds-1st-desi-breed-in-pms-spg-squad/articleshow/93625830.cms (accessed 18 May 2023).

39. Yamini Narayanan, 'Animating Caste: Visceral Geographies of Pigs, Caste, and Violent Nationalisms in Chennai City', *Urban Geography* 44, no. 10 (2021): 2185-205, DOI: 10.1080/02723638.2021.1890954.

40. Indian Council of Agricultural Research, *NBAGR Newsletter, July–Dec 2020* (2020), 281, krishi.icar.gov.in/jspui/bitstream/123456789/69410/1/NBAGR_NWSLTR_Jul-Dec2020.pdf, accessed 29 September 2024.

41. Aaron Skabelund, 'Can the Subaltern Bark? Imperialism, Civilization, and Canine Cultures in Nineteenth-century Japan', *JAPANimals: History and Culture in Japan's Animal Life* (2005): 195–243.

42. Maneesha Deckha's pithy argument regarding anti-cruelty laws – that it is welfarist and imperial – is important here.

43. Anand Pandian, *Crooked Stalks: Cultivating Virtue in South India* (Durham and London: Duke University Press, 2009).

44. Vanja Hamzić, 'The (Un)Conscious Pariah: Canine and Gender Outcasts of the British Raj', *Australian Feminist Law Journal* 40, no. 2 (2014): 185–98, DOI: 10.1080/13200968.2014.985774.

45. Hamzić, 'The (Un)Conscious Pariah', 194.

46. Yamini Narayanan, 'Animating Caste: Visceral Geographies of Pigs, Caste, and Violent Nationalisms in Chennai City', *Urban Geography* 44, no. 10 (2021): 2185–205, DOI: 10.1080/02723638.2021.1890954.

47. Raja K. N., P. K. Singh, A. K. Mishra, I. Ganguly and P. Devendran. 'A New Methodology for Characterization of Dog Genetic Resources of India', *Journal of Livestock Biodiversity* 6, no. 2 (2016): 87–96.

48. Phenotypic characterisation is the practice of systematically documenting the observed characteristics, geographical distribution, production environment and utility of these resources. FAO, *Phenotypic Characterization of Animal Genetic Resources.* FAO Animal Production and Health Guidelines No. 11 (Rome, 2012).

49. Vikhar Ahmed Sayeed, 'The Hounds of Mudhol', *Frontline*, 24 April 2018, frontline.thehindu.com/other/the-hounds-of-mudhol/article7298432.ece (accessed 29 September 2024).

50. Ironically, such enterprises rely on a standardisation that must meet western kennel club criteria for it to gain credibility and validation. The Fédération Cynologique Internationale, the apex body which governs classification of dog breeds, has not recognized a single Indian breed.

51. S. Theodore Baskaran, *The Book of Indian Dogs* (New Delhi: Aleph, 2017).

52. Indian Council of Agricultural Research, *NBAGR Newsletter, July–Dec 2020*, 2020, krishi.icar.gov.in/jspui/bitstream/123456789/69410/1/NBAGR_NWSLTR_Jul-Dec2020.pdf, accessed 29 September 2024.

53. Waman Vishwanath Soman, *The Indian Dog* (Bombay: Popular Prakashan, 1963).

54. The chapter opens with long quotes from: (*a*) *The New Book of the Dog* (1907) by Robert Leighton, who argues that all the pariah dogs are mongrels because of interbreeding and that we should not mistake a local character for type, although this is precisely the argument that Rajashree Khalap will make by claiming the Indog to be a landrace and not a unique breed. (*b*) *The Domestic Dog* by Brian Versey Fitzgerald (1957), who claims that the ownerless street dogs or the town dogs are not pariahs and that pariahs are not mongrels. (*c*) *Observations on the Pariah Dog* (1948) by R. Menzel and R. Menzel, who argue that the pariah dog is not a mongrel stray because it is a group of different natural breeds.

55. Soman, *The Indian Dog*, 30.

56. Skabelund, 'Can the Subaltern Bark?' 199.

57. Skabelund identifies such a trend in colonies and pinpoints this as a gendering of Orientalism. Charu Gupta's work may be useful here to think about how indigenous breeds are gendered.

58. Instead of a traditional notion of agency that relies on autonomous subject and intention, Despret defines interagency, or *agencement*, as an assemblage of forces that can produce agency as shared between living beings where each being has a power to affect and be affected. Vinciane Despret, 'From Secret Agents to Interagency', *History and Theory* 52, no. 4 (2013): 29–44.

59. Gopal Guru and Sundar Sarukkai, *The Cracked Mirror: An Indian Debate on Experience and Theory* (New Delhi: Oxford University Press, 2018).

60. Maurice Merleau-Ponty, *The Visible and the Invisible: Followed by Working Notes* (Evanston, IL: Northwestern University Press, 1968).

61. Guru and Sarukkai, *The Cracked Mirror*, 43

62. David Abram, *The Spell of the Sensuous: Perception and Language in a More-than-human World* (New York: Vintage, 2012).

63. See Dominique Lestel, Jeffrey Bussolini and Matthew Chrulew, 'The Phenomenology of Animal Life', *Environmental Humanities* 5, no. 1 (2014): 125–48.

64. Gopal Guru, 'Archaeology of Untouchability', *Economic and Political Weekly* 44, no. 37 (2009): 49–56.

13

Animals in Poems

Dalits and Their Relations with Non-humans

Gautam Vegda

Marginalised communities, and Dalits in particular, have faced exclusion from access to public natural resources due to their social position. As they are a historically oppressed community, it is important to analyse their experiences and interactions with specific animals, birds, plants and other living beings because these associations arise from caste-based occupations imposed on them. The social evil of untouchability compelled them to live outside the social interaction of the dominant groups, forcing them to carry out certain duties such as handling dead animals, tanning animal skins and cleaning. The particular social space that Dalits occupy not only disables them from having access to a clean and safe environment but also forces on them the proximity of animals and birds considered impure and inauspicious. As a result, despite environmental hazards, Dalits have survived as a scavenger community for centuries, sharing space with vultures, dogs, pigs and crows.

The lived experiences of Dalit lives with animals speak of the community's environmental history, which has not been documented fully. Speaking for myself, disposing of dead animals and scavenging were part of my family history, which lasted until the end of the twentieth century. My poems heavily bank on these stories of our environmental engagements with birds and animals like vultures, dead cattle, pigs and crows. The everyday stories and images of vultures I got to know as a child still reappear in my mind's eye whenever I hear the word 'vultures'.

I use the images of these animals in my poems. Poetry, for me, is a repository of our lived history. I write so that these can be conserved and recited repeatedly to express our past realities. The environmental worldview of Dalits remains unknown, despite their survival eked out in adverse socio-geographic circumstances, but is very much connected to ecology. Therefore, using ecological imagery as a literary device in my poems is my way of countering our unspeakable realities and opening up a new world for Dalits.

Dalits were assigned a restricted space on the outskirts of our village, where they shared the same kind of food among themselves, which was at variance with the rest of the community. My family was closely engaged with vultures on a daily basis due to the imposed caste-based work of scavenging. Vultures, for us, are both competitors and companions. Both of us competed for the flesh of carcasses, and even bones; in our case, the skin too, to make leather. We desperately needed the meat, and my parents would find ways to preserve it for future use. Seeing my parents dragging dead cattle around has left a painful and long-lasting impression on me. These are the indelible memories that still haunt me.

Many Dalit communities hold memories of past vulnerabilities, which often fade away with time due to changes in socio-political and environmental consciousness. However, those memories now demand acknowledgement, as they hold within them a dark and unknown world. I have attempted to narrate these age-old environmental vulnerabilities and social obligations to create a poetic archive of Dalits' survival, oppression and resilience. Using environmental motifs in my poems allows me to personify and give them voice, something that has never been allowed because we are always considered the Environmental Other. In the interminable cave of darkness I saw first-hand, generations of my people had roved for centuries, and it has fallen upon my generation to tell their stories that no one has ever told and write their history that was never written down. The environmental othering of animals, birds and Dalits by mainstream society is central to my writings. I write poems to present to the world a perspective that had hitherto remained invisible. One of my poems is on vultures:

> The ear tearing yells and massive proportions
> Of vultures hush up ancient agonies;
> Their narrow throats gulp down the world …
> The bones are still haunted by their shrieks,
> As the vultures rest on a barren tree
> Their deeds raise a stink to the high heavens.[1]

Sometimes, the vultures get nothing from a food-deprived community such as that of the Dalits, since the entire carcass of the dead cattle is divided into equal shares and distributed among community members. Even the horns and hooves of the cattle are not thrown away. Only if the cattle died of some disease, or if the carcass was of a cat or a dog, would they become available to the vultures. Our community can precisely decipher the aviation intelligence of vultures. Their non-stop hovering in the sky indicates to us the presence of potential dead animals in the vicinity. We decode signs such as these to trace the bodies of unknown dead cattle. The spaces where Dalits gather to skin dead cattle and carve off large chunks of meat are often also shared by vultures. Coexisting in the same space makes for an extremely intimate experience, which helps us gain exclusive knowledge of vultures.

My family and I could see all this happen in the exclusive, dark world of my childhood, one which no one even thought to pass by due to the unbearable stink and social aversion to our community. Today, the populations of vultures, porcupines and such animals, along with the stories around them, seem to have faded from Dalit life, due to their declining population but also due to shrinking opportunities for scavenging. The Dalit epistemologies related to food, animals and survival remain unrecorded and, as such, unheard. It is indeed essential to define the relationship between the marginal identities of Dalits and the ecologies they are involved in. The vulture population has declined now, yet the horror of those times still haunts, and the experiences demand to be documented, not only for their own sake but also to showcase the darker side of the glorious narratives that have been built up about the country.

When I started exploring the area of literary studies and environment, it was Mukul Sharma's *Caste and Nature*[2] that provided me with a much-needed conceptual framework to pursue my research. The concepts of environmental justice and environmental casteism appealed to me a lot. To study and interpret birds, animals, plants and other elements of ecology, these notions furnished a much-needed framework. Using Sharma's works and the works of other scholars who write about Dalits' lives, I started exploring my lived environmental experiences with birds and animals.

The relationship between humans and animals carries multiple meanings in various cultures worldwide, but culture has also consigned certain animals to an utmost inferior place in certain societies owing to their close association with subordinate social groups that are considered impure and even lower than the animals themselves. The struggle to humanise themselves and raise themselves from their lower-than-animal status has been a never-ending process for these marginalised groups. Their historical subordination has compelled them to continue associating with animals considered 'inferior' due to their distinct social locations. One such example is the vulture.

The novel titled *Gidh* (Vultures)[3] by Dalpat Chauhan opened an avenue for me to express myself as a writer. He describes the complexities of rural Dalit lives in relation to vultures, against the backdrop of a violent caste-based society in Gujarat. The work encouraged me to write about my lived experiences and my community by writing about vultures. It also invoked a sense of Dalit aesthetics of literature in me, compelling me to pen poetry of resistance and realism. The use of uncommon animal and bird imagery in the Dalit literary tradition has helped shape a distinct environmental angle to my poetry.

The vulture is a frequent image that appears and reappears in my poems since it is a powerful embodiment of our environmental history. The symbol is not posited here as a merely aesthetic one but as Dalit testimonies personified. Our identification with the animals and birds we coexisted with helps us voice our life experiences through them.

> He has a man's hands, feet and torso,
> Some shreds of clothing to cover his body,
> But his head is that of a vulture,
> His hunger too, is a vulture's hunger,
> This biped walks, but in zigzag like a vulture.
> Tearing,
> Pulling,
> Hubbub,
> From age to age,
> Generation to generation,
> He was born in fetters, condemned
> To suck the marrow off discarded bones,
> To prosper the earth for others.
> What incarnation is this?[4]

Our image of the vulture stands in contrast to the image of Jatayu, the mythical vulture that appears in the Ramayana. Jatayu is quite different from the actual vultures we have lived with. The vulture in this epic possesses divine attributes and is shown attacking humans. Jatayu has the power to articulate language and attack the king Ravana with his powerful claws, behaviour totally in contrast with the vultures we encountered. In our world, vultures do not attack humans. As Shashtri states:

> 'Uttering these harsh words, the valiant Jatayu swooped on the ten-headed demon and, seizing him in his claws, tore his flesh like the rider of a restive elephant. Inflicting deep wounds, he plunged his beak into his back and tore his hair with his talons. Thus assailed by the Vulture King, the titan, trembling with rage, pressing Vaidehi to his left side, foaming with anger, struck Jatayu with the palm of his hand, whereupon the mighty vulture Jatayu, the Destroyer of his Foes, hurled himself on Dashagriva and with his beak tore off his ten left arms.'[5]

Our vulture does not assault people, nor does it display any awareness of the binary of good and evil established by the Hindu religion or any other moral agency. This image is imaginary, while ours is entirely experiential. Those who have not experienced the presence of vultures closely would not propose the image of a 'divine' vulture. Dalits have direct experiences with vultures; we know what they look like, what size they are, what they eat and how they walk. All these may be subjective, but these experiences emerged from lives deeply entangled with the lives of vultures, and they unfailingly produce a collective memory.

My poem 'Nargidh' (Half-human-half-vulture) challenges the idea of the deification of a particular kind of animal or bird. The hybrid human–animal image of Narsinha (*nar* refers to man and *sinha* to lion) is a half-human-half-lion figure deified in mythological accounts. In contrast to it, I posit Nargidh as an alternative argument to acknowledge the perspectives of the Dalits who seek to attain human status. It also reminds me of the half-human status or, indeed, the non-human existence of the Dalits in the Hindu social structure. Fellow Dalit poets and writers have used such non-human or semi-human symbols to contest the historically imposed vulnerability of Dalits and the subhumanity that was forced on them. Therefore, Nargidh refutes the image of Narsinha's incarnation and challenges the religious meanings attached to the Hindu god.

In Hinduism, animals such as lions, tigers and elephants are considered auspicious and associated with many gods like Indra, Shiva and Vishnu as well as many goddesses. Even semi-human deities have been worshipped and their bodily 'deformities' embraced by the devout. However, for Dalits, we embody vultures and other animals in a bare human form, having been forced for generations to live like vultures and other animals subjected to perennial humiliation and subjugation. At times, the bodies of Dalits and vultures appear to be one as we share food and space. The experience of vultures clamouring, trying to sneak away a chunk of flesh or fat from the carved human shares of meat, while others wait impatiently for us to leave the site to collect any leftovers, describes for us the horror inflicted on us by India's caste structure. I wrote the following poem to recollect the faint childhood images of my family's interactions with vultures, which I find more ghastly in hindsight.

But who fixed
These clumsy wings
On our human bodies?
Who made us bury our beaks
Into motile lumps of flesh?
Who poured corrosive acid
Into our stomachs
That burns even cholera and rabies?
Can one evolve from
Gyps Indicus to Homo sapiens?
We are not vultures.[6]

The poem 'Gyps Indicus' condemns the oppression and the severe effects of the environmental hazards inflicted upon the bodies of Dalits by the Hindu caste order, which compelled the marginalised sections to survive through unhygienic and inhuman livelihoods. Vultures easily digest the meat of dead cattle despite the multiplying bacterial growth in it. Similarly, Dalits too share the same food, eating and digesting rotten food with ease. There is an anecdote told by my mother about my grandfather, who was fond of the liver of cattle. The first thing he would do when disembowelling an animal was to pluck out its liver and eat it uncooked on the spot. Dalpat Chauhan's novel *Vulture* also describes how Dalits grew impatient and excited to eat the meat of a dead buffalo that was shared among them. What made them risk their health or become accustomed to such risky food habits? What is the difference between vultures and human beings? The issue of refusal of humane treatment to Dalits is questioned in this poem since it explicitly condemns the fact that the caste order pushed them into a site where they were forced to live out their vulture-like existence.

Similarly, Namdeo Dhasal's poem 'Kamatipura'[7] left an everlasting impact on my writing. His reference to porcupine happens to be my preferred subject to talk about marginality and resilience. Here is a part of my poem 'Porcupine':

> The walls of caste were impossible to climb,
> What was left for us was to skin a tree,
> We chewed and chewed and chewed.
> Rattle and chomp synced for ages.
> But then our quills caught fire
> That lit the path of freedom,
> Burning barbed quills
> Pierced the wall,
> Some light sidled through holes.
> Our due share of water, land, dignity
> Too followed.
> Our quills got more pointed
> And our feet faster.
> They were already bigger than
> Your fangs,
> And sharp enough to retaliate.[8]

This poem largely refers to the Dalits' historical state of repression through the biological characteristics of a porcupine. The poem's focal points are the sense of retaliation and resilience in the face of caste atrocities. During the rule of the Peshwas in India, untouchable communities were condemned to hang an earthen pot from their necks in front to collect their spittle, and a broom on their backs to erase the footsteps they left behind, lest someone from a dominant caste got polluted by accidentally stepping on them. The porcupine personifies the historical Dalit body, since it possesses a broom-like bunch of quills. The agony of being nocturnal in historically dark times is portrayed through this symbol. The idea of quills forming a broom connotes subjugation and helplessness; however, later in the poem, it is developed into a weapon to retaliate, a defence mechanism. This poem encapsulates Dalit consciousness and resistance against the characteristic forms of caste violence.

Traditional society and its role in making a fellow human being endure such grave environmental hazards is particularly egregious since such stratification of occupations by caste, such as scavenging for Dalits, have been sanctified by so-called religious teaching. The practice of scavenging among Dalits as a profession was imposed through socio-religious means of oppression, so as to keep them enslaved and far removed from the circles of progress and dignified life that the dominant castes enjoyed as a birthright. The caste laws are deemed 'natural' and created by God. The Bhagvad Gita, in Chapter 4, Shloka 13, explicitly proclaims that the four classes of occupation were created by Krishna himself (the incarnation of God). Such religious legitimacy granted it ensured that the *varna* system prevailed throughout the historical ages and is still prevalent in contemporary times.

My unpublished poem 'Hyena' employs the symbol of this nocturnal animal to refer to the occupational trait of Dalits as bone collectors. Dalits indulged in the occupation of bone collection to earn some livelihood for the bonemeal industry as a livelihood, which happens to this day. Like Dalits, the hyena, as part of its survival mechanism, collects bones. The hyena's stripes may be compared to the historical wounds of caste cruelty, which was necessary to keep such an exploitative system intact.

What happened after the Una incident, when a group of Dalit youth were flogged publicly on 11 July 2016 in Gujarat, is remarkable. Hundreds of Dalits came forward to publicly denounce and reject their caste occupation of disposing dead cattle and demanded self-respect for their community. This led to a massive nationwide protest against the accused, who had performed the brutal act on the Dalit youth for the 'sin' of skinning dead cattle, even though this very occupation had been imposed on Dalits by stringent caste rules. In Surendranagar district, Dalits dumped dead cattle on roads, government offices and public places. Bones were also laid on the tables of the offices to symbolically reject the idea of being forced to live off leftovers.

Dalpat Chauhan rightly hit the mood of this poem in *Vultures*: 'If these Hyenas pounce on the whole buffalo, it will vanish in a few moments.'[9] The hyena in my poem refers to Dalits who do not want to remain untouchable bone collectors or accept leftovers but demand equal social, economic and educational status.

> My body has been lashed
> And slashed,
> Cicatrix still subsists,
> In the shape of stripes and spots
> As if a hyena.
> Everyday a new scar emerges.
> Our fault was to demand our share,
> That is iniquitous, you say
> But hurling our clans into the nocturnal world wasn't?
> What about condemning us
> To feed on leftovers?
> Your rancor keeps us migrating,
> Nocturnal and down and out.
> Fleshless black bones take everything of ours,
> In reaching the marrow.
> Our throats are like the trunks of palm trees,
> And our tongues are parched.
> But our clan now hunts huge prey,
> Our feet sturdy, don't wobble anymore.
> We are no more bone collectors.
> Our stripe marks won't keep us
> From snatching that hunk.
> The meat will nourish us,
> And heal us too.[10]

I wrote this poem by recollecting my childhood memories of playing with the horns of dead cattle by tying them with a string and dragging them about. In our innocence, we would cross over from our *mohalla* (ghetto) and enter the areas where the dominant castes resided. On such occasions, we would encounter their abuses and their eyes fuming with anger and aversion. Reading the first Gujarati Dalit autobiography, *The Whole Truth and Nothing but the Truth,* by B. Kesharshivam inspired this poem. In his life narrative, Kesharshivam recalls his childhood experiences of playing with hooves and horns of cattle since his family worked in a factory that processed animal bones.

We had to find our toys around the place where our parents worked for their livelihood. In the bonemeal factory, we played with cattle's hooves, bones, and horns.[11]

After being exposed to literature written by marginalised communities in India and in Africa, by women, Dalits and indigenous people, I realised that I had to find my place as a writer, where I truly belonged. Dalit poetry enabled me to write and express my lived experiences, the vulnerable self-making itself heard as a collective voice. My sense of belonging was discovered through literature and poetry. Dalit poets like Neerav Patel, Dalpat Chauhan, Namdeo Dhasal, Pravin Gadhavi, Om Prakash Valmiki and Sukirtharani appealed to me extraordinarily since their work extensively featured animal and bird symbolism, such as vultures, wild boars and porcupines. Dalit literature is the literature of resistance, but also of harsh reality and of pain; ultimately though, it strengthens Dalit consciousness and aspirations for equal status as humans. My everyday experience of caste discrimination which contrasted with narratives around me that attempted to portray caste oppression as mere myth, and which therefore had to be constantly contested, compelled me to document my own caste history, which, incidentally, also had a lot to do with nature. Dalit writings depict a certain form of human–environmental connection, which is deeply intimate, demonstrating powerful resistance to discrimination and injustice, noted by Sharma[12] as follows:

> It is equally important to note that Dalit critiques of present environmentalism, including their perspectives on labour, natural resources, village communities, public spaces, food, animals, vegetarianism and development, have not been integrated into environmental studies and politics.[13]

The ecology we have been engaging with is linked to our experiences, and the worldview is yet to be acknowledged. Nature is romanticised and mythicised by *savarnas*,[14] a cultural project that has long overshadowed our own aesthetics, which is derived from how we live with animals and how we understand nature. The environmental elements are often deified, masking their real-life significance and understanding. Vultures, boars and crows are showcased as having supernatural attributions, conceptions that are not based on any 'real life' lived experience of coexistence with them. Human–animal

Figure 13.1   Living with vultures

relations and their interactions are inseparable from Dalit realities. Therefore, in our literature, it is reflected in a starkly different form compared to the literature of the *savarnas*.

My determination to document Dalit environmental history through poetry from a caste perspective has enabled me to verify (and to create in verse form) the animal–bird testimonies of the communities. The everydayness of caste oppression and notable atrocities like the Una flogging compelled me to pen anti-caste poems. This is my way of coping with atrocities that happen to my community on an everyday basis. My writing not only reflects the present realities but also helps me to unearth the haunting collective past hovering over our memories, shaping the identities of my people. Poetry is both a medium of resistance and a vehicle to carry forward the resistance from one generation to another. Therefore, for me, poems are a tool to strengthen my voice against injustice and to seek justice and the right to be acknowledged as human, and to be treated as one, which have also been denied to my community, along with the form of environmental deprivation that has been imposed on us.

Notes

1. Gautam Vegda, *Vultures* (Bilaspur: Evincepub Publishing, 2018), 35.
2. Mukul Sharma, *Caste and Nature: Dalits and Indian Environmental Politics* (New Delhi: Oxford University Press, 2017).
3. Dalpat Chauhan, *Gidh* (Ahmedabad: Gurjar Sahitya Bhavan, 2011), 46.
4. Gautam Vegda, 'Nargidh', 2020 (unpublished manuscript).
5. Hari Prashad Shashtri, *The Ramayana of Valmiki* (Bristol: The Burleigh Press, 1952), 108–9.
6. Gautam Vegda, 'Gyps Indicus', 2020 (unpublished manuscript).
7. Namdeo Dhasal, *Namdeo Dhasal: Poet of the Underworld (Poems 1972–2006)*, trans. Dilip Chitre (Chennai: Navayana, 2007).
8. Gautam Vegda, 'Porcupine', 2020 (unpublished manuscript).
9. Chauhan, *Gidh*, 46.
10. Gautam Vegda, 'Hyena', 2020 (unpublished manuscript).
11. B. Kesharshivam, *The Whole Truth and Nothing but the Truth: A Dalit's Life*, trans. Gita Chaudhari (Kolkata: Samya, 2008), 7.
12. Mukul Sharma, 'Dalits and Indian Environmental Politics', *Economic and Political Weekly* 47, no. 23 (2012): 46–52.
13. Sharma, 'Dalits and Indian Environmental Politics', 50.
14. *Savarnas* are the upper three of the four caste groups of the Hindu hierarchical system who avail privileges merely by being born in the upper castes.

About the Contributors

Shibangi Dash is pursuing PhD in English Literature at the University of Delhi. Her primary research interest lies in an intersectional study of caste in India, women's writings, food studies and Odia literature. Her MPhil dissertation focused on exploring caste consciousness in medieval *puranic* texts from Odisha. She has published papers on Dalit writings from different regions in India and has presented papers in various national and international conferences. She is also pursuing her PhD from the Department of English, University of Delhi, where she analyses the changing expressions of caste oppression in Odisha, focusing particularly on the post-independence period.

Rachan Daimary is Assistant Professor in the Department of Journalism and Mass Communication at Manipal University, Jaipur, India. Rachan is a science and technology studies (STS) researcher working on science communication, biodiversity and wildlife conservation. He holds a PhD in studies in science, technology and innovation policy from the Central University of Gujarat, Gandhinagar. He was also a visiting fellow at the IAS-STS Unit, Graz University of Technology, Austria. His long-term work investigates the relationship between conservation scientists and the public at large for effective wildlife conservation management in India. At present, his research interest is in the area of human–nature relationships to further his understanding of STS and science communication.

Deepak is an Assistant Professor in the Department of Arts and Humanities at SGT University, Gurugram. He holds an MPhil from the University of

Delhi as a UGC Junior Research Fellow and is pursuing PhD at the Centre for English Studies, Jawaharlal Nehru University. A dedicated translator and scholar with works showcased at the Conflictorium Museum, Kanpur, and in peer-reviewed articles. He has delivered several invited lectures on Dalit literature and Dr B. R. Ambedkar's writings. He served as the Convener of the 2024 National Conference on 'Human Rights, Language and Literature: Advancements in Contemporary Times' at SGT University.

R. Samuel Gnanaraj is Assistant Professor of English at Bishop Heber College (affiliated to Bharathidasan University, Tiruchirappalli). His research concentrates on integrating human rights and trauma studies in the life narratives of the Sri Lankan war. His areas of research interest include human rights literature, life narratives and trauma studies. He has presented research papers at various national and international conferences and seminars and has also published several research papers in reputed journals.

Susan Haris is an Assistant Professor of English at GITAM University, Hyderabad, and the co-founder of the Indian Animal Studies Collective. Her writing has appeared in the *Economic and Political Weekly, Culture, Theory and Critique* and the *Journal of Applied Animal Welfare Science*.

Ashwini Labde is a first-generation learner from the Dhangar community. She completed her master's in Dalit and tribal studies and action from the Tata Institute of Social Sciences, Mumbai. At present, she is a Steering Committee member at the South Asian Pastoral Alliance. She has been working with pastoral communities in Maharashtra for the last three years. She is interested in field-based studies and in devising sustainable policies that incorporate native or subaltern understanding from pastoral communities in general, but especially from the women. In addition to this, she has a more general research interest in pastoralism, nomadic tribes, gender and livelihood.

Greeshma Mohan is an Assistant Professor, English, in the School of Arts and Sciences, Azim Premji University, Bhopal. She holds a PhD, MPhil and MA from the Centre for English Studies (CES), Jawaharlal Nehru University. Formerly she taught literature, humanities electives and academic writing at Mahindra University, Hyderabad, and at Krea University, Sci City. She is interested in caste, affect, the novel, autobiography and life writing.

Khriengunuo Mepfhuo is currently working as a scientist at the Indian Council of Agricultural Research–National Research Centre on Yak (ICAR-NRCY), Dirang. She has travelled extensively to the yak-rearing tracts across India. Through her research, she hopes to highlight the unique features of yak rearing as well as those of its herders.

Purnachandra Naik holds a PhD from the School of Arts and Humanities, Nottingham Trent University (UK). In his thesis titled 'Reading the Rejected', he examines 'dirt' in Dalit literature. He has published research papers and book reviews in the *Economic and Political Weekly*. He has contributed the chapter 'Studying Caste Up: Yashica Dutt's Coming Out as Dalit' in the edited book *Subalternities in India and Latin America: Dalit Autobiographies and the Testimonio* (Routledge, 2022). He is interested in Indian cinema and the caste question from an anti-caste perspective.

Mihir Sarkar is presently the Director at ICAR-NRCY. He started his career as a scientist at this institute and is well versed in yak husbandry and its many facets. He has to his credit many publications in international and national journals. He has also guided a good number of postgraduate and doctoral candidates while working as a scientist at ICAR-Indian Veterinary Research Institute (IVRI) (Deemed University).

Akshay Sawant is a PhD scholar in sociology at Indian Institute of Technology Bombay. He is currently working on the life and career of the Marathas in contemporary Maharashtra. He has worked on Maratha identity formation in the early twentieth century for his MPhil thesis. Anti-caste movements, caste in India, transactions between caste and gender and castes' psychological aspects are his areas of interest.

Abhishruti Sarma is currently pursuing her PhD in the Department of Sociology and Anthropology at Ashoka University, Sonipat. Her research explores human–non-human relations in the forested landscapes of India's northeast. Before joining Ashoka, she worked as a Research Associate on multiple projects in the North Eastern Social Research Centre in Guwahati and co-authored a book titled *Changing Affinities: Ecologies of Human Mithun Relationships in Northeast India* (2023).

Gautam Vegda is an anti-caste poet and research scholar. He has published poetry collections, namely *Vultures and Other Poems* (2018) and *A Strange*

Case of Flesh and Bones (2019). He is currently pursuing PhD in the Central University of Gujarat and his research focuses on eco-semiotics and human–animal relations.

Saravanan Velusamy is a PhD scholar at the Center for the Study of Social Systems, Jawaharlal Nehru University, New Delhi. His research interests are in the sociology of education and youth studies. His works mainly focus on the issues of access and equity in education, employment and entrepreneurship in India. Nevertheless, he keeps an ear to the ground on events that are sociologically significant, for he knows he bears witness to the history that is unfolding in his times.

Index